New Perspectives for Bank Directors

New Perspectives
For Bank Directors

Edited by
RICHARD B. JOHNSON

SMU PRESS • DALLAS

© 1977 · SOUTHERN METHODIST UNIVERSITY PRESS · DALLAS

This is the fourth of a series on financial matters sponsored by the Foundation of the Southwestern Graduate School of Banking.

Library of Congress Cataloging in Publication Data
Main entry under title:

New perspectives for bank directors.

    Bibliography: p.
    1. Bank directors—Addresses, essays, lectures.
2. Banks and banking—Addresses, essays, lectures.
3. Bank management—Addresses, essays, lectures.
I. Johnson, Richard Buhmann, 1913-   ed.
HG1591.N68   658'.91'332   77-12973
ISBN 0-87074-168-3
ISBN 0-87074-167-5 pbk.

Contents

PREFACE — vii

DUTIES AND RESPONSIBILITIES OF BANK DIRECTORS — 3
    William H. Bowen (President, Commercial National Bank, Little Rock, Arkansas)

RECENT DEVELOPMENTS IN DIRECTOR LIABILITY — 19
    Edward B. Close, Jr. (Partner, Hughes and Dorsey: Attorneys at Law, Denver, Colorado)

WHAT MANAGEMENT EXPECTS OF BANK DIRECTORS — 27
    Kenneth L. Roberts (President, First American National Bank, Nashville, Tennessee)

WHAT BANK DIRECTORS EXPECT OF MANAGEMENT — 35
    Edwin Jones (President, J. A. Jones Construction Company, Charlotte, North Carolina)

WHAT A BANK SUPERVISOR EXPECTS OF DIRECTORS — 40
    John G. Hensel (Regional Administrator of National Banks, Twelfth National Bank Region, San Francisco, California)

THE FUNCTIONS AND CONTRIBUTIONS OF REGULATION — 46
    Robert E. Barnett (Kutac, Rock, Huie, Brown and Ide: Attorneys at Law, Washington, D.C.—Chairman of FDIC 1976-77)

EVALUATING THE QUALITY OF BANK MANAGEMENT 61
   Eugene L. Swearingen (Chairman and Chief Executive Officer, Bank of Oklahoma, Tulsa, Oklahoma)

EVALUATING MANAGEMENT 70
   Frank A. Plummer (Chairman and Chief Executive Officer, First Alabama Bancshares, Inc., Montgomery, Alabama)

BOARD FUNCTIONS AND COMMITTEE ORGANIZATION 74
   B. Finley Vinson (Chairman of the Board, First National Bank, Little Rock, Arkansas)

ANALYZING BANK OPERATIONS 81
   Gerald R. Sprong (President, The American National Bank, St. Joseph, Missouri)

PLANNING, BUDGETING, AND CONTROL: A BANK DIRECTOR'S PERSPECTIVE 88
   Phillip F. Searle (Chairman and Chief Executive Officer, Flagship Banks, Inc., Miami Beach, Florida)

MANAGEMENT REPORTS TO DIRECTORS 99
   Phillip F. Searle (Chairman and Chief Executive Officer, Flagship Banks, Inc., Miami Beach, Florida)

MARKETING AND THE BANK DIRECTOR 113
   C. C. Cameron (Chief Executive Officer, First Union National Bank of North Carolina, Charlotte, North Carolina)

THE MARKETING FUNCTION AND THE BANK DIRECTOR 116
   Terry E. Renaud (Chairman and President, The Twin City Bank, North Little Rock, Arkansas)

THE CHANGING FINANCIAL STRUCTURE 124
   John H. Perkins (President, Continental Illinois National Bank and Trust Company, Chicago, Illinois)

CONTENTS vii

APPRAISAL AND PLANNING 132
    Philip E. Coldwell (Member, Board of Governors, Federal
        Reserve System, Washington, D.C.)

CAPITAL NEEDS AND PLANNING 138
    James S. Hall (President, First Arkansas Bankstock
        Corporation, Little Rock, Arkansas)

CAPITAL ADEQUACY, ACCESS TO CAPITAL MARKETS,
AND FINANCIAL PLANNING 147
    William H. Dougherty, Jr. (President, North Carolina
        National Bank Corporation, Charlotte, North Carolina)

CAPITAL NEEDS IN BANKING 155
    Frederick Deane, Jr. (Chairman of the Board, Bank of
        Virginia Company, Richmond, Virginia)

MANAGING BANK INVESTMENTS 162
    Harold R. Hollister (Senior Vice President, United Missouri
        Bank of Kansas City, N.A., Kansas City, Missouri)

REAL ESTATE PROBLEM LOANS AND THE FUTURE 174
    Richard L. Kattel (Chairman and President, Citizens and
        Southern National Bank, Atlanta, Georgia)

TRUST BUSINESS 182
    Leonard W. Huck (Executive Vice President, Valley National
        Bank, Phoenix, Arizona)

THE TRUST DEPARTMENT AND THE BOARD OF DIRECTORS 194
    Richard B. Johnson (President, The Foundation of the
        Southwestern Graduate School of Banking, Southern
        Methodist University, Dallas, Texas)

EFTS AND ITS IMPLICATIONS 208
    J. D. Schiermeyer (Chairman of the Board, Bradford
        Investment Company, Fremont, Nebraska)

HOLDING COMPANIES: ONE- AND MULTI-BANK 216
    Charles E. Rice (President and Chief Executive Officer,
        Barnett Banks of Florida, Inc., Jacksonville, Florida)

NATIONAL AND INTERNATIONAL BANKING STRUCTURES 226
    Harry W. Albright, Jr. (President, The Dime Savings Bank,
        New York, New York)

APPENDIX A: CODES OF CONDUCT 233

APPENDIX B: SPECIMEN OF A STATEMENT OF LENDING POLICIES 238
        AND PROCEDURES

Preface

IN 1974, the Foundation of the Southwestern Graduate School of Banking published selected talks from the first fifteen of the Assemblies for Bank Directors. The book, *The Bank Director*, still is relevant and in demand. Since its publication, however, the scope of Assembly topics has been widened and greater emphasis has been placed on contributions which bank directors can make. The talks presented to the Assemblies of 1974-77 therefore provide materials for bank directors which usefully augment the earlier publication.

We have selected twenty-five talks from the presentations of the Sixteenth through the Twenty-sixth Assemblies. To them we have added a paper prepared for publication by the American Bankers Association, "The Trust Department and the Board of Directors," which is included in this volume with the permission of the ABA, and specimen codes of conduct and a statement of lending policies which were distributed to an Assembly as examples of policy statements.

The talks in this book were presented to Assemblies by men who head national and state bank regulatory agencies, major banks, and large industrial concerns. The success of the Assemblies, and the reflection of this success in this book, are the result of the generous contributions made by these diligent men to the Assemblies, and reflect their commitment to the highest purposes of the banking industry.

RICHARD B. JOHNSON

The Foundation of the
Southwestern Graduate School of Banking
Southern Methodist University
September, 1977

ns for Bank Directors

WILLIAM H. BOWEN

Duties and Responsibilities of Bank Directors

THE ANSWER IS IMPRECISE to the question of whether a bank director has a higher duty than his business corporation counterpart, but the circumstances of his selection, his qualification, and his duties suggest that he does. First, it is clear that banking is different from other businesses. The initial formation of a banking operation is restricted to organizing stockholders who "have the confidence of the community, are financially able to discharge the obligation resting upon [them] . . . [and who prove] that there exists a public necessity" for the bank.[1] When chartered, banks are examined in the public interest from once a year to three times in two years. They are not allowed to experience the rigors of unrestrained competition for fear that the patrons and the entire community will suffer. A vast web of legal restraints governs the nature of the business in which a bank may engage, what assets it may acquire, how much it may loan, what it may invest, what interest it may charge, and what interest it may pay. Even such a simple business promotion as premiums offered for new business is subject to a thicket of regulatory limitations. To add to the confusion, the regulations of supervisory agents who share control and supervision of banks are not always in agreement.

Consider the following differences between service on a bank board and service on a regular corporate business board.

1. Bank directors take an oath of office; business corporation directors do not (12 USC 73).

2. Bank directors have residence and citizenship requirements; their peers in business may, but often do not.[2]

3. Investment bankers may not serve as bank directors (12 USC 78); no such barrier exists in business corporations.

4. A bank director must have a financial commitment in stock own-

ership (12 USC 72); business corporate law typically exacts no such requirement of its directors.

5. Statutory machinery exists for summary prohibition of unsafe or unsound practices which bank directors permit or even are about to permit. Additionally, the bank director may be removed from office for these practices with recited statutory liability for damages that may result from willful violation of the laws—12 USC 1818 (b)(1) and (e)(2). Vague or less summary procedures, if any at all, appear in the typical business corporation codes.

6. With exceptions, national bank directors may not serve on more than one national bank board (15 USC 19); there is no such general prohibition in nonbanking corporations.

7. Criminal laws abound which expressly prohibit certain acts by bankers—embezzlement (18 USC 656), making false entries (18 USC 1005), taking fees for loans (18 USC 215), falsely certifying checks (18 USC 1004), making or granting a loan or gratuity to a bank examiner (18 USC 212), and borrowing funds entrusted to a bank under its trust powers. No such direct targeting of criminal laws confronts the business corporate director.

Clearly, the bank director is set apart for different attention, and it may be argued that a higher duty of performance and behavior is expected of him than of his business corporation peer.

Elements of the Bank Director's Duty

An understanding of the director's duty begins with his oath of office. A national bank director, in language adopted in 1864, must swear that he will "so far as the duty devolves on him, diligently and honestly administer the affairs of . . . [the bank] . . . and will not knowingly violate or willingly permit to be violated . . . provisions of the National Banking Act" (12 USC 73). Oaths of directors of state chartered banks typically track this language.

A companion provision of the National Banking Act provides that a director who knowingly violates or knowingly permits the violation of the act "shall be held liable in his person and individual capacity for all damages which . . . shall have been sustained in consequence of such violation" (12 USC 93). The oath of office and this statute create the foundation of the statutory duty and responsibility of the national bank director.[3]

Statutory Guidelines

The statutory duty of the director prohibits "knowingly" breaking the law, which, if proven, makes the director personally liable for damages that result. Breach of this duty has been declared to require "proof of something more than negligence . . . ; that is, that the violation must in effect be intentional."[4]

In *FDIC* v. *Mason*, 115 F 2nd 548 (3rd Cir. 1940), the court confronted a director's argument that he did not know dividends had been paid out of capital in breach of the law. Defalcations by officers of the bank, of which the director admitted general awareness, exceeded profits and surplus. The court noted that the bank had suffered previous embezzlements which were clear warnings of the need for a thorough and complete audit. The court decided that because the directors deliberately refrained from employing independent auditors to locate and define the extent of the losses, they "knowingly" violated the statute. Thus the rule of this case is clear. A director cannot hide behind a statutory requirement of a known violation if he deliberately turns his back on his duty to investigate facts—e.g., *Corsicana National Bank* v. *Johnson*, 251 U.S. 68, 71-72 (1919).

Common Law Burdens

The common law is ordinarily understood to embrace those principles, usages, and rules of behavior applicable in both the public and private sectors which do not rest for their authority upon any express and positive declarations of the legislature. Suits against directors quite often incorporate a broad enough charge of dereliction of duty to include a claim of common law negligence along with an allegation of statutory violations. *Bowerman* v. *Hamner*, 250 U.S. 504 (1919), was such a case. The suit alleged unlawful and negligent management of the bank. Bowerman was an outside director and the bank's largest stockholder. Three overline loans were made on which large losses were sustained, and the bank failed. Bowerman, a banker, was a director throughout the entire five-and-a-half-year life of the bank and never attended a single directors' meeting, regular or special. His justification—and the only one offered—was that he lived two hundred miles away and communication was difficult.

The evidence made clear that the bylaws requiring review by the board of bank loans were flagrantly disregarded and that the bank was grossly mismanaged. Bowerman defended on the ground that there was no evidence that he knowingly consented to the three illegal loans. Acknowledging that intentional violation of the law forbidding excess loans was not shown and had to be proven to show breach of Bowerman's statutory duty, the court continued: "While the statute furnishes the exclusive rule for determining whether its provisions have been violated or not, this does not prevent the application of the common law rule for measuring violation of common law duties."

Concluding, the court summarized:

> That ordinarily prudent and diligent men, accepting election to membership in a bank directorate, would not willfully absent themselves from directors meetings for years together, as Bowerman did, cannot be doubted; that a director who never makes or causes to be made any examination whatever of the books or papers of the bank to determine its condition, and the way in which it is being conducted, does not exercise ordinary care and prudence in the management of the affairs of the bank is equally clear; and that Bowerman, when guilty of neglect in both of these respects, did not exercise the diligence which prudent men will usually exercise in ascertaining the condition of the business of the bank, or of reasonable control and supervision over its affairs and officers, is likewise beyond discussion. He cannot be shielded from liability because of want of knowledge of wrongdoing on his part since that ignorance was the result of gross inattention in the discharge of his voluntary assumed and proper duty.

Nor is ill health an excuse for failure to attend meetings of the board. J. C. Penney, founder of the great store chain and a paragon of honesty, learned this to his sorrow. Penney was a substantial stockholder and a board member of a Florida bank which fell victim to the Florida real estate depression that led the nation into the great depression. He bought substantial amounts of preferred stock to undergird the ailing bank. On June 11, 1930, a run developed and Penney loaned the bank $880,000 to tide it over the crisis. That storm was weathered, but another developed on December 20, 1930, and the bank closed. Penney's loan had been repaid in the summer, but his deposits were increased from $171,602.13 to $485,500.87 by December 20.

Of thirty-one regular and special meetings of the bank's board of directors during Penney's service, he attended only three. He argued ill health of both himself and his wife. He pointed out his loss of very large sums of money in his attempt to save the bank without personal gain of any kind, either through dividends or otherwise. Nor was there ever a claim made against him of intentional wrongdoing. Nevertheless, the court with some sadness ruled against Mr. Penney:

The picture of the bank disclosed by the record is that of a comparatively small institution, which during its brief existence engaged in a continuing struggle against the deepening gloom of the Florida real estate depression. Hindsight suggests that it was doomed from the beginning. Nevertheless, certain of the losses should never have been incurred. One cannot be a national bank director in absentia, and we cannot condone defendant's failure to attend to the duties of an office voluntarily accepted or relieve him of responsibility for losses to the avoidance of which he should have devoted his best thought and endeavor.

In a suit against the directors of a national bank in Little Rock, Arkansas, which failed in 1894, the court summarized the learning of the cases, the common law rule, in language with a very contemporary ring:

Briefly summarized, I understand the law of this subject to be as follows:

(1) Directors are charged with the duty of reasonable supervision over the affairs of the bank. It is their duty to use ordinary diligence in ascertaining the condition of its business, and to exercise reasonable control and supervision over its affairs.

(2) They are not insurers or guarantors of the fidelity and proper conduct of the executive officers of the bank, and they are not responsible for losses resulting from their wrongful acts or omissions, provided they have exercised ordinary care in the discharge of their own duties as directors.

(3) Ordinary care in the matter as in other departments of the law, means that degree of care which ordinarily prudent and diligent men would exercise under similar circumstances.

(4) The degree of care required further depends upon the subject to which it is to be applied, and each case must be determined in view of all the circumstances.

(5) If nothing has come to the knowledge to awaken suspicion that something is going wrong, ordinary attention to the affairs of the institution is sufficient. If, upon the other hand, directors know, or by the exercise of ordinary care should have known, any facts which would awaken suspicion and put a prudent man on his guard, then a degree of care commensurate with the evil to be avoided is required, and a want of that care makes them responsible. Directors cannot, in justice to those who deal with the bank, shut their eyes to what is going on around them.

(6) Directors are not expected to watch the routine of everyday's business, but they ought to have a general knowledge of the manner in which the bank's business is conducted, and upon what securities its larger lines of credit are given and generally to know of and give direction to the important and general affairs of the bank.

(7) It is incumbent upon bank directors in the exercise of ordinary prudence, and as a part of their duty of general supervision, to cause an examination of the condition and resources of the bank to be made with reasonable frequency.[5]

Avoidance of Self-Dealing

Alfred F. Conrad, professor of law of the University of Michigan Law School, says there are two great commandments which should continuously guide a director: "To manage the company, and to act for its benefit."[6] A succinct and appropriate recitation of this second commandment appears in the monograph of the Administrator of National Banks entitled *Duties and Liabilities of Directors of National Banks* (revised June, 1972):

> Directors of a national bank are under a duty to conduct the affairs of the bank with the utmost loyalty. Breach of their duty of loyalty or good faith from which the offending directors benefit personally to the detriment of a bank exposes such directors to personal liability for the harm done the bank. Such conflicts of interest encompass the receipt by directors in their operation of the bank of personal benefits not shared with other directors of the bank.

The duty of the director to avoid self-dealing is confirmed in *Barber v. Kolowich*, 283 Mich. 97, 277 NW 189 (1930). Kolowich was president and principal stockholder of the bank. He had borrowed to his loan limit and then, by deception, caused additional money to be borrowed for his benefit without revealing to the bank the true nature of the transaction. Finding him guilty of fraud and responsible for the loss to the bank occasioned by the loan, the court ruled:

> The legislature has seen fit to permit officers and directors of a bank to borrow from that bank; . . . however, the directors and officers of any corporation stand in a fiduciary position and must deal with the corporation only in good faith, with all material facts made known to the other directors. . . . The director has the burden of proving the fairness and honesty of his dealings with the corporation. . . . These rules should be applied even more stringently to an officer and director of a bank who should be concerned with the welfare of depositors as well as that of customers and stockholders.

Measure of Damages

By statute a director is "liable in his personal and individual capacity for all damages which the association [bank], its stockholders, or any other person shall have sustained" by reason of his violation of the law (12 USC 93). At common law a director is responsible for damages which flow from his imprudent and negligent acts or omissions.[7] If, for example, the loan limit for an individual is $20,000 and he has already borrowed $20,000, then the extension of another $100,000 loan violates the law immediately upon disbursement of the funds. The measure of damages will not be limited to the excess portion but may include the whole amount plus interest less any recovery on the loans.[8]

Suppose the loan limit was $167,584.20 and loans of $20,353.89 and $10,164.31 were made the same day, when the borrower already owed $156,578.33. In *First National Bank of Lincolnwood* v. *Keller*, 318 F Supp. 339, 347 (DC 1970), the court ruled that the total of recoverable damages was the difference between the greatest amount of loans made when overline and the balance of loans outstanding before the series of overline loans was made.

In all areas of responsibility, the measure of a director's exposure to damages is typically a question of fact. Some members of a board may be exonerated because of noninvolvement or creditable behavior, while others are found guilty of negligence and subject to damages because of their imprudent errors or omissions.

JURY TRIAL DEVELOPMENTS

Willful disregard of the law makes a director expressly liable for damages that result. Negligent acts or omissions determined under common law rules make him accountable for damages that accrue because of his behavior. The suit or cause of action filed to reduce these damages to judgment are actions at law as distinguished from proceedings in equity.

Suppose a bank director for a commission or a fee uses his influence to cause a loan to be made by his bank. This breaches the law if done directly or indirectly.[9] Next, assume that a stockholder requests that the bank seek recovery of the illegal fee or commission paid to the director who had caused the loan to be made, but that the bank, subject to his control, would undertake no such action. What is the stockholder's remedy?

These simple facts provide the framework of a so-called minority stockholder's derivative suit, viewed as a suit to enforce a corporate cause of action against its officers, directors, and third parties which the corporation refused to initiate. The right to bring the suit is universally recognized as an equitable matter. Historically, the cause of action in behalf of the corporation has also been viewed as equitable in nature and not an action of law. In 1970 the United States Supreme

Court confronted the question squarely for the first time. The question specifically presented was whether the corporate right, pursued by the minority stockholder, was a common law action for which a right of jury was guaranteed by the Seventh Amendment to the Constitution.

Only one case had previously held that a jury trial was available in a minority stockholder suit—*De Pinto* v. *Provident Security Life Ins. Co.*, 323 F 2d 826 (CA 9th 1963), Certiorari Denied, 376 U.S. 950 (1964). The Supreme Court reasoned that there are two elements to a minority stockholder's suit. First, he must establish a right to sue on behalf of the corporation, which the corporation has refused to exercise. This the court confirmed was an equitable remedy. Second, when it is shown that a cause of action exists, then that action must be examined to determine whether, if brought by the corporation, it would have been a common law or equitable proceeding. If the action recognized was one traditionally brought at common law, then right to a jury trial exists.[10] A simple suit for recovery of the illegal commission is provided for by statute and would appear to be at common law. Therefore, under the *Ross* v. *Bernard* rationale it would seem that a minority stockholder could demand and obtain a jury trial in a suit for recovery of illegal commissions earned by a director.

The De Pinto case illustrates the expansion of risk, not legal exposure, that grows out of a jury trial. An advisory jury was utilized in the first De Pinto trial. That jury exonerated him. The trial judge set the verdict aside and entered a $314,794 judgment against De Pinto and other directors. This judgment was reversed on appeal and remanded for a new trial. The second jury trial was ordered by the same appellate court as of right, and this time the jury returned a verdict against De Pinto of $314,794, which was affirmed on appeal. "It appears, however, that sometime between the second and third appeals, De Pinto [a physician] went into bankruptcy—possibly because of the high costs entailed in defending the multiplicity of legal proceedings."[11]

CASE STUDIES

Negligent errors and omissions of bank directors typically occur in hurried meetings resulting from a crowded agenda, which is usually marked by dull statistical reviews of a month's operations. These errors, however, are examined by the courts in the cold leisurely hindsight of judicial review and tested in the light of what the prudent man would have done under those circumstances. The cases illustrate the jeopardy.

Direction of Management

A cardinal duty of the board of directors is the selection of management. The National Banking Laws authorize the board of directors to appoint the officers of the bank and define their duties (12 USC 24 P.Fifth). These laws anticipate that this duty shall be fulfilled each year at the organizational meeting of the board (Comptroller Interpretative Ruling 7.4400) and make clear that the board is not delegating its duties but assigning their performance (Ruling 7.4425). State banking laws are parallel.

But the board's duty does not stop there. The Supreme Court of Utah made this clear in the case of *Warren v. Robison*, 57 Pac. 287, 289 (Utah 1899):

> It does not follow that the responsibility of the board, or of the individual director, ends with the appointment of honest men to the executive offices. . . . The directors were not intended to be mere figureheads without duty or responsibility. . . . It is incumbent upon the board of directors to possess a general knowledge of the character of the transactions [of the bank] and of the manner in which they are made.

Consider this illustration of the board's duty to establish and implement operating procedures. The First National Bank of Sutton, West Virginia, was closed by the comptroller in 1914 because of insolvency, which was due in large measure to embezzlement and fraud by a vice-president who also made excessive and unwarranted loans to himself and his family. It was found that the board of directors had adopted bylaws requiring a periodic audit of the bank's affairs; but the board had failed to implement the bylaws, had failed to pass upon loans either in discount committee or in regular board meetings, and had failed to require the vice-president to be bonded for faithful performance, which was contrary to the bylaws the board had adopted.

Holding that the directors were responsible for the losses, the court ruled that mere adoption of bylaws and procedures was not enough; the board was responsible for the reasonable implementation of them.[12]

Directors Are Not Insurers

Although it is responsible for the employment of officers it believes to be competent, and while it has a continuing duty of providing direction and policy guidelines for these officers, a bank board is not an insurer of satisfactory performance. In *Hoehn v. Crews*, 144 F 2d 665, 673 (CA 10th 1944), this rule was affirmed by the following language:

> At common law directors must exercise such care as ordinarily prudent men would exercise in the administration and management of such an institution, and they will be held to a high degree of care, both to the stockholders and the general public. But a director is not an insurer and is not liable for losses resulting from his inattention. He is liable only for loss that results from his negligence.

Director's Use of Insider Knowledge

Along with the director's duty not to break the law willfully or be negligent in guiding the affairs of the bank is his duty to avoid self-dealing in his relationship with his bank. The reach of this rule was illustrated by the insolvency and failure of the Manufacturer's National Bank & Trust Company of Rockford, Illinois. On June 13, 1931, this bank closed its doors. As early as January 8 of that year the comptroller had alerted the board to the bank's unsatisfactory condition. In a letter dated May 31 he characterized the bank as being in dangerous condition. On June 12 a national bank examiner met with the board to discuss this threatened insolvency and advised that a run was likely the following Monday.

Eric S. Ekstrom was a director of this bank. He was president of the Mechanics Universal Joint Company, which patronized the bank. On June 12 his company had checking balances in the bank of $65,224.30. He drew a company check payable to a neighboring bank for $42,761.12 of this amount, which cleared the next day. Shortly after the bank closed on June 13 a receiver was appointed. He sued Ekstrom and his company and recovered a judgment, joint and several, between Ekstrom and his company, for depletion of the assets of the bank to the extent of the withdrawn funds.

Justice Brandeis delivered the opinion of the United States Supreme Court upholding the judgment:

> It is true that ordinarily a payment made by a bank to a depositor in the usual course of business is not recoverable, even though the bank was then clearly insolvent. But the payment here in question was not made in the usual course of

business; and the company was not a stranger. Its president and manager was a director of the bank; as such acquired in confidence, knowledge of its perilous condition and in violation of a statutory duty as director, used that knowledge for the purpose of preferring his company.[13]

INDEMNIFICATION

Common Law

At common law the cases are in disagreement as to the authority of a corporation to indemnify directors for the cost they incur in successfully defending a suit claiming breach of duty. An early decision from Wisconsin held that it was not improper for the corporation to pay for the defense of its directors and officers if they were not guilty of misconduct.[14] A contrary rule was announced in *New York Dry Dock Commission* v. *McCollom*, 16 NY S 2d 844 (NY Sup. Ct. 1939). The latter court reasoned that no benefit which might have been a basis for indemnity had accrued to the corporation. Some authorities view the *Dry Dock* case as an aberration, but cite little convincing authority to the contrary.[15]

Statutory Authority for Indemnification

Right or wrong, the *New York Dry Dock* case precipitated corrective legislative action. New York adopted in 1941 the first indemnification statute in the country. It was followed in 1943 by Delaware. Other states followed slowly. Arkansas incorporated a provision authorizing indemnity for litigation expenses in its corporation code adopted in 1965. The Arkansas provision was closely patterned after California and North Carolina statutes.

Two conditions are incorporated in the Arkansas statute, both of which must be satisfied before indemnity is proper: (1) The director must be successful in whole or in part in the action against him or in any compromise thereof; and (2) the court must find that his conduct fairly and equitably merits a relief.

Indemnification provisions in some state laws, as is true in Arkansas, are specifically applicable to business corporations as part of a business corporation code. The director of a state chartered bank must satisfy himself that the law of his state permits indemnification.

National Banks Have Authority

By comptroller ruling, national banks are authorized either to provide for indemnification of expenses of litigation or to expend bank funds to pay premiums with which director and officer liability insurance may be purchased. Interpretative Ruling 7.5217 reads:

> In order to secure and retain competent personnel, a national bank may amend its articles of association to provide for the indemnification of directors, officers, and other employees against legal and other expenses incurred in defending law suits brought against them by reason of the performance of their official duties.
>
> Payment of premiums for insurance covering such indemnification of officers, directors, and other employees is a permissible expense.
>
> It should be understood, however, that in order to preserve incentives for sound banking principles neither the bank's articles of association, bylaws, shareholder resolutions nor insurance shall provide for the indemnification of bank personnel who are adjudged guilty of, or liable for, willful misconduct, gross neglect of duty, or criminal acts.

Limit of Protection

Assuming that national banks have the authority to indemnify the director and to advance the legal expense incurred, there is another question having to do with the limitation of indemnification. Most statutes expressly exclude protection where a willful breach of law, civil or criminal, is involved, or where the director is found grossly negligent. Moreover, these statutes typically limit protection to payment of the director's litigation expenses. Arkansas imposes these limitations.

What about compromised settlements? Most of these derivative actions against directors are settled. Suppose the director is charged with a law violation plus common law negligence, sued for one hundred thousand dollars, and after protracted pretrial procedures and discovery—during which legal expenses mounted—the case is settled at the courthouse just before trial for ten thousand dollars. Is this settlement an oblique admission by the director that he was guilty of dereliction of duty, which would bar payment even of his expenses under a bylaw or charter provision?

There is some comfort for the director under Arkansas law, which provides for reimbursement or indemnification if he is successful in whole or in part in the action or "in any compromise thereof." The comptroller's ruling does not expressly mention protection in the event of compromise of litigation. It is believed that clarification of this particular question in the Office of the Comptroller can be obtained by a private letter ruling.

Insurance—Availability and Cost

Insurance is available to protect directors and officers within the framework permitted by law and regulation. The cost is high and is spiraling upward. Standardized rating is virtually impossible because of the complexity and variability of underwriting factors.

A well-advised bank director does not seek special advantages from his bank for his company or for the conducting of his personal business. His fee for service on the board is small and typically is payable only if he attends. He is expected to bring his business to the bank and aid in selling bank services to his friends and customers. His selection for board service is prestigious in his community and proof of his integrity and financial acumen. On balance, this recognition of leadership is the director's major reward for bank board service.

On the other hand, his correlative duties have been described as awesome. But if the same discipline, motivation, and skill which propelled him into leadership in his chosen business or profession are brought to his bank board duties, he will meet them well, and his exposure to legal liability will be slight. The following guidelines will, if observed, assure this result.

1. He must share the direction of and maintain general supervision over the bank's affairs. This direction may not be delegated, only assigned. A principal duty is the employment of a qualified chief executive officer, who is then supported in his job. Charles Agemian, chief executive officer of the Garden State National Bank, Hackensack, New Jersey, says humorously but thoughtfully that the board at each meeting should ask itself two questions: "Should we fire the president and, if so, with whom should he be replaced? If the decision is not to fire him, the next question is how could we be helpful to him in his job?"

2. Under the guidance of senior management, policies and procedures should be adopted which guarantee promotion of the well-being of the bank and, equally important, provide a full flow and complete revelation to the board of facts pertinent to happenings in the bank. The cases make clear that a director is not an ornament. If he is to serve well he must have a continuing flow of data upon which to make policy and judge management. For example, Frank Plummer, chairman of the board and chief executive officer of the

First National Bank, Montgomery, Alabama, requires his commercial loan department to maintain a list of the top twenty most troublesome loans in the bank. He presents from three to five of them to his board at each meeting, with a general status report on the loan portfolio. This contrasts with the policy of many executive officers who simply reveal a list of all loans made, with little or no detail, for after-the-fact ratification by the board.

3. An appropriate audit of the bank's operation should be provided on a regular basis. This will supplement the examination of supervisory agents. While directors are not expected to watch minutely the daily routine of the bank, they are responsible for establishment, through management, of a routine which safeguards funds of the public and investors entrusted to them. When audit and supervisory examination reports are received, they should be thoroughly reviewed by an audit or examination committee.

4. A check list of yardsticks for measuring the performance of management should be regularly reviewed. These will reveal the adequacy or inadequacy of capital funds—whether loans are proportionate to deposits, whether the investment portfolio is sound and serving its functions, whether salaries are in line with assets and operating revenues and those paid by banks in the market area of like size and circumstance, whether the return on capital is fair, and whether loan losses are reasonable or excessive. If management feels put upon by requests for ways and means to measure its performance, then perhaps Mr. Agemian's first question should be answered affirmatively and a search for a new chief executive officer begun.

5. In all circumstances, the director must be satisfied in light of his experience that proposals submitted to the bank board for approval make common sense. The directors and management can and will make mistakes. These mistakes do not constitute negligence. But where a course of action violates rules of common sense and prudent behavior, a warning should be expressed.

6. A director at all times must avoid self-dealing. "He should not, for example, seek a loan at less than going rate; nor should he seek an unsound loan from the bank at any interest rate. He should not collect from the bank unjustified fees, salaries, or other payments for services or goods. He should eschew 'insider trading.'"[16]

7. Making policy and administering it are different. Directors cannot and should not manage the bank. Their duty is to employ sound

management, provide for succession, and give management a reasonably free hand (with their support) in executing policy. The sound and reasonable director will have little trouble knowing where to draw the line between interference with management and abdication of duty to guide.

8. Banking laws must be understood and observed. A periodic legal review of policies and procedures is a help and safeguard against an unwitting violation.

9. A bank charter is a license to serve a community and beneficially influence its economy. A discerning director will work at maintaining a balanced view of his responsibility to investor, depositor, and community, insuring on the whole that the economic well-being of all is served.

Why does the bank director serve? Because his reward comes from personal satisfaction of a job well done, the supportive friendship of his peers on the board, and the knowledge that his service is viewed in his community as evidence of business and professional leadership. An awareness of his legal duty and liability should motivate him to work at this important job and will not deter him from service.

Notes

1. *Ark. Stats. Anno.* Sec. 67-303.1; *Acts of Arkansas* (1969), Act 179, Sec. 1.

2. "Directors need not be residents of the State or shareholders of the corporation unless the articles of corporation or bylaws so require." *Ark. Stats. Anno.* (1947), Sec. 64-301.

3. As a general proposition, the varied state laws detailing responsibility of bank directors of state chartered banks are comparable. This statutory duty is one of at least two bases of liability. Another basis is one at common law "for failure to exercise that degree of care which ordinarily diligent and prudent men would exercise under the circumstances"—Michelson v. Penny, 135 F. 2d 409, 417 (2d Cir. 1943). A third basis seems to invoke a little higher duty than either of the first two, and that is the duty of the director to avoid self-dealing with his bank. See Barber v. Kolowich, 282 Mich. 143, 277 NW 189 (1938).

4. Yates v. Jones National Bank, 206 U.S. 158, 160 (1906).

5. Rankin v. Cooper, 149 F 1010, 1013 (W.D. Ark. 1907).

6. Conard, Mace, Blough, and Gibson, "Functions of Directors under the Existing System," *Business Lawyer*, February 1972, pp. 23, 25.

7. Rankin v. Cooper, 149 F 1010, 1017 (8th Cir. 1907).

8. Corsicana National Bank v. Johnson, 251 U.S. 68, 87-88 (1919).

9. 18 USC 215. United States v. Harlan Lane, 464 F 2d. 593 (CA 8th 1972).

10. Ross v. Bernard, 396 U.S. 531 (1970).

11. Cary and Harris, "Standards of Conduct under Common Law, Present Day Statutes and the Model Act," *Business Lawyer*, February 1972, pp. 61, 69.

12. Gamble v. Brown, 29 F 2d. 366 (CA 4th 1928).
13. Mechanics Universal Joint Co. v. Culhane, 229 U.S. 51, 56-57 (1936).
14. Figge v. Bergenthal, 110 NW 798 (Wisc. 1906).
15. Klink, Chalif, Bishop, and Arsht, "Liabilities Which Can Be Covered under State Statutes and Corporate Bylaws," *Business Lawyer*, February 1972, p. 107.
16. "A Bank Director's Job," *Banking*, 13th ed. (Washington, D.C.: American Bankers Association, 1970), pp. 8-9.

EDWARD B. CLOSE, JR.

Recent Developments in Director Liability

PAYING ATTENTION to the job of being a bank director and finding out on a continuing basis what is expected of a director are the first important steps in practicing preventive law, as far as our own prospective liability and that of our company is concerned. Because of the tremendous increase in litigation to which both corporations and directors have been subjected, preventive law has become more and more important in the minds of today's top management. We are currently in a very litigious period in our history, a period of the coming of age of Section 10(b) and of class actions, shareholders derivative suits, and litigation inspired by consumers, equal rights, etc. Even if in the United States the basic theories of director liability have not really changed all that much over the last fifty years or so—and a pretty good argument can be made for this opinion—the exposure, the chance of getting hit, and the expense in defending lawsuits have all increased so greatly that in order to protect ourselves and our corporations we as directors must view our duties and responsibilities, and their discharge, in this modern context. If we do not, our occupations as corporate board members will indeed be dangerous.

In recent years there have been a few civil cases and a good many criminal cases under the federal banking laws involving bank directors' liability, yet none of these cases would qualify as a landmark case or one which has significantly changed the law regarding the civil or criminal liability of bank directors. None of several articles I have found—such as Jack Chambers's "Legal Responsibilities of Bank Directors" in *Selected Talks from the 21st and 22nd Assemblies for Bank Directors* (1975), or Gerald T. Dunne and Robert H. Fabian on the same subject in *The Bank Director* (1974)—which summarize the responsibilities, rights, liabilities, etc., of bank directors, mention any recent cases as being especially significant. Dunne, in the March 1976 issue of the *Banking Law Journal*, does state, however, that the old standby and celebrated 1891 case of *Briggs* v. *Spaulding* is "rapidly tottering." If so, the blow which will make it fall has not yet been struck. In the *Briggs* case, the United States Supreme Court established the "reasonable directors test" in determining the liability of national bank directors for other than willful and knowing violations of the law. This test is apparently also used by most state courts for their state banks. The case refered to in the article by Dunne is the 1967 case of *Heit* v. *Bisby*, but that is not a bank directors' case. *Heit* v. *Bisby* holds that although a director of a corporation is not normally liable for misconduct by a codirector where he has not participated in the misconduct, he may be liable when he totally abdicates his duties to codirectors. Reliance on the apparent trustworthiness of his codirectors may not be a defense for such negligence. In fact, there has been very little printed recently concerning the civil liability of bank directors. But, of course, what happens to nonbank directors is vitally important to us.

Probably the most significant securities case of 1976, which many commentators believe will have considerable impact, is *Ernst & Ernst* v. *Hochfelder*, decided by the United States Supreme Court in March, 1976. Briefly, the case involves an action against the well-known public accounting firm of Ernst & Ernst, alleging that the firm was negligent in auditing First Securities Company and thus aided its president in his fraudulent activities. These fraudulent activities consisted primarily of his not investing customers' funds where he said they had been invested. Plaintiffs sued Ernst & Ernst under Section 10(b) of the Securities Exchange Act of 1934, and Rule 10b-5 promulgated thereunder. Prior to the decision in this case, the tendency of the courts was to disregard intent and accept mere negligence on the part of a defendant as sufficient to make him liable in a private Section 10(b) case. The Supreme Court made it pretty clear, however, that for a plaintiff to recover under Section 10(b) or Rule 10b-5 he must prove that defendant had an intent to defraud, manipulate, or deceive. Certainly, defendant Ernst & Ernst was not a director, but an outside, independent professional. Also, the court left open the question of whether in some circumstances reckless behavior would be sufficient to evidence a "mental state embracing intent to deceive, manipulate or defraud." For the time being, at least, it seems that there should be fewer plaintiffs' suits under 10(b) without proof of such mental state embracing intent to deceive. I say fewer with some apprehension, because many plaintiff suits against corporations and/or their directors and officers are filed not with the expectation that the case will be tried on its merits, but for the purpose of effecting a settlement prior to such trial.

Another very important case decided by the United States Supreme Court on June 14, 1976, was *TSC Industries, Inc. v. Northway, Inc.* This case determined the standard of materiality as it applies to the proxy rules of the 1934 Exchange Act prohibiting the issuance of a proxy statement which is false or misleading with respect to any material fact. In its decision in this case the court stated that the general standard of materiality which comports with the policies of the proxy rule is that

> an omitted fact is material if there is substantial likelihood that a reasonable shareholder would consider it important in deciding how to vote. . . . It does not require proof of a substantial likelihood that disclosure of the omitted fact would have caused the reasonable investor to change his vote. What the standard does contemplate is a showing of a substantial likelihood that, under all the circumstances, the omitted fact would have assumed actual significance in the deliberations of the reasonable shareholder. Put another way, there must be a substantial likelihood that the disclosure of the omitted fact would have been viewed by the reasonable investor as having significantly altered the "total mix" of information made available.

The court also stated:

> The potential liability for a violation can be great indeed, and if the standard of materiality is unnecessarily low, not only may the corporation and its management be subjected to liability for insignificant omissions or misstatements, but also management's fear of exposing itself to substantial liability may cause it simply to bury the shareholder in an avalanche of trivial information—a result which is hardly conducive to informed decision making. These dangers are presented, we think, by the definition of a material fact adopted by the Court of Appeals in this case—a fact which a reasonable shareholder might consider important. We agree with Judge Friendly, speaking for the Court of Appeals in the *Gerstle* case that "might" is too suggestive of mere possibility, however unlikely.

This definition of materiality is very welcome and must be considered a plus in the area of limiting potential director liability.

The recent 1976 case of *Kamin v. American Express* is also helpful.

This case basically stands for the proposition that if stockholders do not approve of the directors' good-faith decisions, they should express their disagreement within the corporation and not burden the courts with expensive time-consuming lawsuits. The court stated that there should not be judicial interference with business decisions unless there is a "clear case made out of fraud, oppression, arbitrary action or breach of trust."

The 1974 Employee Retirement Income Security Act has created new areas of responsibility. ERISA, as it is called, is the federal law intended to protect millions of employees and their dependents covered by several hundred thousand private pension plans. Many, if not all, banks have some form of pension plan and trust. The problem here for directors is that so far there are virtually no precedents to guide us. We are therefore at the mercy of the particular judge before whom we may find ourselves, answering and defending against allegations of violations of the act. This should be fertile ground for plaintiffs seeking to recoup from wealthy directors what they may have lost as a result of a down market, such as the one recently experienced. Undoubtedly, most of your pension plans have been amended to conform to ERISA. But, if you are like me, that is about all you have done, and you have not yet gotten around to finding out whether as a director you are among that group of fiduciaries upon which ERISA imposes a uniform standard to discharge certain duties. For instance, the Act provides in Section 404 that "a fiduciary must discharge his duties . . . for the exclusive purpose of providing benefits . . . with the care, skill, prudence and diligence . . . that a prudent man acting in a like capacity and familiar with such matters would use in the conduct of an enterprise of a like character and a like aim. . . ." If you are such a fiduciary, then you had better find out what those duties are that you must carry out in such an exacting manner. And how about those words "familiar with such matters." As one commentator has expressed it, "Does it mean familiar with your primary duty as a director of choosing the trustee, or does it mean familiar with formulating investment policies of pension funds?" I don't know the answer, and it is possible that only a court can give us the answer unless the act is amended by Congress.

Dealing with the matter of exculpatory provisions and insurance, Section 410 of the act provided that, with certain exceptions,

(a) Any provision in an agreement or instrument which purports to relieve a fiduciary from responsibility or liability for any responsibility, obligation, or duty under this part shall be void as against public policy. (b) Nothing in this subpart shall preclude (1) a pension plan from purchasing insurance for its fiduciaries or for itself to cover liability or losses occurring by reason of the act or omission of a fiduciary, if such insurance permits recourse by the insurer against the fiduciary in the case of a breach of a fiduciary obligation by such fiduciary; (2) a fiduciary from purchasing insurance to cover liability under this part from and for his own account; or (3) an employer or an employee organization from purchasing insurance to cover potential liability of one or more persons who serve in a fiduciary capacity with regard to an employee benefit plan.

There is also (Sec. 405 of the act) liability on a fiduciary for breach of fiduciary responsibility of a co-fiduciary if he knowingly participates in, undertakes to conceal an improper act of such co-fiduciary, or if he, in effect, through negligence enables such co-fiduciary to commit a breach; or if he has knowledge of a breach by such co-fiduciary, unless he makes reasonable efforts under the circumstances to remedy the breach. Since the majority of directors' and officers' liability policies today exclude liabilities arising under ERISA, most banks are now purchasing surcharge liability policies to protect the bank and bank officers and directors against alleged wrongful acts in acting as bank trustee under "outside" plans. Also, banks are purchasing fiduciary employee benefit liability insurance to protect the administration of the bank's own pension plan. This would normally also include protection for all other benefit plans, such as group life insurance. These policies are expensive and carry a deductible of from $10,000 to $50,000 per loss, depending on the type of insurance and other factors.

Another recent development which could affect a director's liability is the adoption by the FDIC of new regulations covering "insider transactions." These regulations became effective May 1, 1976, and are designed to curb abuses which might occur in transactions between an insured state nonmember commercial bank and insiders of the bank. This was brought about, according to the FDIC, because abusive self-dealing has been a significant contributing factor in more than half of all the banks that have collapsed since 1960, and because a review of existing and past problem bank cases indicates that such self-dealing is a significant source of difficulty. The regulation establishes procedures to insure that bank boards of directors supervise such transactions effectively to enable the FDIC examiners to identify and analyze such transactions. It was reported in *Federal Banking Law Reports* that Congressman Henry Reuss of the House Banking, Currency, and Housing Committee in Washington, while praising the FDIC for adopting the regulation, criticized the attitude of the Federal Reserve Board and the comptroller of the currency as "complacent and lackadaisical" on insider transactions by banks.

According to the FDIC, the new regulations cover loans or other extensions of credit, purchases of assets or services from the bank, sale of assets or services to the bank, use of the bank's real or personal property or personnel, leases of property to or from the bank, payment of commissions and fees by the bank for brokerage, management services, consulting or legal or architectural services, and interest payments on deposits of $100,000 or more. These activities are all subject to board review and management reporting procedures, and the list may be expanded from time to time.

A transaction with an insider must be reviewed and approved by the board of directors if it involves assets or services of more than $20,000 for banks of up to $100 million in total assets; $50,000 for those with assets between $100 million and $500 million; and $100,000 for those with more than $500 million in total assets. Transactions must be shown to be arm's length in nature, and the bank will have to maintain records which will be readily accessible to examiners.

Developments also increase the need to be aware of the responsibility to "disclose." The comptroller of the currency has proposed regulations establishing minimum standards of disclosure applicable to all public offerings and sales of securities by national banks. The proposal would substantially expand the existing disclosure requirements of the comptroller's regulations, requiring that detailed offering circulars acompany equity and debt issues of new and existing national banks. Acording to the comptroller, "the proposed disclosure guideline standards are intended to accommodate and facilitate their utilization by smaller banks seeking to avail themselves of the public capital markets." Apparently the comptroller has stated that use of the circulars would not impose undue burdens on smaller banks. It is true that an exemption from the regulation is provided for "a public offering by a bank of its securities where the offering, when aggregated with the amount of all offerings of the bank's securities in the immediately preceding twelve-month period, does not exceed $100,000." This presumably will help very small banks. But in other cases where there is no exemption provided, the preparation of the circular will be a relatively major expense to small banks seeking the public capital markets. The present regulations are not applicable to the offer and sale of equity securities by existing banks; they apply only to debt securities. If the proposed regulations are adopted, however, a public offering of its equity securities by a national bank will result in additional expense. Whether, in a particular case, this will translate itself into "an undue burden," only time will tell, but I suspect that it will.

The proposed substantial expansion of existing disclosure requirements is very healthy and should be looked upon by bank directors as being helpful, in a preventative way, in avoiding liability. As the comptroller has pointed out, while securities of banks are exempt from registration requirements of Section 5 of the Securities Act of 1933, the offer and sale of such securities are nevertheless subject to the antifraud provision of Section 7(a) of the 1933 Act, and, of course, Section 10(b) of the Exchange Act of 1934 and Rule 10b-5 thereunder.

Directors and Officers Liability Insurance also deserves consideration. The comptroller of the currency authorizes, as a permissible expense, the payment of premiums for insurance covering indemnification if such director, officer, or other employee is adjudged guilty of, or liable for, willful misconduct, gross neglect of duty, or criminal acts. There are still five markets available for the purchase of such insurance, all situated to a large extent in London. The policies are still being written for three years, although they are cancelable at any time by the underwriter on short notice. The usual policy actually consists of two inseparable policies. One reimburses the bank whenever it indemnifies its directors and officers for their losses, including legal fees entailed when they are sued for doing—or not doing—something in the course of their business activities. The other policy reimburses the directors and officers for such losses whenever those executives are not indemnified by the bank.

Not so very long ago it was possible to shop around at policy renewal time for a lower premium, even with the same company. This is certainly not so true today. The best way to obtain or renew such a policy is to pick a good knowledgeable broker in the field and have that broker negotiate for the policy, rather than ask for bids based on a set of specifications. But however this insurance is obtained, obtaining it is extremely important today. The defense costs alone of defending a class action, even only up to the point where a judge decides whether the case should be tried as a class action, are very large. Without this type of insurance I shudder to guess how many honest, competent men and women would desert the boardroom, and this would not do business or our country any good at all.

The average payment to successful claimants under D&O policies rose to $865,000 in 1975, up about $100,000 from 1974, according to a Wyatt Company study. According to a report, there has been a general trend toward a tightening of the market for D&O. The banks have a special problem. Some banks have been involved in situations where municipalities have verged on bankruptcy. Loans have been in default; some banks have sponsored REITS and as a result premiums for renewal have been high, and, according to one source, the capacity of the market has been limited. In a recent New York placement, a $50 million policy which had expired could only be renewed to the extent of $25 million. Any excess above this would command, if available, much higher premiums. Also, the tendency may well be to impose more and more restrictive terms and conditions. For instance, the D&O excludes anything having to do with ERISA and there is now apparently and understandably the exclusion of claims in the area of illegal foreign payoffs, etc.

Where does all this leave us today? No one has to reach out too far to scare anybody into wondering whether being a bank director or a director of any public corporation is worth it. Articles like "The 'Legal Explosion' Has Left Business Shell-Shocked" in *Fortune Magazine* (1973) are not untrue, and perhaps not even exaggerated. But we have not seen a vast exodus of the people who serve the boards of our great corporations. We have all heard corporate counsel tell us about the staggering liabilities which can befall us for such things as material misstatements and omissions in proxy statements, registration statements, and the like. BarCris is still with us, and probably always will be. But if a person serving as a director knows his duties and obligations, refuses to be passive in carrying them out, carries them out with common sense, is honest and fair and reasonable, refuses to rubber stamp everything or blindly go along with management, and, of course, is adequately covered by D&O and other insurance, then—putting it all in perspective—the odds are way in his favor.

KENNETH L. ROBERTS

What Management Expects of Bank Directors

FROM THE PERSPECTIVE of an inside director and chief executive of a bank with more than $1 billion in deposits, I see in such an organization the roles of inside and outside directors as being perhaps more formalized than those in a smaller bank; but regardless of the size of the institution, there are certain underlying principles which should guide the actions of directors. Perhaps some of the greatest frictions that develop between managers and their outside directors result from a failure of either or both to appreciate properly their respective roles. Thus, the first thing that each should expect from the other is a proper understanding of those roles. What are the legal distinctions between management (members of senior management who are also inside directors) and outside directors? While my point of view is from the standpoint of the national banker, I believe the precepts governing state banks are similar.

Directors of national banks are charged by 12 U.S.C.71 to manage their affairs as follows: "The affairs of each association shall be managed by not less than five directors. . . . The directors shall hold office for one year, and until their successors are elected and have qualified."

While this statement indicates that directors shall manage, nevertheless, 12 U.S.C.24 permits the exercise of corporate powers through duly authorized officers and agents: "Seventh. To exercise by its Board of Directors or its duly elected officers or agents, subject to law, all such incidental powers as shall be necessary to carry on the business of banking. . . ."

Further, the comptroller of the currency, in Interpretative Ruling 7.4425, allows the following assignments of directors' responsibilities: "The president of the bank shall be a member of the board and shall be the chairman thereof, but the board may designate a director in lieu of the president to be chairman of the board, who shall perform such duties as may be designated by the board."

Taken together, these statements are generally understood to mean that while directors (inside and outside) collectively have the ultimate responsibility for the management of the bank, they should select from among their number a president, who would then be the equivalent of managing director. The president, along with other officers and agents designated by him, would be assigned the responsibilities of the managerial functions necessary to carry on the business of banking. The president is accountable to his fellow members on the full board for the performance of these duties.

The guidelines also signify that the role of the president is not antagonistic to the board; rather, his first responsibility is that of a director; his second that of an officer. This leads to several conclusions concerning the respective roles of inside and outside directors:

The president and other officers should manage, i.e., plan, control, organize, and lead; the board should oversee management in the performance of these duties.

A good president remembers that his first obligation is to his board, and he sees to it that his fellow board members are provided with sufficient information to assure themselves that their duties, which have been assigned to the president, are being effectively performed.

Good outside directors remember that they have assigned managerial responsibilities to the president and do not undertake to involve themselves directly in management unless they individually or collectively wish to challenge the president in the performance of his assigned duties. Rather, they involve themselves in formulating general policy and monitoring and overseeing management's performance.

Regardless of the size of the institution, failure to understand and observe these distinctions will result in conflict and a poorly managed bank. Conversely, a proper observance of these distinctions by both inside and outside directors will lead to mutual respect and successful management.

Problems generally arise when outside directors seek to involve themselves directly in operating matters, because (a) such actions have the effect of undermining management in the performance of its duties; and (b) such actions make the director, not management, accountable, therefore tending to expose the director to a greater potential liability than he has been informed about or is prepared to accept.

For example, while the board is certainly responsible for policies governing asset management (principally the extension of credit and the making of investments) it should not involve itself in direct credit or investment decisions that have been otherwise designated within management's authority. It can review, criticize, and monitor conformance to policy, and it can even repeal authority; but if board members, individually or collectively, seek to make specific credit or investment decisions that are otherwise within management's authority, this will lead to ineffective and uninformed decisions.

While the board, or an appropriate committee, is responsible for overall personnel policies and direction, it should not involve itself directly in personnel administration. The outside director who seeks to hire, fire, promote, punish, reward, or otherwise direct or influence the activities of the personnel of the organization (other than through duly authorized management) has transcended his responsibilities and assumed the duties of management.

While the board is clearly interested in the external communications and image of the bank, the board member who presumes to speak for the bank or commit the bank to outsiders for any reason, or to mold the image of the bank to his own liking, without the clear direction of the board, has assumed a role directly contrary to that of management.

There are other examples. The point is that while management expects direction from the board, it does not expect the board to intermeddle in managerial functions which have been assigned to it. If the board does not agree with management's actions in these and other areas, it should either cause management to take corrective action or replace management.

On the other hand, conflicts also arise when management forgets its responsibility to the board and presumes to act autonomously. For example, the executive who acts, for whatever reason, beyond his duly delegated authority in any area has violated his obligation to the board. The president who, even though technically acting within authority, assumes a course he knows contradicts the policies and direction approved by the board will precipitate unneeded conflict. The manager who does not recommend policies to his board, preferring to act without policy constraints, has undermined the responsibility of his fellow directors. He should assist the board in formulating policy where it is not clear.

Here also there are other examples, but the point is that while the outside directors should expect and permit their designated managers to manage, they should not expect or permit them to act autocratically and contrary to policy.

The first thing, then, that both outside and inside directors should expect from each other is a proper understanding of their roles. They should appreciate both their common obligations as board members and the distinctions between them as outside and inside directors. Both inside and outside directors of a bank should constantly assay the performance of their respective roles by asking themselves (a) am I properly performing the particular duties and responsibilities expected of me? and (b) if not, why should I not be asked to resign?

The character of a bank is, to a large extent, exemplified by the characteristics of its directors. The director must have a strong orientation to community service and an appreciation for the responsibilities inherent therein. A bank is a unique organization in its community. While it is organized for profit, it is significantly different from other business organizations. It has the high responsibility of receiving the resources of the community and then reallocating them. Therefore, it is clearly affected with a public interest and accordingly is highly regulated. The director must be prepared to accept this regulation. In fact, he takes an oath to this end.

The foundation of successful banking is integrity. People expect their bankers to be sound, upright, honest persons. The most essential characteristic of any bank director, therefore, is that he be a person of the highest integrity. He should have an unblemished reputation. All of his actions should be open, honest, and above reproach. I have heard it expressed that a good test for the conduct of any bank director is whether or not he would be willing to have any of his actions or words with respect to the bank described in the local newspaper. Would they reflect discredit upon himself or the bank? While this may be too difficult a test, nevertheless it should be a guideline for all our actions. A bank director must submit himself to the public view, to a higher degree than directors of other institutions.

In many respects, bank directors are fiduciaries rather than simply business directors. They hold the resources of their community in trust. Thus, they, more than most business and professional men, should expect to be held to high standards of conduct.

It goes without saying that a bank director should possess no interest which would conflict, in either a general or specific way, with his role as director. In the event that such an interest or activity should arise, he should immediately excuse himself from any board action which would raise even the remotest question that his decision might be hampered by conflict of interest.

Good bank directors must be men of objectivity and courage. They must be willing to face hard facts realistically and have the courage to make tough decisions with respect to those facts, regardless of the unpleasantness that may be involved. Particularly, they must prevent bias from entering into any of their decisions. Of course, they should be conservative and prudent men. A bank by its very nature should reflect conservatism and prudence, and this is best exemplified by the characteristics of the directors. This does not mean stodgy. While being conservative, a good director can, and should, at the same time be progressive. That is, he should be alert to the changes going on in business, in community life, and in the realm of banking. He should be willing to advance his own ideas and support sound new ideas advanced by management. He should not simply allude to the way things were done in the past. With the fluidity and dynamism of modern banking, a flexible mind is probably one of the most important attributes of a bank director. Today, if you just try to keep up with new developments, you are probably already way behind.

Confidentiality is one of the keystones of an effective banking business. Bank directors must be men who know how to keep confidential the vital information to which they are exposed in board and committee meetings. A person who cannot maintain a confidence has absolutely no place on a bank board.

A good bank director should be a man of restraint. While a position on a major bank's board is generally one of prestige in the community, this should not lead to an inflated ego on the part of the person serving as a director. Board members should not take advantage of their positions to seek any special treatment from either the bank or the community. They should not seek to use their board positions for self-enhancement.

Of course, the director should be a financially responsible person who maintains his own and his company's affairs in excellent order. If the director cannot do this, how can he set the example of financial responsibility that is clearly necessary for the bank to be successful?

The director should be a strong, vigorous person capable of exercising his faculties to the fullest in the furtherance of the bank's interest. If the director cannot be alert and give the time and energy necessary to support the bank's activities, he should not participate. In no sense should a director outlive his usefulness. This is not determined by age alone. I know some people who are senile at forty and others who are vigorous at seventy.

While these characteristics and attributes may sound impossible to achieve, I believe they represent certain basic standards by which all directors, both inside and outside, should compare themselves. I, therefore, expect directors to have these attributes, and they should expect the same of me in even higher degree.

What should management expect from outside directors with respect to their knowledge, involvement, and activity in the affairs of the bank? The director should be knowledgeable about the objectives of the bank, as they are presented by management, and express his approval or disapproval thereof. If the majority of the directors does not agree with the goals and objectives of the bank, the board should cause either the objectives or management to be changed. Conversely, if a board member cannot agree with the majority of his fellow directors on what those goals should be, he should either accommodate himself to them or resign.

However expressed, it is my personal belief that the philosophy undergirding all bank objectives should be a commitment to excellence. Simply stated, this means that in whatever the bank undertakes it should seek to do its best. It should not try to be all things to all people if doing so leads to mediocrity in some areas. Within this framework the essential objectives of any banking organization should be first, soundness; second, profitability; and third, growth. In a well-managed organization there can be an optimum balance of these areas which can lead to superior results in all three.

Whenever conflict arises among these three objectives, however, priorities should clearly be in the order indicated. If the bank's soundness is assured, it will be able to reflect the public confidence necessary for it to profit and grow. If it maintains consistent profitability, it will further enhance its soundness through the addition of retained earnings to capital. If it is both sound and consistently profitable, its continued growth should follow. Why? Because soundness and profitability cannot be maintained without good management and a commitment to excellent services. These factors will clearly lead to continued growth. Management should lead its directors to understand the delicate balance between these objectives on all critical issues.

A director should be in regular attendance at board and committee meetings. If he is not, how can he exercise his responsibilities? Further, he should be willing to spend enough time at meetings or between meetings to assure himself that he is knowledgeable about the direction and policies of the bank. At meetings the director should be alert, attentive, and, where appropriate, he should ask questions. The director who asks relevant, direct questions can perform a great service, both to management and to his fellow board members. On the other hand, the director who asks gossipy and irrelevant questions generally confuses and delays the meetings. Directors should keep management on its toes by being critics, but they should always preserve the fine line between constructive and negative criticism. The outside director who is antagonistic for the sake of building up his own self-esteem generally demeans himself rather than management. I also expect directors to be good listeners as well as good questioners. If management makes good presentations to the board, directors can learn much if they listen. Managers must also listen and be willing to accept constructive criticism.

The director should learn as much as he possibly can about the business of banking. This knowledge is achieved by asking questions, reading relevant materials, and attending seminars. It is the responsibility of management to provide the directors with sufficient data to help broaden their knowledge of banking. The directors, however, should not expect to be, or hold themselves out as, professional bankers. Directors should know their own business well and know the difference between that business and banking. A director who brings constructive ideas from his own activities to assist in the better management of the bank makes a valuable contribution. The director, however, who fails or refuses to see the difference between his business and that of banking can render a disservice if he pushes too hard the point: "This is the way we do it."

The director, of course, must be a shareholder and should be as large a one as possible. As a representative of other shareholders he should reflect a significant awareness of their interests. We should remember, however, that his main mission as a director is to advance the cause of the bank and not his own investment in it. He should never act from the motive of enhancing his own investment if it would not otherwise be a sound action for the bank. The director should promote the bank. He should be a salesman for the bank and comment favorably upon it at all times to all parties where appropriate. He should, of course, have his own business with the bank, do his best to bring other businesses into it, and generally advance its cause. If a director cannot speak well of the bank, he should not speak ill. If he has negative comments about the bank, he should, in the board or committee meetings, direct them toward constructive actions to eliminate the reasons for those comments. He should never carry negativism outside the bank to the public. If he cannot resolve his objections, he should resign.

I believe management and directors should get to know each other on a personal basis. Each needs to know what is on the other's mind. If they are to work together as a team, they should understand each others' philosophies, attitudes, and approaches. They should share problems with each other, thereby assisting each other to perform their respective roles more effectively.

In summary, if management and outside directors understand and respect the other's role; if they openly, honestly, and constructively seek to help each other meet their responsibilities; if they conduct themselves at all times with the highest integrity; if they always expect the best of each other; then, while there may be conflicts, they should not be deep-seated ones. Rather, they should be able to work collectively as a successful team to meet their full responsibilities to the public at large, to their shareholders, to their customers, and to their employees. When this happy situation occurs, the bank should be assured of continued soundness, profitability, and growth.

EDWIN JONES

What Bank Directors Expect of Management

HAVING SERVED on the boards of three banks, one of them a small local bank, I have seen the different attitudes and approaches that management takes in informing its directors and using their talents. It is one of management's major responsibilities to stockholders to select as strong a board of directors as possible. An effective board is not a figurehead but a functioning group of capable, sensible, and successful people elected because of their qualifications and experience. Management does not need friends and yes-men as directors. I am not giving idle advice in making this statement. Last year in our company (J. A. Jones Construction Company) the first three outside directors were elected. None of them were close friends with anyone in our organization. All were chosen because of the expertise and experience that they brought to the board. All of them were men that I felt would have the courage to challenge management and vote their own convictions. Be assured that it took some courage on my part to nominate these men. It was the right thing to do, and I look forward to adding more outside directors to our board.

It is a responsibility of management to indoctrinate new directors, and I judge management by the degree of thoroughness with which it carries out indoctrination. At the time he is asked to serve and prior to his being elected to the board, a new director should be informed of the liabilities and responsibilities of a bank director. In this way he will know what is expected of him so that there will be no surprises for him or for management later on. A complete indoctrination should take place soon after he is elected and should include (1) a complete and thorough review of the bank's organizational structure (if it is a bank holding company, the review should include the subsidiaries as well as the holding company); (2) the distribution of copies of all policies so that the director may become familiar with them and understand the reasons behind them; (3) a discussion of the organization of the board of directors and the function of each committee; (4) a quick summary of each department's operations, going into as much detail as the new director has time for and interest in; and (5) a discussion and analysis of the most recent bank examiner's report.

The new director should know that committee work is necessary to review the actions of officers and to formulate policies to guide the officers. Committees also have the responsibility to see that sufficient reports are brought to the full board so that all members are thoroughly familiar with the bank's operations and can intelligently approve new policies. In addition to being told the functions of the various committees during the first year, the new director would benefit if he could sit in as observer on at least one meeting of each committee.

One of management's greatest challenges is to use the talents of the board effectively. Directors can contribute in a number of significant ways without overstepping their role. With this in mind, management should utilize board meetings to inform the directors, as well as to seek their guidance. But in utilizing the talents of its directors, management should not confine itself strictly to board meetings. Management is not expected to check with one or more directors before making a decision, but why not use directors' knowledge whenever it would be appropriate and helpful to do so? For instance, management is missing a golden opportunity if it fails to use directors to help solicit key accounts, select new directors, advise on whether to work out a loan or just write it off, or consult on matters of policy that are being considered—all matters in which an individual director's knowledge and experience would be helpful.

All agenda should be in the hands of board members at least seven days prior to a meeting. Copies of all resolutions, along with adequate backup information, should also be provided in advance. If directors are not given such information at least a week ahead of time, any action on the matter should be postponed until the next meeting. It is crucial that management furnish full and complete information in advance of the meeting. Otherwise it is asking the board to make decisions without having ample time to study and research the matter. Management has often taken weeks, months, and sometimes years to develop the case for a recommended action, yet directors are often asked to think for a few minutes and then vote on it. This is not a sensible way to do things. Moreover, the board's function is not to witness a dog and pony show and then routinely rubber-stamp the recommendations of management.

There are, of course, potential problems in providing information ahead of time. Sensitive or confidential material could be involved. There is the possibility of inside trading. Neither of these possibilities will occur if management has done a proper job in selecting qualified board members, for the honesty and integrity of directors must be stressed before election. Furthermore, the initial indoctrination of a director will have made it clear that management will automatically seek the removal of and take legal action against any director found guilty either of misconduct involving the leaking of information to others or of inside trading based on confidential information.

Another item that should be included in board meetings has to do with the bank's personnel. Meetings should be planned so that every department has the opportunity to present its story at least once a year. A least two representatives from each department should participate in this presentation. This will give the directors knowledge of the operations and some idea of the depth of talent in various departments. It will also give the employees an excellent opportunity to know the director and to learn more about the board and its function. The opportunity to meet in this way with the board should be rotated among appropriate individuals and the younger officers in various departments.

While the suggestions I have made thus far would probably not create strong disagreement, my recommendations having to do with disclosure are very likely to be the most controversial. I believe that the board should be furnished explicit information on these lines of credit and the use thereof by each director and top officer of the bank. This disclosure would extend to family members as well as to any companies or partnerships with which directors and officers have significant ties.

Disclosure information would include the minimum net worth of each individual, the repayment schedule of any loans, the status of loans (are they current?), and the minimum income or earnings. I said minimum with regard to earnings because I recognize that individuals with substantial wealth or income might not wish to disclose their full worth. However, if substantial unsecured loans are being made to individuals or to their companies, all directors should be made aware of this so that they will be in a better position to evaluate and guide the decisions and actions of management.

The policies of the bank should be developed by management and approved by the board. Specifically, they should include:

1. Retirement of directors.
2. Attendance required of directors.
3. Ground rules for loans. The loan policy should provide for diversification and should be designed to serve the community's needs as well as those of the bank. The bank should pursue collection of loans charged off. In establishing a loan policy, a bank should take into consideration the size and skills of the bank, the location of the bank and, therefore, the needs of the community served by the bank.

Limits on loan authority need to be set and reviewed on a regular basis to make sure that the limits reflect the abilities of loan officers and the size of the bank. Loan limits are usually designated, based generally on experience and ability. Some banks assign loan limits by title, some on the geographic or industry area to be covered, and others on the consideration of the type of responsibility required in each lending person's assignment. Sometimes limits are based purely on personnel's proven ability regardless of title. I like the latter approach.

Some banks will allow a group of lending officers to combine their lending authorities to approve a prescribed total amount, while others insist that subordinates obtain greater authority as needed by having someone with larger limits authorize the loan in question. Whatever policy is followed, prompt decisions should be made as soon as the necessary information is available to the loan officer.

4. Procedures for the review of loans.
5. Interest charges and who will be entitled to prime interest.
6. Credit requirements for each borrower.
7. Credit analysis of individual accounts—when they will be reviewed, by whom, and how substantive the analysis will be.
8. Percent of each major type of loan.
9. Ratio of loans to deposits.
10. Guidelines for the trust department.
11. Ground rules for investment practices, capital formation, and dividends.
12. The type of business that management may consider developing as a subsidiary, if the bank is a holding company.

13. An audit committee, one of the most important committees. The committee needs to have its own guidelines or policies to guide it in its work. Of first priority would be a yearly review of all loan policies and the updating of same.

14. Lists of commitments bank employees or officers can make in politics, civic affairs, and religious organizations. Bank officers should be involved in the community. I especially encourage bankers to help all of us teach the young generation about the free enterprise system, emphasizing that profit is necessary and not a dirty word.

Any bank, regardless of its size and scope of operations, should have policies that are clearly spelled out and followed. Furthermore, the directors need to see that the bank's policies are properly communicated and understood by the officers and employees.

15. A long-range plan updated annually.

16. Policy reference ratio of total lines of credit and deposits. This should be reviewed quarterly by the directors and more often by the executive committee.

Regardless of the situation in which we find ourselves, whether as a member of the management team or a member of the board, we are not living up to our responsibilities unless we are trying to improve upon what we are already doing. Let each of us try to make our bank number one. Let us not strive for zero loan losses, but work to build stronger banks and a stronger free enterprise system that will keep America free.

JOHN G. HENSEL

What a Bank Supervisor Expects of Directors

TO BE CANDID, as a regional administrator of national banks I expect a great deal from all directors of banks and bank holding companies, particularly those who serve national banks. In addition to being generally familiar with and knowledgeable about the host of laws, rules, regulations, interpretations, opinions, and civil law responsibilities, directors should be expected to keep abreast of changes within their respective banks and to keep their fingers on the very pulse of the bank they represent.

Directors are charged with the duty to exercise general supervision over the bank's affairs and to direct and control its officers and employees. It has been demonstrated in recent years that directors not only have a responsibility to stockholders, but have a certain, not yet clearly defined, responsibility to depositors and to society. When a regulator invites himself to meet with an executive committee or a full board of directors, it may generally be assumed that problems of more than the usual variety have surfaced or have been uncovered by an examiner. At such meetings, directors are admonished for ignoring their responsibilities, for being neglectful, for not managing their banks in a safe, sound, and prudent manner. Unfortunately, regulators sometimes find directors to be uninformed, disinterested, and anxious to be rid of this uninvited intruder. In other situations, however, regulators—myself included—often find directors willing to rekindle their interest. Many admit that far too much dependence has been placed upon executive officers, and quite often directors will "take charge" under adverse conditions, when pressures are great and when the most critical of decisions must be made. Such meetings and experiences are rewarding. What is discouraging and somewhat disgusting is a group of directors who cannot or will not face reality, who are split among themselves, who tend to be self-serving, who are inclined to play politics, and who fail to take away authority and responsibility from executive officers who have been derelict in the sound management of their respective banks.

To guide directors there are the comptroller's thirty-one page, four-part pamphlet entitled *Duties and Liabilities of Directors of National Banks* and many essays or discussions of a director's role which deal with tangible subjects. Topics covered in various director-oriented talks and publications include such important matters as (1) the selection, development, and evaluation of management personnel; (2) the establishment of executive policies, especially with regard to the making of loans, investments, internal controls, etc.; (3) problems of bank organization and expansion; (4) the nature and importance of trust business; and (5) other very practical, timely, and important subjects.

But among the various treatments of the director's role that have come to my attention, relatively few provide the emphasis and balance that seem most appropriate to me. Certain exceptions to this generalization appear in the Southern Methodist University Press publication entitled *The Bank Director* (1974), edited by Richard B. Johnson. This book is a collection of papers presented at other assemblies for bank directors. The first four articles in the volume are entitled "The Director and the Banking System," "Moral Responsibilities in Banking," "Moral Standards and Standards of Ethics in Commercial Banking," and "Integrity, the Cornerstone of Banking." These are excellent articles and discussions, and I can recommend them and the entire book. However, they still do not present the full scope or vitality of the director's role as I feel it should be developed, nor do they describe the director's potential influence in the dimensions that seem to be demanded by today's challenges in banking.

The results of directors' participation in banking or the lack thereof are significantly involved in many of the problems that I deal with on a day-to-day basis. But to give major emphasis to the directors' part in day-to-day operations is to limit and distort seriously the director's total role. An approach from the opposite point of view, that is, one emphasizing the director's participation in and impact upon long-range trends and developments, is much more accurate. Directors are not day-to-day practitioners of banking. They are the philosophers of the profession. They have a primary responsibility to see the business of banking in its broadest, its most vital, and its most essential terms.

Banking's primary task is to meet an almost universal need for financial assistance to initiate, maintain, and/or expand economically sound projects. Consumers, business firms, and agencies of government are all subject to this need. The power to meet such needs, to supply funds that create jobs and produce goods, is really an awesome power. To misuse such power for personal gain, or to permit such a misuse when means are at hand to prevent it, is a serious breach of moral standards which sooner or later is bound to have very serious consequences.

When we employ new examining personnel from colleges and universities in our region, there is so much I would like to tell them about the importance of the job for which they seek qualification that it is difficult to know where to begin. Even when we bring in our most experienced examiners, men and women who have developed a deep appreciation for banking as a unique service to our economic society, and a service which can function properly only by adhering to the highest possible code of ethics, the impression left with the trainees inevitably falls short of the goal of communicating this high ethical purpose.

I am confident it is the same with many bank trainees. Limited experience and the tendency of the young to emphasize the material benefits they desire from the job make it difficult for them to see the full implications of what they can do for the system and themselves through their jobs. How can they see from their level of perception that the competition (about which they may have some misgivings) channels resources (including their own) into the most productive jobs that they are capable of handling, in a relative sense, with their present motivation and training? How can they be expected to see the nature and scope of banking's contribution to economic progress? How can they comprehend the opportunities that banking offers to those who diligently participate in its provision of vital financial services, success in which, properly understood, brings a satisfying sense of accomplishment as well as potential for economic rewards?

Personnel training and motivation are two of the most difficult aspects of successful enterprise. One of the vital functions that directors must perform is using their experience and influence to build a healthy, trustful, and creative atmosphere within our banking organizations. In my view, two principal approaches may be used to accomplish this. The first is to develop clear, concise policy statements dealing with personnel matters, including qualifications, duties, responsibilities, privileges, compensation, and opportunities for advancement covering all personnel. The single most important responsibility of directors is to select sound management and thereafter to monitor its performance. To have sound management, however, banks must deal fairly with their staffs so that first-class talent can and will be attracted and retained. The second is to promote good interpersonal relationships and to foster effective communications within the organization, so that each employee may develop sound and healthy working relationships with fellow employees and supervisors. Directors must know their organizations well enough to evaluate these factors and to see that steps are taken as needed to maintain effective working relationships.

Heading the list, then, I expect bank directors to be men and women of broad vision, whose personal accomplishments enable them to coordinate all facets of banking enterprise, and who think creatively, innovatively, and philosophically about banking. This emphasis on the philosophical may seem archaic, but it is especially needed to offset the nearsighted attention to immediate goals that has come to dominate some banking organizations.

I try to keep informed about the latest approaches to management theory and practice. New phrases are coined from time to time which give a new look and sometimes new content to the ancient art of directing a productive enterprise. Science has greatly improved our data collecting and record keeping activities, but human nature and motivation have not changed very much in a long, long time. What passes for modern management technique may end up being the manipulation of people, conning them into certain patterns of behavior without really enrolling them as intelligent, willing, and understanding participants in a purposefully creative process.

The root definition of the word philosophy is "love of wisdom." The person who expresses a love of wisdom in his style of life is a philosopher and fills a most important role. His concern is for truth and virtue, and for principles of ethical behavior which evolve from and further promote the highest human traits. He comprehends the deep purposes and possibilities of human life in terms of a search for such qualities as knowledge, imagination, honesty, kindness, sensitivity to others, calmness under pressure, harmonious attitudes, strength of character, and all other personal and social qualities that contribute to the unity and effectiveness of an organization. The philosopher-director finds the greatest challenge and potential for achievement in helping individuals and institutions to set the best goals they are capable of reaching, and in laying out for them the best plans to achieve such goals. This is the vital role in banking organizations in which directors must actively participate.

It is not traditional in many banks for directors to be on a personal acquaintance basis with employees below the middle and upper executive levels. More extensive acquaintances are desirable for directors so that they may develop a broader, firsthand knowledge and exert firsthand influence in ways that will promote the future strength of the bank. Management succession, for instance, must always be a challenge; it is a major supervisory concern. This applies to small, midsized, and larger banks alike. Wider personal acquaintances can give directors a much needed personal perspective on the present qualifications and potential for growth and development within the existing staff. Directors' meetings are by tradition scheduled and highly organized in many instances. They are designed to conduct business efficiently, but efficiency does not necessarily coincide with effectiveness, knowledge, and the exercise of one's responsibilities. Directors must learn for themselves what the situation is in the banks they serve.

There seems to be a great deal of cynicism in people these days. It is an infectious kind of cynicism that goes deeper than the concept of assuming hidden motives behind every good deed. Today's cynicism can become an exercise in self-justification, and the cynic not only disbelieves the apparent kindness and generosity behind other people's motives but draws encouragement from his disbelief for his own self-serving plans and activities. Modern cynicism frequently remains hidden until some unexpected turn of events reveals its corrosive presence. Think of how many news stories lately reveal the extent of this cynicism and the carelessness, confusion, and dishonesty that its presence encourages, even justifies, in some mixed-up minds. Sometimes, even in a reasonable mind, desirable ends may seem to justify unethical means.

Leaders, particularly directors, cannot ignore unethical, questionable, or dishonest events, but must respond to them verbally and actively. Many people are deeply influenced by events which they themselves are not really capable of evaluating. They require leadership.

The original cynics were philosophers of ancient Greece whose basic belief was that truth and happiness are achieved in the pursuit of goodness and virtue, rather than in the pursuit of pleasure. The cynics in their day represented a reaction against the hedonistic practices and philosophies of the times. Their criticisms of society at large, however, became more and more bitter and less and less rational until they established a reputation for being unable to see or believe anything good about anyone. They lost both their objectivity and their effectiveness.

Modern society produces a number of ambivalent people who are capable of moving in many directions, depending on what pressures they feel and what motives capture their attention and enlist their loyalties. Such a situation calls for strong leadership based on sound principles effectively stated and clearly demonstrated in practice and policy.

Directors' responsibilities reach from the top down through the organization and outward to the stockholders and the public. Directors must not only select competent and effective administrators, but they themselves must keep informed about current problems, both internal and external. And they must participate actively in finding workable solutions. Directors must resist any tendency to recognize as dominant any one influence on their thinking. They have been elected by the shareholders for the purpose of overseeing the operations of a bank, which automatically requires their sensitivity to the public interest. In behalf of the stockholders and for the purpose of serving the public profitably, directors must select top administrative officers to whom decision-making powers are delegated. Directors must be certain that their relations with management remain fluid and well balanced so that each respects the authority and seeks the counsel of the other. Directors are expected to provide banks with their special areas of expertise. But their fundamental ability to establish a general atmosphere of trust, confidence, enthusiasm, and understanding—an atmosphere in which the bank's work can be effectively carried forward— is their most important responsibility.

ROBERT E. BARNETT

The Functions and Contributions of Regulation

THE OUTLOOK FOR BANKING and the economy, the FDIC's problem bank list, the performance of regulators during the past difficult years, and the role of bank directors in the present economic and regulatory environment deserve careful consideration. Economic forecasting is always a hazardous activity, especially when it is done for a short period of time, i.e., for six months or a year. Not only is it easy for forecasters to be way off, but people tend to remember incorrect forecasts. My comments, therefore, must be viewed as the best guesses of the Office of Corporate Planning at the FDIC and somewhat outside the areas of the corporation's primary expertise.

Those making short-term modifications of forecasts had their problems in 1976. Real GNP rose by a surprising 9.2 percent in the first quarter of 1975, after a sluggish performance in the fourth quarter of 1974. The first quarter GNP increase in 1976 combined with an increase in the price level of only about 3 percent persuaded some forecasters to up their projections. The second quarter performance, however, turned out to be disappointing: only a 4.3 percent real increase in GNP (not very good considering the extent of unused resources in the economy) and about a 5 percent increase in the price level. The latter figure and the most recent (1976) rate of about 6 percent was helped by relatively stable-to-declining food prices. Most forecasters expect that GNP figures for the third quarter of 1976 will not be better than those for the second quarter.

The unemployment rate fell dramatically during the first several months of 1976, from 8.3 percent at the end of 1975 to 7.3 percent in May, 1976. That translates into a decline of about one million in unemployment. As a result, some forecasters projected a fall in the unemployment rate to less than 7 percent by year-end. In the summer of 1976, however, unemployment rose considerably; the August figure was 7.9 percent.

Few economists expect any reversal of the upward movement of the economy before 1978. The economy rarely moves in a smooth, consistent way, with everything conforming to a single scenario. The real world just does not work that way, and the variations that exist may be exacerbated by data collection and measurement problems. Certainly, the rapid up and down movement in employment statistics suggests that seasonal adjustments and labor force estimates probably exaggerated the decline and the subsequent increase in the unemployment rate early in 1976. As for the dramatic change in the GNP increases between the first and second quarters of 1976, much can be explained by the large increase in inventory accumulation in the first quarter. The increase in final sales was about the same for each quarter. Also, auto sales rose substantially in the first quarter and, while the level has been maintained in the second and third quarters, there was no further increase.

It is easy to be "whipsawed" if one focuses too much on monthly variations in statistical series. But what about the general economic outlook and what it means for banks? Our Office of Corporate Planning expects real increases in GNP to average almost 6 percent for the second half of 1976 and all of 1977, though there may be considerable variation from quarter to quarter. This would bring about a gradual, but not dramatic, reduction in unemployment to a level below 7 percent by the second half of 1977.

Capital spending should rise considerably next year. This, combined with a moderate increase in housing starts and business inventories, should increase bank loan demand. The level of bank loans has been almost flat since the end of 1974. The prime rate should go up moderately along with short-term interest rates, while the movement in longer-term rates will depend in an important way on the inflation rate. So long as the inflation rate remains in the moderate range (around 5 percent or so) there should not be much of an increase in long-term rates. Higher short-term rates and somewhat less liquidity in the economy will probably result in more modest gains in savings and other consumer time deposits than there have been during the past twenty months.

Banks should experience considerable lessening of loan losses in 1977 if substantial REIT losses do not spill over into 1977. Loan losses in 1976 may approximate the very high level of 1975, although the basic strength of loan portfolios is probably improving more than these figures suggest. In assessing loan loss figures, several factors should be kept in mind:

1. While the cyclical low point in economic activity occurred in April, 1975, the depth of the decline was such that the economy did not get back to prerecession levels in real output until almost a year later, i.e., early 1976.

2. There is some discretion in loan writeoffs, and some of the 1976 writeoffs reflect situations that occurred and were recognized and partially accounted for earlier.

3. A lot of the bank loan problems have been real estate related, and while there is evidence of improvement in several areas of the country, some of these loan problems are taking a long time to work out.

Our Office of Corporate Planning expects bank earnings for 1976 in the aggregate to be about the same as those for 1975. The year-to-year comparisons, however, will be favorable in the second half of the year, and banks generally will go into 1977 with rising earnings. Earnings should increase considerably in 1977.

We have found in recent analyses of bank loan losses and changes in our problem list that there is a definite connection between those bank problems and the general state of the economy. The problems develop and show up in our examination reports, but there is a lag which in the past has averaged about twelve months. That is, the number of banks on our problem list generally does not start rising until the business decline is well under way, and it continues to rise well into the recovery period, in most cases approximately twelve months into it. Similarly, the size of the list depends in great part on the depth of the trough of the preceding business cycle.

The change in our problem list and its relation to the business cycle can be seen most vividly with respect to our most recent recession, which was the most severe since the Great Depression of the 1930s. In this case, perhaps because of the severity of the recession, the nature of the credits extended by banks during this period, and the time required to process the reports of the large number of banks involved, the time lag between the depth of the cycle and the peak of our problem list is even longer. Thus, although we are over a year past the low point in the recession, our problem list is at its highest level in 25 years. The number of banks on the list has been increasing since the spring of 1973, but the increase of net additions has dropped dramatically in the last 6 months. For example, the number of banks on the FDIC problem list has increased by only 18 during the 8 months since January 1, 1976, compared with an increase of 76 during the previous 6 months and an increase of 176 during the previous year. The total number of banks on the list now appears to be leveling off.

As of August 31, 1976, there were 377 FDIC insured banks on our problem list. This number is only about 2.5 percent of all insured banks. Said another way, 97.5 percent of the nation's banks are not in even the least serious of our problem categories. Of those on the list, about two-thirds are in our least serious category of problem banks.

The problem list in 1976, as distinct from the one a few years ago, includes a few large banks—banks with over $500 million in deposits— and a few very large banks, those with over $1 billion in deposits. That, incidentally, is one reason for the longer time lag. It simply takes longer to conduct and review the examination of a large bank. There are many explanations possible in answer to the question, "Why are so many banks on the problem list now?" One mechanical answer is that now more than ever before there are a lot more banks with over $500 million or $1 billion in deposits (even though the share of the domestic deposits of the top fifty has decreased). A more complete answer must discuss the increased risk assumed by larger banks on both sides of their balance sheets, and the inevitable result of a severe recession for the industry which finances the economy. In any case, it is clear that my remarks apply to directors of large banks as well as small.

Problems of the banking system have gotten considerable attention over the last year or two, and so has the bank supervisory system. There are those who say or imply that inadequate bank regulation was the cause of so many banks being on problem lists. That misses the point, however, since it is good bank regulation and supervision that spot the banks that are in trouble and put them on lists for closer supervision. The questions then might be, Could better regulation and supervision have prevented banks from reaching a condition which required closer supervision by bank regulators? What are the implications of this relationship between the economic cycle and bank problems for bank supervision?

It is my view that bank supervision as we know it in the United

States, as opposed to its characteristics in other countries, such as Japan, is limited in its ability to dictate the soundness of the banking system. It appears that many of the bank problems of the last couple of years (1974-76) have been brought on by the general state of the economy. That is clearly a matter beyond the control of the process of bank supervision. Some of the problems have been the result of specific unpredictable events, such as the rapid increase in oil prices and a subsequent decline in the demand for oil and oil tankers. It would have been nice if we had been able to anticipate and prevent the debacle of the REITs, for example. In view of the vast number of financial experts who failed to foresee these problems, it is not surprising that bank supervisors failed also.

There is one area, however, in which we do have an ability to lessen the impact of the business cycle. We must be very careful in this area, for it is the one covering bank attitudes toward risk and the willingness of bankers to increase loan ratios and decrease capital. We are giving more attention to these matters at the present time, and we will continue to demand more capital from banks inadequately capitalized, as well as demand that loan, investment, and operating policies and practices be reasonable ones. We are analyzing trends, rather than static pictures, much more intently than we did in the past. Computers are whirring constantly as we try to find ways to discover problems sooner. In the FDIC we have three separate early warning systems in operation. We are looking much harder at management and are willing to step in quicker with formal orders requiring action on management's part. During the first eight months of 1976, the FDIC has already issued or authorized our lawyers to begin the process of issuing twenty-seven cease and desist orders, as compared with an average of only seven a year during the past five years. We have asked Congress for more powers to deal with not only dishonest bankers but grossly negligent ones.

We recognize, however, that banking is a risk-taking business and we must rely on market forces, management, owners, and particularly directors, in addition to our supervisory judgment, to determine the appropriate degree of risk for individual banks. I do not believe that even the most outspoken critics of banking and bank regulators want the regulators rather than the bankers to run the banks. That is not our function. In some cases, government policy has encouraged a shift toward a riskier banking posture. We have issued regulations on "leeway investments" which have broadened the types of investments that can be made. By our disapproval of redlining and promoting the concept of equal credit opportunity, we have actively pushed banks into lending that they may feel (though I do not necessarily agree) is more risky. The FDIC has been in the vanguard of those who insist that the Bank Merger Act be interpreted to permit more competition between banks; this approach has as its corollary an unwillingness to protect competitors from the results of competition—i.e., one wins, one loses. I feel the same way about restrictions on EFT developments that are designed primarily to protect less efficient banks.

Frankly, I believe that the FDIC and the other regulators have done an excellent job of bank supervision during the past two or three years after the magnitude of the problems became apparent to us. Very large bank failures have been resolved by the Corporation working closely with the comptroller of the currency and the Federal Reserve System, without the loss of a dime to any deposior and with only minimum disruption in the communities affected. For example, in two banks, Franklin National Bank and U.S. National Bank, nearly one million depositors were totally protected—they had their entire deposit accounts always available to them without loss of even a day's banking services—even though these huge banks failed. Compare that wtih the result of the bank panics in the twenties or early thirties. The Corporation and the other regulators should be praised, not berated, for this part of their performance.

The jury is still out, however, on the question of prevention. Somehow, the regulators must do a better job of carrying out the full range of responsibilities given to them by Congress; they must spot problem situations earlier and must be willing and able to move more quickly with effective enforcement action. But I want this to be done primarily within a framework of reliance on our free enterprise system. We must recognize that our economy needs the initiative, ingenuity, and aggressiveness of free enterprise and competitive banking. Compatibility of those objectives with safe and sound banking rests only in part with the supervisory agencies. Success is more dependent on the efforts, dedication, and wisdom of bank directors. In the final analysis, bank directors, not the regulators, bear the primary responsibility for the safety and soundness of the banks they direct.

As Chairman of the FDIC (1976-77), I have a direct interest in bank directors' being alerted to the dangers of lawsuits resulting from failure to carry out their legal responsibilities. The legal responsibilities of directors are of particular interest to us, since the FDIC is the plaintiff in many suits against directors. In most bank failures we end up with a suit against some or all of the directors of the closed bank; and in the suit we claim that the directors were negligent in meeting their responsibilities.

Some cases of bank failures are a result of embezzlements that cannot be detected in time, even though the directors are diligent in meeting their responsibilities. But usually bank failures result from imprudent or self-serving action that directors could have and should have discovered and remedied. In some cases, the directors are directly involved in and benefiting from self-serving bank policies that result in failure. Obviously, we hope to recover all we can from those guilty of such malfeasance. More commonly, however, we find directors simply guilty of nonfeasance, of not paying sufficient attention to the condition of the bank, the policies and actions of the bank, and the condition of the bank. While we may feel some sympathy for the plight of those directors who may have been duped by management or other directors, nevertheless, as a receiver, we have a legal obligation as a representative of the creditors of the bank to seek recovery for losses from directors who did not meet their legal responsibilities. As a supervisor, the FDIC is insisting that directors pay more attention to their responsibilities. We have recently promulgated regulations covering insider transactions, for example, so that now no director can attempt to argue that he did not know that transactions of this sort were occurring.

The demise of the U.S. National Bank in San Diego, which helped awaken the country to the fact that a $1 billion bank could fail, served to focus the attention of the public and bank regulators on the problem of insider abuse. The USNB insolvency was caused by the extension of between $400 million and $450 million in loans to persons and more than two hundred entities controlled by or associated with C. Arnholt Smith.

Prompted by the U.S. National failure, the FDIC began a review of the matter of insider abuse and FDIC policies and practices with respect to it. Upon review, abusive self-dealing was found to be a significant contributing factor in more than half of all bank failures since 1960. Losses to the deposit insurance fund as a result of these failures are likely to exceed $175 million. Moreover, a review of existing and past problem bank cases revealed a high incidence of abusive self-dealing as a source of serious difficulty. In addition to these clearly quantifiable effects, even where the immediate result is not a bank's failure or its designation as a problem bank, a transaction that is not effected on an arms-length basis may lead to a diminution of the bank's earnings and an erosion of its capital, increasing the risk of loss to depositors and minority shareholders and, ultimately, to the deposit insurance fund. Such transactions represent a diversion to insiders of resources that properly belong to all shareholders on a pro rata basis; they also represent a misallocation of the community's deposited funds. In short, the review indicated a need for more vigorous supervision of insider transactions by both the boards of directors of banks and the FDIC.

Based upon this review, the FDIC adopted a regulation governing insider transactions effective May 1, 1976. The regulation requires that the board of directors of each insured nonmember bank review and approve each insider transaction involving assets or services having a fair market value greater than a specified amount which varies with the size of the bank. The purpose of this provision is to insure that boards of directors police insider transactions, making sure that they are both sound and in the bank's best interest. In addition to the review and approval requirements of the regulation, certain record-keeping requirements are spelled out which are intended to foster effective internal controls over such transactions by the bank itself and to facilitate examiner review of such transactions.

The regulation covers not only transactions between a bank and its insiders and their corporate interest and related persons, but also transactions between an insured nonmember bank and its holding company parent or other members of a holding company system. This coverage is based upon recent experience which indicates that all too often banks within a holding company system blindly enter into transactions which are not in the individual bank's best interest and which are not properly scrutinized by the board of directors of the bank in question. While it might be argued that an entire holding company system should be allowed to function as an integrated business entity, the legal framework of bank regulation and our deposit insurance system mandates that we, as bank regulators, focus upon the safety and soundness of each individual banking institution. Moreover, the fiduciary duties of the director of an individual bank also demand that his loyalty lie with the individual banking institution and not with the holding company system.

In addition to spelling out review and approval and record-keeping requirements, the regulation makes it clear that formal compliance with these requirements neither relieves the bank of its duty to conduct its operations in a safe and sound manner nor prevents the Corporation from taking appropriate supervisory action with respect to any insider transaction. The regulation makes it clear that appropriate supervisory action, including legal action under Section 8 in the Federal Deposit Insurance Act, will be taken where an insider transaction represents unsafe and unsound banking practices.

Although the Corporation has determined that insider transactions require special supervision by bank boards of directors and close scrutiny by the Corporation's examiners in order to insure their fairness, we have carefully sought to avoid unrealistic prohibitions or unduly burdensome recording requirements. Instead, the Corporation has attempted to develop requirements which will place responsibility where it belongs—in the hands of the bank's directors—and to strengthen existing bank and supervisory procedures for policing insider transactions. In doing so, we hope to correct a serious and continuing source of abuse without incurring excessive bank or regulatory costs.

In the several months since the adoption of the regulation, we at the Corporation have attempted to monitor its operation carefully by seeking feedback from our own examiners and from bankers. We have been pleasantly surprised. It appears that most of the banks we regulate have been able to implement the requirements of this regulation without undue burden or cost, and many feel that it has certain salutary benefits from their point of view, a novelty in our experience with the adoption of new regulations. In some cases, management has told us that the regulation makes it easier to turn down unreasonable proposals of insiders for favorable treatment. This is not to say, of course, that compliance is perfect or that the regulation cannot be improved. Examiners in some regions report a significant number of violations of the review, approval, and record-keeping requirements of the regulation—a phenomenon experienced early in the life of any new regulation. A few bankers have complained about some aspects of the regulation, most particularly about the inclusion of large deposits in the covered transactions and the coverage of foreign bank holding companies. The FDIC staff is in the process of evaluating banker and examiner criticism of the various facets of the regulation, and I would expect this evaluation to result in at least some modification of the regulation, probably in the coverage by the regulation of large certificates of deposit.

When a newly chartered bank seeks deposit insurance, we have something to say about the selection of directors of the bank. In general, however, we do not have any legal authority to determine who is or is not a bank director. We do not expect or want all directors to be bankers by profession, but bank directors must make some effort to take their jobs seriously and learn about banking. We are troubled by situations where directors serve solely because of the honor or prestige attached to being a bank director, and where the person so honored does not intend to be an independent force in forming the policies of the bank. We want informed directors.

The selection and continuous evaluation of management is, in my opinion, the single most important task of directors. The job of directors is to direct and the job of managers is to manage; and I agree with the view that directors should not be running the bank on a day-to-day basis. But the board cannot escape responsibility for management of the bank. Once a top management team is in place, the board must give adequate consideration to working with it in outlining specific goals and objectives for the bank. We see many problem banks that result from nebulous goals and objectives, from contradictory goals and objectives, and from a divergence between the board and the chief executive officer as to what are appropriate goals and objectives. Occasionally, the chief executive officer and other officers are interested in quick but nonenduring results which, while they may dress up the financial statements and make good quotations for their résumés, create serious future problems. Often the problems brought on by these hotshots do not appear until after their departure. Directors cannot escape the responsibility for those management mistakes, however, so be sure you do not become mesmerized by discussions of P/E multiples and leverage. Remember that you are a director of a bank, not of an industrial corporation.

Once these goals are established and agreed upon, top management should be asked to prepare policy and procedure statements to implement them. These objectives must be reviewed by the board to insure consistency and reasonableness; continuous control and measurement devices must be built into the system. It is highly important that progress be monitored continually, not on a one-shot or once-a-year budget review basis.

This leads into the evaluation of top management performance. Performance evaluation cannot be an afterthought, done in a ritualistic manner. It must start by insuring that the bank's goals and policies be written and understood, and that they provide the necessary specific guidance for the top management of the bank. The performance of management must be measured by these specifics. In a sense, then, these statements become an agreement which will be discussed with the officer at frequent intervals. Approached this way, evaluation of management can be fair, objective, and thorough.

A primary responsibility of directors is simply to know what is going on. That is easy when management makes an effort to see that directors are kept informed, but, unfortunately, that is not the universal situation. Even when management is not doing what it should to see that directors are kept informed, it is possible, even for a nonbanker director, to be knowledgeable if he asks the right questions and knows where to look for information. In banking, to a greater extent than in other businesses, there are sources of information that ease the job of knowing how your bank is doing and what condition it is in.

Obviously, we regard the bank examination process as playing a key role in keeping directors informed. The bank examination, whether by the FDIC, the Federal Reserve, the comptroller of the currency, or the state supervisory authorities, provides a wealth of information and an excellent, even if usually a somewhat critical, picture of the condition of the bank. These examinations are intended to be useful to the bank, and we think they are. Most managements feel the same way. Obviously, then, directors should review the report of examination carefully. One way to be sure that you have ample time and opportunity to do so is to insist upon a copy of the examination report for your own use; and do not be content with just a summary.

In some cases, the examiners will seek a meeting with the board of directors to review the report, though agency policies on such meetings vary. FDIC examiners at the present time do not routinely meet with boards of directors following every examination, but they do attempt to arrange such meetings if the examiner feels the bank's condition is particularly weak. I understand that the comptroller of the currency does follow a policy of having national bank examiners meet with the board of directors following each examination of a national bank. The FDIC attempted to introduce that requirement a number of years ago but discovered that in many cases it was unproductive. Nevertheless, we feel that it is appropriate to consider that policy once again. In any case, it is a responsibility of the director to find out the substance of the examiner's comments; he should not simply assume that, because nothing has been brought to his attention, there is no need for him to investigate the report.

Incidentally, we do not officially notify a bank when it is placed on our problem list. This is a hoary tradition in the Corporation. As far as I can gather, it exists because we are afraid that directors will talk about the news with others not on the board, and, if that happens, everyone will attempt to withdraw their funds from the bank, thereby precipitating a bank failure. While this may prove to be the result, we cannot say for certain that it would be. In the past few years, banks have made more and more voluntary and involuntary disclosure of information that would have been judged highly sensitive (in fact, perhaps fatally sensitive) only a few years ago. In most cases, the disclosure has not proved disastrous or even particularly difficult for the affected bank. Whether it has proved beneficial to the bank or, on balance, to the public, is a subject which has not been sufficiently explored, and one which must be thoroughly explored before any problem bank names should be published. It may well be, however, that the time will come when the FDIC will feel relaxed enough about the potential side effects to insist on the board of directors knowing that the bank it is directing is having difficulties sufficient to place it on the Corporation's problem list.

Regardless of whether or not the board of directors of a bank on our problem list is specifically told that it is on such a list, every director of every nonmember bank that is on the list should know that the FDIC is unhappy with the condition and management practices of the bank. Board meetings, CPA audits, officers' reports, progress reports requested, the content of the examination report, and supervisory letters—indeed, the entire tone and emphasis of our supervisory efforts—should leave no doubt in the mind of the director of a problem bank that his bank is a matter of serious concern to the FDIC. When we turn down an application for a branch on the basis of the financial condition or management weakness of the bank, or even when in a most extreme situation we close the bank, a diligent director has no justification for being surprised. He has had ample opportunity to find out that the FDIC and others, such as independent auditors, think his bank is in difficulty; and he has had equally ample opportunity to acquaint himself with its condition.

When FDIC officials speak about the responsibility of directors, we usually talk about responsibility for the safety and soundness of the bank. But, without in any way understating the importance of safety and soundness, I want to remind you of your responsibility to see that the bank is run profitably. A good deal of research in recent years has led to the conclusion that sound, prudently generated bank profitability is crucial to the future soundness of the bank. We feel this strongly at the FDIC. In our economic system, profitability is not a dirty word; in fact, it is to be encouraged. We have been doing some work on the development of statistical early warning systems at the FDIC (we have three different ones in operation), and we have come to the conclusion—a conclusion that has been defended by leading bank stock analysts for some time—that the most important key to the future of a bank is to be found in its income statement and in its bottom line. This represents a change from the traditional view that the balance sheet and bank capital ratios are the sole reliable indicators of bank soundness.

Now this creates some difficulties for the director because, to a considerable extent, the earnings of a bank are not an accurate reflection of the skill and quality of management. To a large degree the earnings performance of a bank depends on external factors, such as the general economy, the competitiveness of the relevant marketplace, Federal Reserve montary policy, etc. But it is possible to compare the performance of your bank with that of other banks subject to these same external forces. To facilitate such comparisons there is a great deal of information made available on a routine basis by the FDIC, the Federal Reserve, several investment firms, and some firms whose major business is providing comparative banking data.

In fact, the problem for the director may be that there are too many financial data available, too many ratios. It may be difficult to see the forest for the trees. We can count on management to point out those areas in which the bank's performance looks good, but the director must take a broader view than that. The FDIC, on a semiannual basis, sends a good deal of comparative financial information to each insured bank. We have found that many banks use this information as a basis for a director's meeting, and we have received many complimentary letters from bankers and directors about the value and usefulness of this information. When we looked into it a little deeper, however, we found that the banks that were pleased with this service, and that were presenting this information to directors, were all banks whose performance looked very good in comparison to banks in their area or other banks of their size. I am afraid that data for the bank whose performance looks bad may simply be thrown in the wastebasket, that the board of directors may not see any of it. If your bank looks poor in comparison with others in the area, or with the banks which you particularly think are comparable to yours, ask why. There may be a reasonable answer. But at least the question should be asked and management should be required to give an explanation.

Since the bank director plays an important role in the success of a bank, the FDIC would like to see the most able people possible selected for positions of bank directors. In view of the responsibilities and risks involved, the best people are not going to be willing to serve unless they are adequately compensated. Our regulation on insider transactions implies that we do not believe directors should receive their compensation in the form of favorable treatment in their dealings with the bank. Our view is that bank directors should be paid openly and directly for their contributions and for their assumption of responsibilities, and that compensation should be in keeping with the contribution.

We do not have a great deal of hard information about the compensation of directors, but we do have some general impressions formed from conversations with bankers, with our bank examiners, and with other experts in the field—such as Richard B. Johnson. Let me just summarize the conclusions which I think are valid but which we cannot document definitively at this time.

First, banks pay directors substantially less than nonbank firms of comparable size. In many cases, the disparity is huge.

Second, many banks do not guarantee directors a compensation that reflects their ongoing responsibility. Instead, compensation is based on attendance at meetings. There may be some logic to this approach as a means of encouraging directors to attend meetings, but the fact needs to be emphasized that directors have an ongoing responsibility whether or not they attend meetings or vote on particular issues. Since there is a continuing responsibility, it may well be that there should be a continuing compensation.

Third, supplementary services provided by directors (such as service on special committees) are generally not compensated for at a reasonable level. In some cases, there is no payment. In other cases, there may be a nominal payment of, say, $20 per meeting, even though preparation for the meeting may involve many hours of homework.

Fourth, there is an extremely wide disparity in the compensation of directors, even among banks of the same size.

It is my strong conviction that directors should be adequately compensated. Our regulation on insider transactions is aimed at preventing directors or insiders from receiving benefits from the bank in a way that we think is inappropriate; it is not aimed at holding down deserved and earned remuneration for directors. Of course, there are a lot of people who are happy to serve as directors of a bank simply because of the prestige involved. In general, however, getting capable bank directors is going to depend on paying them adequately.

The job of a bank director is not an easy one, and the task of sorting out economic predictions, determining their impact on the bank and the actual condition of the bank, is not an easy one. There are techniques and material available that will make the task possible, however, and all directors should make use of them.

EUGENE L. SWEARINGEN

Evaluating the Quality of Bank Management

A VERY WISE BANK PRESIDENT once said that the first item on the agenda of every board of directors' meeting should be the question, "Shall we retain the chief executive officer?" If the answer is "No," he went on to say, the next question should be, "What procedure shall we use to select the new chief executive officer, and who will be on the committee to make the selection?" If the answer is, on the other hand, "Yes, we shall retain the chief executive officer," the next item to be considered should be, "How can we help him to do his job?"

What we are talking about is the number one job of every board of directors. If the directors have the wrong president, it is their responsibility to correct that situation. If they have the right man, their faith in the quality of that person will make many of their other problems much less difficult to solve.

I should like to pose twenty questions which, if you are a director, you can use to evaluate your chief executive officer. If you are yourself the chief executive officer, you can use them to evaluate your own performance. And if you are in the position of having to go out and find a chief executive officer, these are the kinds of questions you should be asking yourself about each person you consider.

1. What qualities do you want in your chief executive officer? This depends upon the area of the country in which your bank is located, upon the size of your bank, and upon an analysis of the job you expect that man to perform. Do you want a person who is primarily a manager, or do you want a person to be your chief loan officer? The primary mistake I have seen in my comparatively brief experience (I have been in banking nine years) is banking's best example of "the Peter Principle"—taking a person who is competent in one job and promoting him to his level of incompetence as president. You tend to do

this because you look around and see a man whose performance as a loan officer has been very good, or one who has more seniority in the bank than anyone else, or one who has been an excellent person to head your trust department, and therefore you think he can be the manager of your bank. Well, I would rather have as my president a person who is a great leader than a person who has proved that he is a great follower of someone else.

Sometimes a person gets into the position of president simply because he has been an excellent Man Friday for the man who was president before him. And so I suggest to you that if you have not read the book *The Peter Principle*, you as a director read both that book and the second one which Dr. Peter wrote, entitled *The Peter Prescription*. Dr. Peter developed the principle that a man tends to get promoted until he reaches his level of incompetence, and then to spend the rest of his life in that position. A lot of people who had read his first book wrote to Dr. Peter asking, "Well, how in the world do we keep from promoting a man to his level of incompetence?" or, "How do I keep from being promoted to my level of incompetence?" And so *The Peter Prescription* was written. It contains some sixty-four suggestions as to how to keep from being promoted into a job where you will be incompetent.

2. How well does this man understand himself? Many years ago Socrates said, "Know thyself." I have heard many people say, "You make me sick." What we really should say is, "I make me sick." You may have behavior that I don't like, but I should be in control of my own behavior. I should control my own adrenal glands. If your behavior causes me to become sick, it is because of me, not because of you. And so if you are thinking of putting a man in charge of your bank, one of the first questions to be asked is, "Is he in control of himself?" I would not want to put a person in charge of a bank who had a reputation for losing control of himself through drinking, or through loss of temper, or for any other cause. If he is not in control of himself, I do not think he would be a very good president of your bank.

3. How cooperative is this man? He is going to have to work with a board, and with other community leaders. He will have to attempt to build a team, and it may be that for the first time in his life he is going to have to get the job done through other people. Now, this is what distinguishes a manager from a man who is just a top loan officer or a top man in some particular niche. In many cases the loan officer

has never supervised anybody but a secretary. Often he sat across the desk from someone who was attempting to sell him on a certain loan. One of his primary abilities was to analyze situations and make good loans. Now he is going to have to turn a lot of this work over to someone else and do the job through teamwork. And so the problem is, is he going to be cooperative?

4. What viewpoint is he going to take in making decisions? I know of a man who was an excellent dean of a school of engineering. But this man never became president of a university because he could never see a problem from the point of view of any other part of the university than the school of engineering. Now, one of the difficulties with banks, as I have seen it, is that we tend to teach a man more and more about less and less. And the bigger we get as a bank, the more we specialize the individual. He starts out as a loan officer; then he becomes a commercial loan officer; then he decides what industry he is going to specialize in; and finally he begins to think that there is nothing more important than making a petroleum loan in his bank. If this man begins to believe that his corner of the office represents the entire corporation, he is not going to make a good president. You need to look for the man who understands that his own point of view has to be broad enough so that he can see a problem from other people's points of view. If the man you are considering has not demonstrated the fact that he can look beyond his own point of view and see when he may be causing trouble for someone else, then he would not make a good president.

5. Does he really like people as individuals? I believe that banking is a people business. To be sure, we are dealing with money. But our money is just like the money of the bank down the street. The difference between one bank and another is primarily in the quality of the people. Ours is a service industry, and we must provide this service in a way that pleases the customer. If we fail to please the customer, we will ultimately go out of business. Profits are the by-products of the efficient rendering of a service which the customer needs. I have heard bankers say, "I am in business to make a profit." I don't think that is what you are in business for. I don't think that justifies your existence as a corporation, or even as an individual. Profits are absolutely necessary. If you do not make them, you cannot stay in business; but the thing that justifies your stay in business is your realization that you have to render a service to people. Therefore, I would want a

person as president who was sensitive to the feelings of other people, a person who liked to deal with other people and to be of service to them.

6. What is his philosophy about the nature of man? There is a familiar cartoon showing a man crouched in a box. The corners of his mouth are turned down, and he is saying, "People are no damn good!" If you believe that people are no damn good, you are not going to make a good bank president. I want my bank president to believe that people are some damn good—that they do amount to something and are worth something. If you believe that most people are basically honest, that they want to be good, that they want to be productive, that they want to meet their obligations, then I think your philosophy of the nature of man is one that will enable you to work well with your employees. I don't think you can be a good supervisor unless you have a great deal of faith in human nature. If your basic belief is that your employees are out to steal from you, that they will cheat on the time they give you whenever they get a chance, then you are not going to inspire these people to produce their best for your organization.

7. Will he give credit to other people? Or does he try to get the glory for everything that is accomplished, and place the blame on everyone else when something goes wrong? A good president has to be a person who will assume the responsibility for something that goes wrong in his organization, but who has enough courage to turn over to other people the jobs that must be done, recognizing the fact that they may make mistakes. The kind of person who will not allow his employees to make a mistake can't run a big organization.

8. What about the integrity of this individual? Recently the newspapers carried a story of a bank president who had stolen money down through the years. Not once did he ever indicate that this was against any of his principles. It seemed that his stealing had been a game. Someone has said, "He who stands for nothing will fall for anything." I would like to ask about any prospective president, what about his character? What kind of person is he? Will he steal from your organization? Not only that, but what kind of person is he in many other ways? A banker has to stand for integrity and character in his bank. When a bank loses its reputation for integrity it is in real trouble. Therefore, the quality of the integrity and leadership of this top man is going to be important to your bank.

9. Will he keep on learning? To ask a man who is forty-five years

old and is being considered for the presidency of your bank what college he attended, what courses he took there, and so on, is about as ridiculous as asking a high school graduate whether he majored in sandbox one or sandbox two. The thing that is important about a man is not what he got in a college program, but whether or not he keeps on learning. The fact is that if his college failed to teach him that he must keep on learning all his life, then he didn't get a very good education. In a very basic sense, we are learning something every day we are in a bank organization, or in any other progressive organization. And anyone who does not keep on learning is soon going to fall behind. So I would want to ask how sincere this person is about studying. It is amazing to me that I spent more hours reading as a bank president than I did when I was a university president. A university president is an ex-scholar; but in a bank there is an astonishing amount of material coming across your desk every day, and you are going to have to try to keep up with your profession.

10. Will this man listen effectively? It is interesting that the farther up you go in an organization, the less chance you have to talk and the more you have to listen. Now, this is contrary to the nature of man. I love to talk, and therefore one of my greatest problems is recognizing the fact that much of the information I must get has to come from other people. I no longer have firsthand contact with all of the problems. I have to listen to an analysis of a loan. I have to listen to a story about a human relations problem. I have to spend a great deal of time listening. Listening is not just a function of the ear. It is a function of the eyes, of the mind—of the heart, if you like. You must have empathy with people. You must be willing to sit back and listen to a person and ask yourself not only what he is saying, but what he means. The ability to listen is extremely important. Can the man you are considering get information accurately by listening?

11. Is he effective in planning? One of the most important roles the chief executive officer must play is to assist in setting the goals and objectives in his organization. He cannot delegate this job to someone else. If you are the chief executive officer, the direction of movement of your bank, its basic philosophy, is your responsibility (working with the board of directors), and there is no way you can get out of this job. Determine, therefore, whether your man has proved himself to be a good planner. Has he set goals for himself and for the organization, and has he measured his performance against

these goals? If he has, then he would probably carry over this practice in his job as president.

It is essential to get people to set goals and objectives and to recognize the fact that these must be continually updated. Both short-range goals and goals in the intermediate range (from three to five years) are needed. When we decided to build a new building we had to ask ourselves whether we were going to own it or lease space in it. We decided we did not want to tie up such a large amount of capital in a building, so we decided to lease space in our new building instead. In order to answer this kind of question we had to look fifteen, twenty, or twenty-five years down the road. Then, you must realize that planning is a process that goes on all the time and is constantly changing. Plans are always subject to review. You have to compare your performance with your plans and ask yourself whether your assumptions are still valid.

Planning imposes a very rigorous discipline upon an organization. For example, in our bank we have about $450 million in loans. If we make our five-year plan, we know we are going to have over $700 million in loans. Now, this tells us something about the number of loan officers we are going to need and about the training we must give the new people we will have to bring in to accomplish this job. Finally, if conditions change, if money becomes tight when we thought it was not going to be so tight, then obviously these changes must be taken into consideration. A bank, therefore, needs a president who is highly effective in planning.

12. *Does he get facts before reaching a conclusion?* I would hope that the person chosen as president would have the reputation of waiting until he got all the information he could assemble. It is true, of course, that you never have all you want. In every loan we make, we wish we knew more about certain things. But there comes a time when you feel that you have all the information that is readily available, and that the man who is requesting the loan must have an answer. (I think banks make a terrible mistake in postponing an answer, particularly one that is going to be unfavorable. This just makes the man angrier than ever when he does get the answer.) Many times we may not make a decision at the right moment; but there are some people who make the decision too quickly, without getting the facts they need. And such a person would not make a good president for a bank.

13. What kind of image will this man project for your bank? There is no escaping the fact that the bank's chief executive officer does project an image. This can be an image of enthusiasm, or one that may cause people to believe your bank is sleepy. I know a bank president whose image is one of a man playing gin almost all day in his bank. If a correspondent banker wants to call upon him, he drops in and they play gin for a while. This bank is not going anywhere at this time, and hasn't for several years. The image that is being projected here is not an image of a dynamic, moving bank.

You can have other kinds of images. What image your bank should have is up to the board of directors. You may want to project the image of a very conservative bank, or you may want to be very dynamic. You may want to be a bank that is interested in growth, or one that is more interested in shareholders' profits. This is for you to decide. But in any case, the man you select to be the chief executive officer will have a great influence on the kind of image your bank projects.

14. Is this man effective in delegation? There is no way to run a big organization except by delegation. But some people will not delegate because they fear that they will lose authority, or that someone will make a mistake and they will be blamed for it. *An insecure man cannot delegate.* Show me a good delegator, and I will show you a man who has faith in himself and faith in his people. If he does not have faith, he cannot turn a job over to someone else. After the job is turned over to someone else, it is necessary to follow through to see that it is being done. One of the main responsibilities of a bank president is to have a control and information system in his organization that enables him to know whether or not a job is being done.

Your president may fear losing job satisfaction. I have seen people who will not turn over the job of making loans primarily because they like making loans and would rather do that than anything else. They are secure in that, but they don't quite understand the job of managing the whole thing. So they keep on doing what they undersand well, which may not be the job they ought to be doing. I would ask of your chief executive officer, is he doing things right, or is he doing the right things? I think we make more mistakes by doing the wrong things right than we do by simply fouling up what we are doing.

This leads to one further point about competence. An organization is never fouled up by a total incompetent. The people who foul up an organization are those who are competent in something and are promoted into doing something else in which they are incompetent. The combination that fouls up an organization is made up of a nice fellow who is incompetent at what he is doing and a manager who doesn't have the guts to remove him from that position.

15. Is this man effective in communication? Can he stand up in front of your Rotary Club and make a talk about your bank? Can he talk about what is going on in the economy? Can he use words effectively? He does not have to have the world's greatest vocabulary. I have known people who could communicate in a few words. That is what is important. Dan Devine tells a story of grabbing a great big tackle off the bench one day and saying, "Get in there and get rambunctious!" The tackle started onto the field and then came back and asked, "What's his number, coach?"

16. What about this man's brainpower and judgment? I don't care what his education is, but I want a man leading my bank who is smart, a man who can understand and analyze an issue and who uses sound judgment in arriving at a decision. "Work smarter, not harder." There is a little poem that is relevant here:

> We have two ends with a common link.
> On one we sit; with one we think.
> Success depends on which we use;
> It's a case of heads we win and tails we lose.

17. Does this man know how to organize a team? And does he know how to organize himself? It is very important that a bank president be able to use his time effectively. There will be a lot of people wanting his time, and he has to decide where he is going to spend this very limited resource, the time that is available to him.

18. Can this man select the right people and correct the mistakes he makes in his selections? I do not expect a chief executive officer always to select the right person. But if he makes a mistake and the person does not work out, then I expect him to have enough guts to correct the mistake he has made. I feel that this is terribly important. The president does have the responsibility for judging the performance of other people. Notice that I said judging the *performance* of other people, not judging *people*. I leave this to the Lord. But judging the performance of people is our job.

19. How do people work with and for this man? How effective is

he in motivating the work of other people? I used to tell students about the track coach who had a lousy pole vaulter. He was so bad that the coach thought he was going to lose the track meet because of him. But the pole vaulter backed into the javelin thrower and won the broad jump. Now, I don't know what it takes to get people motivated. More and more I have come to feel that it is what psychologists call self-actualization or self-fulfillment. I do know this: you cannot depend just upon the threat of firing the person. You will never get the best response from people unless somehow or other you can analyze what makes the man tick. What does he want out of life? What is it that will cause him to turn on for this organization?

20. Finally, is this man flexible? Can he adjust to change? There is a story of a ninety-year-old man who was asked at his birthday party whether he had seen a lot of changes in his life. He replied, "Yes, and I have been against every damn one of them!" There are people like this, who don't want to adjust to change. And such a person is not the one you will want as president of your bank.

FRANK A. PLUMMER

Evaluating Management

AS CONCERNED BANK DIRECTORS we would like to have the best of two worlds: the energy and decisiveness of a strong chief executive and the balancing involvement of a thoughtful and informed board of directors. An outside director should evaluate management on a gut level by asking the primary question, Does management guide, help, and protect the board as it resolves its problems in primary areas of responsibility?—namely, (1) the operation of a sound bank, (2) the operation of a profitable bank, (3) bank service to the community, (4) management succession, and (5) administrative evaluation. There is a cord of communality connecting all four areas.

THE OPERATION OF A SOUND BANK

Management should understand both sides of the ledger sheet and indoctrinate the board in all the characteristics of the balance sheet. In order to provide proper liquidity, management should thoroughly understand the necessity of matching maturities of deposits and other liabilities with loans and investments. Surprisingly, many of the large bank failures in recent years have occurred in banks with adequate capital; these institutions failed to provide liquidity. Obviously the attribute of soundness comes from high quality loan and investment portfolios.

Management and directors must frequently review and revise policy and, more importantly, monitor loan policy. Some of the most disastrous credit situations that developed in 1974 and 1975 were the result of loan officers ignoring well-conceived policies. Make certain auditors check this diligently; otherwise, it will be like a fifty-five-mile-an-hour speed limit with no cops. Accidents will continue to occur.

In the area of investments, which is merely another category of loans, there is an added ingredient: the middleman. Evaluate your management on its ability to select a sound investor adviser, whether the adviser is a brokerage dealer or a correspondent bank. A wheeling-dealing adviser can quickly wreck an otherwise sound bank.

Check your management on its ability to explain your capital position. Does it have capital adequacy plans, a good dividend policy, and sufficient reserves? Good management should assist in the education of directors in these areas.

The Operation of a Profitable Bank

We all understand the need for profits. Profits provide reserves to counter the vicissitudes of banking; profits provide capital for growth and expansion; profits pay dividends and provide funds for building the marketplace; profits attract a strong managerial team. Your management should establish profit goals at least a year in advance and provide a budget and a plan for attaining the desired objectives. As a director, I would question management that was not aiming for the following levels of earnings:

Earnings on Assets after Taxes
(In Millions of Dollars)

SIZE OF BANK	EARNINGS ON ASSETS, IN %
0-25	1.35
25-35	1.3
35-50	1.25
50-150	1.2

For example, a $20 million asset bank would earn $270,000 after taxes, before security gains or losses. I know of many banks exceeding the above stated levels.

In checking the progress of the bank during the year, directors should ask management to present financial data so that they can recognize interest expense, income, and interest margins. Noninterest expense items should be segregated. With this data, management can point out trends and the board can determine policy action. Armed with these tools, directors can determine whether management is earning growth with better service, or buying growth. It is easy to obtain growth by paying more for deposits than the market price, or by selling money at bargain rates.

Directors should check management on the pricing of services. Does management know the costs of your product line? Don't let the bank down the street set your price schedules; be aware of competition, but price from knowledge of your costs.

Bank Service to the Community

Directors should have a thorough understanding of management's philosophy and approach to community service. When legitimate needs of convenience and services are supplied by the bank, success is certain to follow; however, when needs are created or anticipated too far in advance, the results can be costly. In this day of escalating costs for personnel, construction, and equipment, a program of branch or facility expansion can wreck the bottom line if the program is designed merely to promote the bank's image.

Usually, the best service you can give the community is proper credit allocation. In today's environment there are powerful forces attempting to gain control of credit allocation at the federal level. The best way to slow or stop this movement is to do a good job at home. Credit allocation is a responsibility of the board of directors, and good management should provide the leadership. Properly allocated credit should keep you in your own marketplace. Many severe credit losses in recent years have resulted from banking in the other fellow's backyard. Surprisingly, a well-allocated loan portfolio leaves very little room for speculative lending.

Finally, if the bank is being operated in a sound and profitable way, management should be in a position to recommend contributions to worthwhile, constructive projects that build the market. It is difficult for a bank to grow in a stagnated market.

Management Succession

Management succession encompasses all facets of the bank's personnel program, and there are a number of questions directors should be asking.

Does management explain to the board its plan for recruitment? Does it request the board's assistance in recruitment under special circumstances? Does management have career paths for potential managers? Has it initiated proper training programs to implement advancement and, at the same time, properly serve your customers? Has management developed techniques for exposing department heads and key officers or potential management to the board so that it can make face-value judgments? Does management bring good individual performance to your attention so that you can personally compliment the young man or woman? Being informed about outstanding personnel is very important. Does the directors' personnel committee have proper information about the individual's performance at the time of review? Today's competitive marketplace does not permit increased compensation for nonproductive personnel, nor does it ignore failure to reward productive staff members.

Administrative Evaluation

Management has the responsibility of directing a well-informed, harmonious board as it strives to establish workable policies. Bank boards have difficulty making intelligent decisions if they are continually surprised by management. If programs have already been accomplished when they are brought to the board, the decision process has been derailed. Make certain management gives ample time to the assessment of material changes in policy or operations.

Directors should be sensitive to the ability of management to provide agendas that properly establish priorities, that utilize the board's limited time and enable it to act as a policy-determining body. It is equally important that management possess the skill to resolve inevitable conflicts outside the boardroom prior to meetings. A successful board does not operate in a climate of continued confrontation.

In the banking industry today we have the best crop of potential managers in several decades. These young men and women need the counsel and guidance that you with your business experience can provide. With this magical, constructive combination, banking is destined for a bright future.

B. FINLEY VINSON

Board Functions and Committee Organization

"I AM A BANK DIRECTOR and I am interested in my job. I have accepted the responsibility with my eyes wide open. I consider it an honor to serve on the board of my bank and I recognize the responsibilities—and the opportunities—that I have assumed." That statement might represent the attitude of most bank directors. But how do we really get a handle on this job?

I am chairman of the board of my bank, an internal director. I have turned over to a younger man the chief executive officer's job, and I am trying to teach my younger associates that they should not fall into the trap of believing that the board is a necessary evil. They should always keep in mind that all management power flows from the board of directors and belongs to the executive in only such measure as the board determines. Some bank executives, and boards, tend to ignore that basic fact. So, what I have to say is from the viewpoint of an outside director.

Our bank is not dominated by one individual, one family, or even a majority group. Our stock ownership is widespread and not under the control of anybody. We meet, we vote, and we act without the potential frustration that anything we do is subject to the overriding vote of some individual or small group. We are fortunate in that respect. If there is in your bank a strong control situation, it is important for every member of your board to know that his or her vote counts, to feel that conviction can be voted and cannot be rejected solely because of majority ownership views.

Now you may say that all banks are different. With qualifications, I can accept that, just as I can accept the fact that all building plans, for instance, are different. On the other hand, I know that there are certain basic similarities found in all buildings. I think this applies to banks as well, regardless of size. We all live under the same kinds of banking regulations and laws—with minor differences.

There must be planned "successor management" for boards of directors. The leadership of banks, the executive officers and the board, should be constantly alert to people in the community who might be considered for membership on the board of directors. A good board of directors should have reasonably full representation for such diverse areas as business, agriculture, the professions, and education. Consumer interests should also be represented, as should women and minority groups. We have a fine young newspaper editor on our board who guards consumer interests with a constant vigilance. How many directors do you have? If you have eight or ten, would you have a more prosperous and helpful community bank if you had fifteen to twenty? Our community deserves different viewpoints on a bank board of directors. A good board of directors will consist of more than just the cronies or close friends of the president or chairman.

I like to have a person around who can ask an executive officer an embarrassing question now and then and make him feel uncomfortable. Most chief executives, of course, do not like that type of director. But a director like that makes me feel more comfortable, because I know that he may keep me out of trouble. Sometimes this director will be a bit of an irritant. Like the cross-eyed discus thrower at the county track meet, he may not break many records, but he sure keeps the crowds alert.

A board of directors must be involved. One of our most experienced and able bankers, oftentimes a member of the SWGSB faculty, Mr. Charles Agemian, tears into me when I talk about committees; but Mr. Agemian is an inside director, and a good one. He is not an outside director seeking a way to be sure that he fulfills his total responsibilities in just the fraction of the time that he is on the job.

So we need outside director involvement—not in management, but in making and then reviewing policy in each major function in which the board must accept responsibility. We need regular review and evaluation of bank operations by outside directors to see whether that policy is being carried out, and to review and update policy as changes occur. Directors should remember that "if we're doing anything the way it was done five years ago in our bank, we're probably ten years behind the times."

The only logical way for an outside director to function is through a group of working board committees. Certainly, by law, we must have an audit or examining committee; a trust committee, if we have a trust department; and a directors' loan committee, unless the board as a whole acts as the loan committee. To avoid any of these—as active participants—is to flirt with legal dynamite.

If a bank has seven or eight directors, the board may act as a committee of the whole, if it has the will and the time. Committee work takes time. I want an officer personnel committee, not just to listen to the president recommend promotions and raises and then pass them on rubber-stamped to the board of directors, but to make certain, through annual or semiannual review with executive officers, for instance, that provision for management succession shall be a prime executive responsibility every year. I like a board committee to review regularly the progress of the young men on the way up in our bank, and this is one good way to do it.

Today, more than ever before, I want an insurance committee to study in detail the insurance and fidelity bond coverage of our bank, not just with the officers of the bank, but with insurance industry representatives who may recommend a better or more thorough way. While most directors are reasonably vigilant in supervising loans, I believe most are negligent in reviewing bank investments. So I want a bank investments committee that reviews investment policy and periodically reviews changes that have been made or that should be made in the investment portfolio. The committee should be one that spends enough time to understand generally the investments of my bank, and one which questions major investment transactions, at least quarterly.

I insist on having a board committee to study at least once a year the long-range capital needs our bank is likely to have, and to report those needs to the board with policy recommendations. This job may be done by the executive committee, but it is too important to leave to management alone. Management will too often consider capital needs only when the examiners drive them to it. In our bank we feel the need for a small board committee to consider stock options and other benefits and to review the retirement policies of the bank; and another to make certain at least quarterly that security measures are current, modern, and being followed. These smaller jobs might be done better by the executive committee, but there is a good chance of their being crowded out by "more important" things.

Our bank has eleven active committees. Some of them meet only once a year, but each has a meeting time (the month of the year, if not the date, is spelled out), written objectives and functions; and each is vital to our board members' knowledge and understanding of their jobs and to the fulfillment of their full legal responsibilities.

I expect the board committees of my bank to help management develop written policies for the major functions of the bank, except operations. And I want brief but regular reports by the director/chairmen of these committees, some monthly, some quarterly, some semiannually or annually. I expect management to help design reports that are readable, understandable, comparable, and meaningful, allowing the director/chairman to review the execution of bank policies when he reports to the board.

Some banks have one or more directors who are careless about attending meetings. Directors should be expected to attend a majority of board meetings, and to be absent only when compelling business prohibits their attendance. A director who does not regularly attend meetings is denying that bank the service of someone else who might contribute more and work harder to meet the needs of today's complex banking world. Most banks have had this problem. It is a tough one, but it is better for the director as well as for the bank if the problem is faced squarely and candidly.

Banks have been notoriously slow in providing for the retirement of board members, although they have done a fairly good job in providing for the retirement of bank personnel. A directors' retirement plan should be a part of the bank's by-laws. It should be carefully devised by a special committee of the board of directors and thoroughly discussed by the board prior to approval. It may "grandfather" in present members, say those over sixty. Most larger banks now have adopted plans which require directors to retire to advisory status either on disability or no later than seventy years of age—some plans call for retirement at sixty-five. Good bank directors are scarce, I know. This makes for a tough job in a small bank with few directors, or in a small town with several banks, but it is a job that should be faced.

As an outside director, you owe your bank a number of things:

1. The courtesy of giving the bank all of your own business, or a major part of it if your firm needs more than one bank. You must feel that it is "your bank."

2. A commitment to work for new business for the bank, and to be alert to new customers who may be prospects for the bank.

3. The good judgment never to carry outside the boardroom confidential bank business or discussion of a customer or a prospect's business. It is sometimes done, but such action is a flagrant breach of trust. It is the chairman's job to police such violations.

4. Your attendance at and participation in board meetings, setting aside enough time to stay for the whole meeting, to attend special meetings if called, and to be diligent in handling board committee assignments.

5. The good sense to conduct your own business and your personal life in a way that will not adversely affect the image of your bank; and you should expect to resign from the board should a situation—business or personal—develop that might embarrass the bank.

6. The good judgment not to ask for or accept special rates, marginal loans, favors, and such. You should know better than to exercise the strength of your position as a director to intimidate or take advantage of a loan officer or any of the personnel of your bank. Such actions can lead to major problems.

7. The courage to stand up against other board members when they meddle in management, or against those who seek to pressure management for their own benefit or that of their friends.

8. A commitment to the public, the shareholders, and the rest of the board to accept the responsibility of never becoming a rubber stamp for the bank's officers.

9. The good sense to stay out of management but to stay involved in policy, and to learn the difference between the two.

No doubt you can add to this list of things which you and I owe our banks, but this could be a starter.

The bank also owes you a few things:

1. Fair compensation for your time in board and committee meetings, even though your acceptance of the responsibility is not for the fees you receive.

2. Written policy statements on all major functions of the bank, with the opportunity to review these statements periodically, to question them, and to suggest changes as needed.

3. An opportunity to hear and see someone besides the president or chairman give oral reports in board meetings. Remember Frank Plummer's recommendation: at least once a year you should want to

see and hear the division heads, the department heads, the principal supporting officers who are carrying out the policies of the board every day. This is a good way to see if these men are growing, to see how they perform before the board of directors, to question them directly, and to see them respond.

4. Regular, meaningful reports—comparisons with other banks in your town, in your area or state, and with banks of your size in the Federal Reserve or FDIC district. These comparisons are available. You deserve to know if your bank operation is as superior as the chairman and president keep telling you it is. You should eyeball it yourself. Different banks make different kinds of reports to the boards. Some of them are so bulky that they are staggering; they cannot possibly be reviewed and understood in the limited time boards meet each month. Some are so skimpy they are meaningless. With a folder before you, or better with a slide on a screen, so that all look at the same page and talk about the same figures at the same time, you should review regularly all important aspects of the bank's business. This does not mean every month for all of them. Some reviews may be made monthly, some quarterly, some annually.

5. An active program of service to the community, not only in business and industry, but also in education, in cultural affairs, and in the political involvement of its personnel. It is pretty hard to separate the interests of bank, customers, and community.

6. Senior officers who are willing to recognize that there has to be a measured amount of "moving over" as they grow older; officers who are willing to delegate responsibility to younger men and help them learn to make decisions; senior officers who truly allow the development of new ideas, new ways, and new people; officers who are willing to supervise them from a little farther off as they mature; to feed in their more conservative influence when needed, but not every day as a matter of course.

7. Executive officers who will counsel with the board of directors but who will, on the other hand, have the stature and fortitude to argue, to present facts and evidence to sustain their position if they feel that it is correct. A chief executive officer who will insist on managing and who will insist on the board staying in its policy-making role, but who may, likewise, gracefully recede, remembering that he, too, is only one board member where bank policy is concerned.

8. The courtesy of giving you time enough in board meetings to

review, question, and understand. This does not mean that you should be allowed to require a board committee to go over again all matters considered in arriving at its recommendation to the board; but you should be allowed to satisfy yourself that the committee has had the facts, has considered them carefully, and has made a policy recommendation that is reasonable, even though you might not have done it exactly the same way.

9. Insurance protection against malicious, unjustified shareholders' suits.

10. Periodic discussions of national trends in bank organization, bank corporate structure, and directions; and information on major legislative proposals which may substantially affect your bank and your investment in it.

11. An opportunity not only to see the examination made by the FDIC or the comptroller or the Federal Reserve, but also to sit in conference with the chief examiner when he completes his work and to discuss with him any matters he reports in the examination, or which he feels will be of help to the board in discharging its responsibilities. Ask your chief executive to notify the examiner that you want to meet with him when he completes the examination. The examiner has instructions to welcome such requests.

The policy guidelines of the comptroller of the currency state: "The directors of a national bank may delegate the day to day routine of conducting the bank's business but they cannot delegate to their officers and employees the responsibility for the consequences resulting from unsound or imprudent policies and practices." The FDIC and state authorities have about the same position as far as state chartered banks are concerned. The language is easily understood.

Such are the things that go along with the honor of serving as a bank director. That is why, as a bank director, you should expect from the executives of your bank an operating structure that will reasonably allow directors to carry out their responsibilities. I submit that an active committee program is the only way this can be accomplished. Directors are the great reserve of strength in the banking business. Banking deserves the unlimited measure of wisdom and guidance that directors can give. Banking is too important to leave to management alone—state and federal laws and the courts have told us that in clear language.

GERALD R. SPRONG

Analyzing Bank Operations

THE PRIMARY REASON a bank is in business is to render service. To render service, it must have a qualified staff and the financial strength to protect depositors. The surest way to preserve financial strength and protect depositors is to have board policies which require management to perform under guidelines consistent with sound banking practices. Paramount among these are loan policies which should control the relationships between the types of deposits and the needs of the customers. If your bank loans money outside your trade territory or deviates significantly from other prescribed loan policy, blow the whistle.

Of nearly equal importance is a good personnel policy, with adequate employee rewards to attract good people and keep them. Knowledge of who your officers are and how they perform is also important. You should know where your officers borrow money. Officers give a report to the board of all their loans with banks. But it is a good policy to require that all borrowing be reported. A periodic and careful audit of the bank, at least annually, by outside auditors is fundamental; and an investment policy that provides for adequate liquidity to meet unexpected deposit outflows and sudden increases in loan demands is equally important.

Every bank should have a written loan policy, as having one and reviewing loans and their adherence to prescribed policy provides an important control. A prudent director who scrutinizes the list of loans with a policy in mind should be able to identify possible improprieties and protect the bank and himself from the consequences of malfeasance and bad credit practices.

Good policies and their enforcement should come first; but a second director responsibility should be the good operating performance of the bank. There are ratios which measure performance and which can guide you in the discharge of your responsibility. The experience in the mid-1970s with bank failures and corresponding shareholder losses should alert the director to the need to know what is going on and how the bank is performing. Proper analysis of financial statements can provide the basis for measuring management performance; it can also provide guidance for corrective actions to improve performance when needed.

In any evaluation of financial performance one needs a base for comparison. I use the ratios of other banks in our market area, but in those instances where there are not enough banks in a market area of comparable size and makeup, I go outside our market area and identify banks of comparable size in comparable markets.

There is a great deal of information concerning bank performance now available to banks that was not available even five years ago. The Bank Administration Institute has several good studies along with excellent data analysis. The FDIC, the comptroller of the currency, the Federal Reserve Banks, and state banking commissions also have ratio information which can provide a base to measure the performance of your bank. The BAI and FRB also have ratios for high performance banks.

Financial ratios facilitate the directors' analysis because they bring the results of operations of all banks to the same common denominator. The greatest difficulty we directors have in looking at financial statements is putting the numbers in the right perspective. It is hard to convert dollar figures into measures of accomplishments. When converted to ratios, they become comparable and more meaningful.

What are the significant ratios a director should use in evaluating the efficiency of the bank? In my view, the most important ratio is the rate of return on average assets; that is, net income after taxes as a percent of average outstanding assets. Average assets, not assets at year end. In determining outstanding balances, daily averages should be used. It is a simple computation to derive the necessary data, and computerized systems can provide the data easily. If your bank has too large a proportion of its funds invested in FED funds, brick and mortar, and correspondent bank balances, or too much in bonds and not enough in loans, the net income will be affected unfavorably. Thus the ratio measures efficiency in use of resources.

The median banks, that is, the average banks, had a rate of return on average assets of .92 percent in 1975. For every $100 of assets they produced a net profit of 92 cents. Just to be average, in my mind, is not an acceptable goal, and I assume that all directors feel the same about their own bank. I find it appropriate to compare our results to those of "high performing banks." The top one-fourth of the high performance banks in 1975 had a return on assets of approximately 1.20 percent.

In using such data you should be aware that return on assets is greatly affected by the banking laws under which the bank is operating. National Banks or FED member banks cannot be expected to earn as much as a state-chartered nonmember FED bank in most states.

In my experience in working with many banks over almost twenty years, it is a common practice to compare the current year's earnings with the prior year's earnings and, if there is a small increase or no decrease, consider that the bank has done a good job. Limiting the evaluation of operating results by comparing them only to results of the previous year is simply not prudent management. The better reference is to comparison with performance of other banks in your geographical area.

A bank's performance might compare very favorably with prior years or with its budget, but the level of performance may not be favorable when compared with other banks. Comparison of small banks with large banks also is an unreliable measure. The small banker usually can say, "Look at the banks in New York, California, or Chicago. They are making only .75 percent on assets and we are making 1.5 percent. We look super." Well, maybe "we" ought to be making 2 percent.

The income statement is an important tool in measuring a bank's performance. The statement is the result of all of management's decisions which influence the bank's performance. It is the end product of decisions regarding quality of assets. If you look at the ratios derived from the income statement and find that your bank has a typical asset distribution, but gross income 25 percent above the rest of the banks in your area, what does that tell you? Does it tell you that you have the smartest bank management in the world? Very likely not. You may be taking more risks than the bank down the street. But it can tell you how effectively the management of the bank is investing funds. If you find that your gross income on a percentage basis of your assets, or your cost of money, or your FED funds' income is low as compared to other banks, you have several questions to ask. For example, Are we properly invested in FED funds or temporary deposits? Is the manager of the bank keeping unnecessary balances with correspondent banks in order to get a low interest rate loan for himself, or is he just not performing well, or are our back office procedures so weak that we cannot really get the money invested promptly? Are the tellers checking out too late? Maybe the tellers should check out at 2:00 P.M. instead of 4:00 P.M. so that the money can be put into use on the fastest availability schedule.

The income statement also forecasts your equity situation. If your bank's net income is low compared to that of other banks, your equity return is going to be low and you need to do something about it. If the situation continues you probably are going to end up with too little capital to support growth. A low earnings ratio is the first indication that an equity problem is ahead. It also gives you an indication of the proper pricing of services. If your bank is operating on lower than average service charge income, return check charges, etc., maybe you are pricing your services too low.

The effectiveness of advertising and promotion is very difficult to measure. However, we need to know how much we spend on such activities, and we should measure these expenses as a percent of assets and operating income. Country bankers have said to me time after time, "Well, we only spend $3,000 a year because we are the only bank in the area; we don't have any competition." They are deluding themselves. There are all kinds of competition in every bank market, including large or small retailers, savings and loan associations, and finance companies. Perhaps they should be spending at least as much as similar banks in other markets.

If your bank is not performing adequately—if the ratios indicate that the bank is doing less than an average job—there may be a dozen or more things that need to be corrected, and your board has the responsibility to cause corrective action to be taken. Sometimes that means telling your best friend, the president, to get off his duff and get to work. Sometimes it is a situation that can only be corrected over a long period of time.

A president who is sufficiently concerned with keeping his directors informed and using their guidance will review performance. We give our board of directors a full report each month, and at each director's meeting the key ratios are reviewed and variances explained completely and in detail.

The ratio I always call to the attention of the directors is the "cash and due from banks" ratio, because it indicates the performance of the back office section of the bank. Our bank had 13.8 percent of its assets in "cash and due" in 1974. That is an average percent; but we reduced the ratio to 10.74 percent in 1975. Any time a director sees this percentage go above 12 percent in a national bank, or above 6 or 7 percent in a state-chartered nonmember FED bank, he can assume there is a problem somewhere with the investment of funds, and the director needs to know why the performance is not better.

Another important ratio is percent of assets invested. We had in our investments, which basically is our bond portfolio plus FED funds, 27 percent of our assets in 1974 and 36 percent in 1975. In 1973 our bank had a lot of money in fifteen-twenty year bonds, and we should not have had, because loan demand fluctuates tremendously in our bank. Our loan-to-deposit ratio is above 60 percent now and can go as high as 75-80 percent for sixty to ninety days almost any time before the farmers go to market. The heavy bond investments forced us to borrow FED funds at times when I was not always sure we could get the funds with which to support the loans, and when the rate on FED funds was high. Therefore, we sought greater liquidity.

Another key percentage is that of total loans as a percent of assets. At the present time our ratio is about 51 percent of assets, as compared to 54 percent for the prior year. Especially in smaller banks this is a key ratio, and a bank director must be aware of what other banks are doing. If that ratio slips to around 40 percent of total assets, you can expect increased competition for loans. The loan ratio should be given a lot of attention.

The expenditure on bank premises is another percentage that I think is very important. Total fixed assets, in our case, is about 1.5 percent of assets. The higher that percentage is, the lower the earnings ratio, usually.

Another key ratio is the demand-to-total-deposits ratio. About 42 percent of our deposits is in demand money and the balance in time money. In our bank this ratio is declining. If it is in your bank, you, as a director, need to give more attention to profit management and how the bank is investing its assets.

Another key ratio is the capital-to-asset ratio. If this ratio starts declining, capital planning should be accelerated. The examiners often talk about this ratio, especially when dealing with rural banks, and may advise that the ratio should be around 8 percent of assets or 9 percent of deposits. If your ratio slips to around 7 percent of assets, your bank needs to begin to give attention to plans to increase capital.

Another key ratio is "Salaries and Wages, Pension Benefits, and Other Employee Benefits" to income. The average bank in Missouri spent 20.7 percent of its gross income on salaries and employee benefits. In our case, the ratio is 19.6 percent. If the ratio is above 20 percent in your bank, you should know why. It is a very important ratio: the percentage of gross income that goes into salaries and employee benefits.

There are many other important ratios, but a presentation of this type cannot review them all. I must review one group of them, however: those which reveal deposit performance. Each time there is a call we analyze our market share in our community of 80,000 people, determining the gain or loss in our share of total deposits and in each deposit category.

If you as a director do not know how your bank is doing in its marketplace, how can you adopt policies that help you meet your community's needs? Remember, your bank's primary reason for existence is to render service to your community.

There are thirteen banks in our holding company, ranging in size from $6 million to $160 million. The smaller banks have been in our holding company only three or four months. But they already have director reports very similar to those of the largest banks which have been in the group several years. We have cut out a few of the fancy charts and graphs, but not the key ratios. You may hear from your president that your bank does not have the data to prepare such a director's report, or that it is too costly to do so, but every single thing I have discussed and more comes from reports and information sent by every bank to the FDIC, or the comptroller of the currency, or some other regulatory agency, and is available in some form as bank performance averages from readily tappable sources. It is a very simple task to assemble and analyze them, a task that will bring amazing results to your bank in analyzing its performance.

The FDIC, the comptroller of the currency, Federal Reserve

Banks, and some state organizations furnish excellent ratio materials. These are published annually, usually about March or April, and probably come to your bank. If you have not seen any of these studies or you are not being exposed to them in your bank, ask for them. You should have them.

PHILIP F. SEARLE

Planning, Budgeting, and Control: A Bank Director's Perspective

WITHOUT DOUBT, contemporary banking and economic environments have brought to bank directors and managers responsibilities that are greater now than at any time since the 1930s. Consideration must be given to bank involvement in any number of challenging and frequently provocative areas: branch expansion, bank charge cards, asset quality, broadened data processing capabilities, capital adequacy, leasing services, installation and/or the competitive impact of customer-bank communication terminals (now better known as CBTCs), a broadened assortment of sources of capital and deposit funds, the possibility and relative advisability of affiliating with bank holding companies, and many other banking activities, functions, or potentialities which are designed to have the effect of increasing the service offerings of banks, or of increasing bank profitableness, or of attaining both of these objectives.

These are not easy times for most banks. In the recent past, the increased reliance of banks on borrowed funds, money market instruments, and an expanded array of relatively high-cost time and savings plans, plus the inherent labor-intensiveness of banking, have resulted in decreased operating margins for banks. These have, in certain instances, contributed toward lessened bank liquidity, lower bank earnings, and a diminished concern over, or attention to, the management of asset risk.

Banking regulatory authorities are, with understandable justification in these times, placing heightened emphasis upon improved capital ratios, enhanced asset quality, and liquidity. In this environment, however, many of those banks with the best long-range planning, and certainly those possessing the optimum flexibility reflecting informed economic probabilities, are prominent among the best performers in the unpleasant and uncomfortable economic and monetary climates of 1974 and early 1975.

There are, to be sure, banks which elected in 1974 to meet loan demand only moderately and instead to invest certain of their liabilities in what were then extraordinarily high-yielding overnight funds. In some instances their 1974 earnings successes were achieved at the expense of meeting deserving requests for loans, the income from which would now be far more attractive to them than the current return on that same previously noncommitted overnight money.

What I am suggesting is that we need to operate our banks with longer-range and better quantified objectives in mind; and this leads more specifically to the broad and obviously interrelated subjects of planning, budgeting, and control. In my almost thirty years of banking I have personally attended about a dozen sessions on planning, three or so on budgeting, and about three-quarters of one, in the aggregate, on control. And yet, these statistics are, in my judgment, wholly misleading.

Planning, per se, has a great deal more sex appeal to it than budgeting or control. In some quarters there seem to be descending levels of intellectual prerequisites for successful participation in the three areas: for planning, a Ph.D.; for budgeting, an M.B.A. or A.B., but certainly a certificate in the appropriate discipline; and for control, whatever in the world that is, some auditor type, with just about any educational and/or experience credentials whatsoever. These perceptions are unfortunate and unproductive. All three functions are interdependent, and without maximum effective, empathetic, and constructive communication and cooperation, none of them can coexist and benefit the organization.

Directors are not expected to be practitioners in the areas of planning, budgeting, or control; these are major responsibilities of your bank's chief executive officer, and you should expect him to report to you on the bank's activities in each of these areas.

Over the years I have accumulated a sizable reference library on the subject of planning. In that collection is a volume entitled *Practical Long-Term Planning for Savings Institutions,* published a few years ago by a branch of our competitors, the Savings Association Marketing Society of America, which includes a classic comment: "Don't start vast projects with half-vast plans." There is much substance to that stipulation.

Planning in banking has now become an industry imperative. Banking is one of the most labor-intensive of all industries. More costly interest-bearing funds are rapidly replacing demand deposits as the prime funds source in commercial banks. Today's lower short-term money market rates cannot be considered as anything but a temporary condition, as banks, for a variety of reasons, will continue to experience a meaningful reduction in the ratio of demand deposits to total deposits. Profitable and prudent employment of these higher-priced funds will require more sophisticated, more timely planning.

Expense control through ardent budgeting and careful profit-planning is essential to the successful operation of banks now and in the future, especially those banks whose optimistic growth potentials demand capital accretions or additions proportionately commensurate with deposit growth expectations.

Bank planning itself can consist of several components. The definition of planning can become confusing, for there is long-range planning (five to seven years), short-range planning (annually), and intermediate planning (somewhere between one and seven years). There are elements of functional planning, such as marketing planning, which can be an important adjunct to, and contained within, overall corporate planning. Many organizations now are engaging in profit planning, which may or may not be meaningfully related to the realities of the corporate long-term plan. Profit planning is usually designed, however, to produce shorter-term advantageous bottom-line results.

The planning process basically is the development of a broad plan and the specific programs that will translate that plan into action. It is fundamental that the plan begin by defining the bank's objectives and setting its goals; it should then present the strategies that will move the bank toward meeting these objectives and goals. Once this rather broad framework has been developed, detailed action programs can then be devised that will stipulate which persons or functional units will perform and/or achieve certain results, and that will establish time frames for the anticipated results.

Planning thus involves not only a scheme of action or procedure, but also includes well-defined programs which stipulate anticipated results as measured against thoughtfully conceived objectives. Furthermore, to be effective, planning must be both total and continuous. Sporadic efforts at solving special problem areas, even if the word *planning* is included in the project designation, do not qualify as acceptable planning. Such efforts tend to be masquerading as planning; in reality they are only programs to beat out one or more of those "brush fires" which beset all of us from time to time.

McKinsey & Company's E. Everett Smith, a leading commentator on bank planning, identifies three distinguishing characteristics of the planning programs of certain leading banks which have been especially successful in their planning activities; i.e., those banks which have fully integrated planning into their management processes.

1. The bank began by identifying precisely what it wanted to plan, and then tailoring a planning process to achieve its specific objectives. Different organizations have different planning needs, so what is appropriate for one bank may not necessarily be suitable for another, even if it is in the same market and/or geographical area.

2. Having created an appropriate planning process, the bank then tailored it to fit the organization's own management process. The significance of this is that all too often in the past banks have attempted to superimpose new management techniques onto existing (and frequent outmoded) management structures and operations. Those banks that have made outstanding accomplishments in planning, Smith points out, are those that have identified the management implications of the kind of planning they are doing, and have then made whatever structural and procedural changes that were required to integrate effective and productive planning into the day-to-day management of the bank.

3. The bank measures the accomplishments of planning by the effects it has on the management process, as well as by the results the plan produces; or, to put it in another way, the principal value of planning does not necessarily exist within the plans that it produces, but rather in the process of producing such plans. The value of planning to managers lies primarily in their participation in and appreciation of the whole planning process, and somewhat less in their use of its end product.

Once you have made a commitment to institute and implement a planning effort, I would caution you to make an effort to be alert to the difference between planning and forecasting. Recent economic, monetary, and fiscal conditions seem to have placed a premium on effective forecasting, especially since consensus economic prognostication has achieved a rather drab track record in recent years. On the one hand, the bank should not be reluctant to take advantage of its own, its correspondents', and its consultants' expertise in developing those economic and interest rate forecasts which will be helpful to the bank in its future activities.

On the other hand, even the most meticulous financial forecast cannot in and of itself be regarded as a viable planning document; it can only be one of the essential elements, which in combination with other basic requirements of the continuing planning process, will benefit the future performance of the bank.

What, then, can an effective planning program do for your bank? It can make more probable the best utilization of your bank's capital and its assets. It can identify in advance information that will be needed for decisions. It can give you an advantage over time in terms of market penetration and performance vis-à-vis that of your competitors, especially if your planning effort is better than theirs. It can contribute toward a continuing improvement of the bank's management structure, organization, and staff as it integrates the thinking and activities of all of those whose suggestions are needed to accomplish complex tasks. It improves communications, and it can instill in the bank's executives a degree of heightened involvement and professionalism which, without a viable planning program, might not occur.

Once directors and managers have become convinced that their bank should engage in more meaningful planning, how do they proceed to encourage the installation and/or the improvement of their bank's planning program? Certainly it is not the director's prerogative to become directly involved in the planning process, but he can, and I believe he should, ask some pertinent questions. Some of these might be: (1) Does the bank have a viable planning program? (2) What time frame does it encompass? (3) What are the sources of information used in the creation of the plan? (4) Does the plan contemplate the use of measurement and control tools, such as profit measurement, work measurement, and standard costs? (5) Is the program broader in scope than just an annual program? (6) Could the program be expanded to provide planning, continually updated, for a five-year period? (7) What would the budgeting consequences of implementing such a program be in comparison with operating only a "seat-of-the-pants" planning program?

Before championing a planning effort in your bank in a "damn the torpedoes, full speed ahead" mode (which I must admit is *not* the reaction my presentations typically receive), you should be aware of some of the pitfalls of sound planning, pointed out by E. Everett Smith, which can befall a bank:

1. There is always the danger of becoming too preoccupied with turning out plans just for the sake of turning them out, rather than with developing a plan and integrating it into the total management process. A corporate (or bank) headquarters planning function could produce little more than impressively and expensively bound planning documents, which all too often might gather dust in senior executives' offices. In such an environment, the plans come to life only on special occasions, possibly when it occurs to someone that the bank ought to determine how close actual performance has come to the objectives set forth in the plan. Another "underuse" of plans occurs when they are only used to monitor performance. Planning makes its greatest contribution to the bank's success when it adds a disciplined time dimension to today's decisions, the perspectives of the past, and the probabilities of the future.

2. Effective planning requires that a decision be made on exactly what it is that the bank needs to plan. Because planning is time-consuming and costly, those few areas which can benefit most from planning should be identified, and a thorough planning effort should be conducted for them. This is better than spreading the entire planning budget and energy thinly over the entire scope of the bank's activities.

3. What the bank wants to plan should determine the kind of planning structure and process it should establish. The earlier pioneering excursions into planning have made it obvious that there is no single correct way to plan. For some banks the emphasis ought to be on budgetary and on budgeting controls. For others, account profitability analysis and key account planning would be the basic elements upon which the planning effort would be based.

4. Planning takes perseverance because the information needed for it may not be readily available. Too few banks have information available on the cost of the services offered; they do not have the information needed for the structuring of planned programs or for measuring or controlling the progress of such programs. As more and more banks install viable management information systems, however, much of the information needed in planning will be produced routinely.

5. A planning effort will identify and/or accentuate some organizational problems that must be resolved before the effort can be effective. There is a direct correlation between realistic structuring of authority and responsibility and any real achievements to be gained from planning. Based upon the experiences of banks that have tried various approaches to planning in recent years, it has been learned that the bank's organizational structure, and the authorities and responsibilities involved, need to be clarified before undertaking a planning effort.

In some banks the appropriate emphasis in planning should be on budgeting and on budgeting control. At the risk of overgeneralization, I am assuming that this is the approach to planning which might very well be undertaken by most, or at least by many, banks. To define budgeting is to define a process that is very much like planning: budgeting is the establishing of what the bank *wants* to happen. This can be compared to forecasting, which is what the bank believes actually *will* happen, once the budget period begins. When the bank has determined what it wants to happen, and where it wishes to go, the budget can be viewed as a guide toward getting there.

The budgeting process is a means of identifying action to be performed in order to achieve the bank's goals and objectives. The budget also serves as a performance measurement tool, to be utilized by lower-level managers in meeting their responsibilities to the organization. It can be used as well by top management to determine the effectiveness of the organization as a whole and of its various components; this function of budgeting is especially important, for it can, through the recognition of deviations from budget, identify the need for corrective action programs.

Thus, budgeting establishes responsibility and invokes a discipline for serious contemplation by senior management as well as by lower level managers throughout the organization. The very fact that a budget must be prepared helps the bank and its departments deal with the basic question of "Where are we going, and how do we get there?" Obviously, budgeting bears a great similarity, although in a somewhat narrower sense, to planning.

Not only can budgeting serve as an important element of the overall planning process, but it is also a valuable management tool. And of no less importance is the fact that an effective budgeting program, sufficiently and effectively reported to the bank's board of directors, can be of material assistance to each director in discharging his directorial responsibilities.

The budget provides the base from which actual performance can be compared to budgeted expectations, but other important managerial and administrative benefits can be by-products of the budgeting program. The budgeting and variance reporting process provides the ability to measure and reward good performance. It also identifies areas of weakness and inferior performance and directs management's attention toward instituting appropriate corrective action. Better control can be exerted over expenditures, a benefit of considerable importance in the current inflationary environment.

In contemplating its budgeting program, your bank should not be discouraged by the fact that banks are not typically organized for budgeting. Even though banking has traditionally come to regard itself as oriented toward a deposit-accepting and lending structure, bank budgeting can be effectively achieved. One approach successfully utilized by a number of banks is to conceptualize the bank as being divided into various "product" or "service line" segments, such as retail, wholesale, automated customer services, trust, international, etc. Within these broad categories, specific services must then be identified.

Just as a budgeting program is mandatory if the overall planning process is to be effective, so also a meaningful organizational structure is needed to define clearly the various levels of responsibility and authority. Without these clear definitions, the disciplines possible within the budgeting process cannot effectively be invoked. The budget discipline must extend up through the lines of authority and responsibility to the chief executive officer, and through him to the board of directors.

It may well be that the actual amount of detailed budget information which is transmitted upward should be diminished at the higher levels of authority; nonetheless, it should be of such integrity and timeliness that an adequate report of actual-vs.-budget figures reaches all higher levels of authority and responsibility, and that all significant variances from budget are readily apparent.

The terms *profit planning* and *budgeting* are often used interchangeably, and they can, in fact, be the same function. Profit planning, however, usually has a more objective-oriented connotation and includes certain elements in addition to classical budgeting which, of course, tends to plan profits for only one year. Profit planning often includes such measures as return on investment, earnings per share, earnings on assets, employee productivity, and possibly a number of other key ratios or indicators derived from the bank's performance.

Profit planning thus tends to be more sophisticated (and complicated) than budgeting. It is likely to cover several years, as contrasted to budgeting, which is primarily a system measuring progress toward achievement of specified goals within a fixed period, usually one year in duration.

Because of the supposed complexities of budgeting, not all banks employ this technique. This seems to be especially true of the smaller banks. Yet there are available articles and publications which can assist and guide even the smallest banks in the design and installation of relatively simple budgeting programs—programs which will bring many advantages to the bank. In today's technical and increasingly competitive banking environment, a bank cannot justify the absence of budgeting as one of the management tools with which it maximizes its performance both in terms of profit and of service.

Assuming that the bank is convinced of the merits of planning and of budgeting, what should be done to insure that these programs work to their maximum effectiveness? Obviously, the answer is in the area of control. The word *control* can be confusing. Some bankers have taken the view, or have created the impression, that control is the enforcement arm of management. According to this interpretation, control involves reviewing performance in order to punish those who do not meet expectations, through such means as cost reductions, lay-offs, and other (sometimes necessary) defensive measures.

This is, of course, an oversimplification of attitudes because control must be integrated into the total management process in such a way that it is progressive rather than regressive, creating and liberating rather than monotonous and confining. Control should be a constructive learning experience. Those who are subject to it should be able to look back and see evidence of progress because control was indeed properly exercised.

The control function starts with the bank's chief executive officer, and descends throughout the bank in accordance with the control structure he devises, or one that is in one way or another developed pursuant to criteria he specifies. Because of the great importance of control to the success of the bank, it is virtually mandatory that the chief executive officer play a major role in the design of the control system, and that he work with it.

Control (and planning, too, for that matter) should be regarded as an operating function and not a "staff" function. There should be no arbitrary lines of demarcation between those who plan, those who operate, and those who control. Moreover, there should be no implication that those who plan and control have any greater or any lesser stature than those who operate.

In devising his planning and control structure, the chief executive officer might choose to place the detailed operation of it in the hands of an executive vice president or a committee of top executives; or he might even operate it from his own office. Fundamentally, it makes no difference how he operates so long as he does not violate the concept that all responsible persons must participate in the planning and control processes.

Some distinctions should be made here between planning and control. Planning might be effective with a minimum of participation by key personnel throughout an organization; however, control cannot be effective unless everyone in an organization participates in the process of having their work reviewed, measured, assessed, evaluated, and, if necessary, redirected. If control becomes distant from day-to-day work, the groundwork has been laid for ensuing difficulties.

Sooner or later persons at all levels will find ways to frustrate any manager who subjects them to what might be thought of as "absentee" control. This does not mean that there is no role for the objective appraisal of results, but such an appraisal must be a cooperative supplement to the control process by which all responsible officials seek to assess performance so that they can move collectively to greater levels of success.

More specifically, here is how one bank exercised a control function with respect to its planning program: a procedure was developed for reviewing performance each month to determine how each profit center was doing; this review was conducted by a senior officer committee appointed by and reporting its findings directly to the chief executive officer.

These reviews covered performance for the month past and the year-to-date, and required the profit-center managers to forecast their performance for the balance of the year. This kept managers constantly mindful of the fact that control relates to the future and is of value only if it provides information that is relevant to decisions on future courses of action.

The work of the review committee was made more meaningful by the development by the bank of certain measurement tools. Because this was a larger bank, these tools were relatively sophisticated: various policies and practices for profit measurement, time standards for most clerical operations, and standard costs for all of the bank's principal functions.

While the foregoing control procedures might be more sophisticated than those in many banks today, they nonetheless demonstrate the fundamental need for control systems in all banks. Control cannot be effective unless everyone in the organization participates in the process of having their work, their achievements, and their failures regularly reviewed, measured, assessed, evaluated, and redirected.

Planning, budgeting, and control are interrelated functionally; each of them individually, but especially all of them in proper combination, can materially benefit your bank. Yet these programs, and particularly planning, will only succeed if there is a strong and continuing commitment of support for them from every member of senior management and from the bank's board of directors. There must be a conviction that the program will contribute importantly to improving the performance of the bank, and that conviction must be clearly and continually enunciated by senior management and by the board.

Beneficial results, again especially in the planning area, will not be apparent quickly in spite of the considerable effort which must be dedicated to the programs. The communication, on a continuing basis, of a strong sense of commitment down through the organization is essential to maintain the necessary momentum. And finally, this commitment of senior management must be matched by a sense of active involvement that generates the feeling that the programs are the products of those who must make them work effectively.

Planning, budgeting, control—these are management tools which have proved their undeniable worth in many banks throughout the nation in recent years. Whatever the size of your bank, there is a version, however truncated, that will benefit it. I urge those who are already utilizing any or all of these techniques to insure that they are as effective and as contemporary as possible; and I urge those whose banks are not taking advantage of every one of these programs, to encourage their bank to give serious consideration to their use.

PHILIP F. SEARLE

Management Reports to Directors

WITHIN THE PAST DECADE, the duties and the responsibilities of bank directors have increased at a faster rate than ever before in the history of banking in America. Directors are asked to consider bank participation in a number of challenging areas, including branch expansion, credit cards, broadened data processing capabilities, leasing services, installation and/or competitive impact of customer/bank communication terminals, a broadened assortment of sources of capital and deposit funds, the possibility of affiliating with holding companies, the sale of gold, and many other banking activities designed to increase the service offerings of banks or to increase bank profitability, or both.

The greater reliance by banks upon borrowed funds, money market instruments, and an expanded array of time and savings plans, together with the inherent labor-intensiveness of banking, have resulted in decreased operating margins for banks, and have in many instances contributed toward lessened bank liquidity. The heightened complexity of banking has not necessarily been accompanied by a commensurate increase in the availability of qualified bank executives and middle management officers; banks today compete more vigorously than ever with each other and with bank-related and nonbank employers for the various executive skills and potentials necessary for successful operation.

The legal responsibilities with respect to one's serving as a bank director have never been more intense. Public and social responsibilities, many of them with their own legal overtones, abound: minority programs, including minority hiring and financing; assistance with urban programs; the maintenance of public confidence; political responsibilities; the necessity for adequate contributions to deserving civic and charitable activities; involvement of the bank's staff in worthwhile community projects; participation in area development efforts—all of these are subjects to which directors must address their thoughtful attention.

In such an environment, the board of directors of any bank, whether state or national, is charged with the responsibility of operating the bank safely—first for the benefit of the depositors, and second for the interest of the stockholders. These duties and responsibilities stem from regulations, from statutes, and from common law interpretations, which have been repeatedly supported in court decisions.

When elected to the board, a bank director assumes a certain moral responsibility to the depositors, the general public, and his fellow shareholders who are affected by the bank's soundness. Businessmen and other prominent community figures who serve as bank directors allow the use of their names as an assurance to the public that they are supervising and in fact are directing the policies and activities of the financial institution. The bank advertises the names of its directors because usually they are among the most prestigious men in the community. These names are used to encourage and maintain the confidence of the people in the stability and the integrity of the institution.

Beyond the directors' moral responsibility lies their legal responsibility under federal and state laws, which requires of each bank director far more visibility than does a usual corporate directorship. The director who does not carry out his responsibilities "with due diligence" subjects himself to financial liability under the law.

Even though directors are permitted to delegate supervision of the functions and activities to the bank's management, they cannot delegate responsibility for the results of bank policies and activities. The board's responsibility lies not so much in doing as it does in seeing that things are accomplished. The directors must determine that safe loan and investment policies are adhered to, and that there is good internal control of all operations for the prevention and detection of losses due to mismanagement and fraud.

It becomes readily apparent that directors need information to maintain their surveillance of the bank's condition and to enable them to determine whether management is alert to its responsibilities. Proper presentation of information presents a challenge and an opportunity for bank management to provide the board with reports that will serve as a basis for the logical appraisal of results of bank operations.

The necessity for adequate and timely management reporting to bank directors has never been greater. It is related not just to the misfortunes which befell Penn Central, BarChris, Gulf Sulphur, and others, and the various relevant allegations of self-dealing, insider information, and directorial negligence which have been lodged in the courts and in the press, but more specifically, insofar as bank directors are concerned, to certain recent major bank failures. A thoughtful observer cannot avoid wondering whether the boards of directors of those banks, had they been in possession of sufficient timely information, would not have taken responsible action which might have averted the demise of those banks. And, conversely, if the directors did not seek and demand such information, what are the limits of their potential liability?

The extent to which directors might be provided complete information is by no means agreed upon among all bankers. Some feel that a distinction should be made between the functions of the board and the functions of operating management. If the board is allowed to go into any type of information, they argue, members might get into operating matters and undermine the authority of those entrusted with the management of the company. Providing directors with certain aspects of confidential customer information is another source of concern for some bankers.

However, as Harold Koontz points out in his excellent text, *The Board of Directors and Effective Management*:

When it is considered that a board member is the highest authority in a company through his election as a representative of the shareholders, it is clear that he should have unlimited access to all kinds of company information. As one company executive stated, "The directors elect the management, so what right does management have to make any rules about access to plans or operating data?"

And Koontz continues:

As for the danger that individual board members may get into operating data of no direct concern to them in handling their functions, this problem can be handled through proper reports to board members, through clarification of the authority of the board versus that of the operating management, and through diplomatic guidance by the chairman to make certain that the board members consider and pass only on items in their province. After all, it is the board members who define this area, and they should be the first to be willing to limit their attention to these matters.

It is thus appropriate that the directors, under their obligation and authority, contemplate that the day-to-day handling of operations must necessarily be delegated by them to the executive officers of the bank. Under this theory, the board of directors should determine broad, general policies, but should not actively involve itself in operating matters. A frequently quoted statement on this subject is, "Let the directors 'direct' and let management 'manage.'"

A sufficient and effective program of providing management information to directors has, therefore, at least the following important elements:

1. The director is well enough informed about the operations of the bank to fulfill his role as a director with maximum competence.

2. The director is kept in a knowledgeable position so that he can make suggestions and proposals to management in the earlier phases of planning, which then can often be helpful rather than destructive, as they might be if presented in the final stages of planning.

3. The director is provided with sufficient meaningful information so that he can meet his legal responsibilities as a bank director, and thus be protected against the possibility of outside legal action against him.

Reports to directors can be submitted at various frequencies: monthly, quarterly, semiannually, annually, and irregularly as needed.

The frequency of submission of any given report, the amount of detail in various reports, and the need for and/or interest in a given report, all are likely to vary from bank to bank. The nature of the bank's business and its market, the relative composite level of business or banking experience represented on the board, the size of the bank, and the level of competency and style of bank management all can have an important bearing on the kinds and the content of reports needed by a board of directors and the scheduling of their presentation.

In my own experience, I have been exposed more or less closely to the reports to directors of several dozen banks, partly through my activities in acquiring thirty or more banks over the years, and partly because my organization operates many banking affiliates. I never cease to be amazed by the striking dissimilarity between reports to directors among many banks, even though banking is a highly regulated business and virtually all of the regulatory requirements for reporting are very consistent. Yet the various differences in boards, banks, and managements to which I have alluded serve as some sort of justification for such variations.

The dissimilarities between these reports are not entirely those of subject matter: the amount of detail incorporated in reports dealing with the same general subject matter can vary widely. Some reports run the risk of losing the nonprofessional reader in a maze of detail, others reduce the substance of the report to only a few meaty statistics, and others strike a compromise by presenting considerable pertinent detail, but including certain readily identifiable conclusive statistical results.

Which of these types of reports management will provide will depend greatly upon the wishes and desires of any particular board. But whatever approach is adopted, I would suggest that all such reports be as consistent in format as possible; that they be designed to facilitate identification and analysis of meaningful trends; and that they be analyzed less as absolute statistics and more as deviations from trends or agreed-upon norms or goals.

Another observation which is based upon my experience is that reports to directors seem to be modernized very little over time, in spite of the changes which are now occurring so rapidly in banking. It seems that all too often a report, once introduced, continues to be presented at regular periodic intervals, in unchanging form. I suspect that a great many banks have not conducted a candid and objective analysis of their board reports for a number of years, in spite of the compelling reasons for doing so on a regular basis.

Hoping that the foregoing will serve as a sufficient caveat, enabling each of you to reject those suggested reports you feel are not appropriate to the needs of your board of directors, or at least to alter their frequency and/or their content, I shall suggest certain reports which I believe are necessary and/or helpful so that board members can discharge intelligently their responsibilities for determining those bank policies and procedures that result in sound and profitable bank operations reflecting responsibility to the community.

Comparative Balance Sheet: This should show a comparison with previous periods, such as the previous month or year or both. Many banks present an average balance sheet showing the accounts on an average basis for the period reported. This is basically the most accurate statement of the bank's operations, since it eliminates daily fluctuations of accounts. If a bank has profit planning and a planned balance sheet, this should be compared with the plan. Brief explanations should be made for large variances. Reading the report can be much simpler when assets and liabilities are detailed by groups, since separate schedules on later pages and back-and-forth references in the report are eliminated; all related information is on a single page.

Comparative Income and Expense Statement: This statement should show income and expenses classified in as many categories as are necessary to give the directors an adequate picture of the results of bank operations. Detailed comparisons of the current period should be made with the previous period, the same period a year ago, and the previous year's total to date. If the bank has a profit plan, a comparison should be made with the plan from the standpoint of management control. Brief explanations should be made for large variances; this is more important in connection with the profit plan than for comparison with previous time periods. A number of banks will build comparisons to budgeted figures into such a report.

Operating Ratios: This report measures the results of bank operations in terms of ratios, such as earnings per share; annualized return on stockholder's equity; annualized return on earning assets; ratios such as capital to deposits, loans to deposits, and capital to loans; price-earnings ratios; dividends as a percent of net profit; dividends as a percent of capital; liquid assets as a percent of total deposits; net income as a percent of gross income; book value per share; yields on investments and loans; and investment and deposit statistical percentages. Some banks present this report quarterly.

A Review and Evaluation of the Bank's Liquidity Positions: This subject has received considerable attention in recent months, and thus I am especially pleased to be able to champion a regular monthly liquidity report to the board of directors.

Investment Report: Securities may be grouped according to recognized classifications such as U.S. Treasury Bills, U.S. Government Bonds, Obligations of State and Political Subdivisions, Corporate Bonds, and so forth. Securities should be listed by maturity, purchase yield, coupon rate, and rating of each bond. The par value, book value, market value, and net market appreciation or depreciation should be indicated by columns with totals. Bond purchases and sales since the previous report should be listed on the report, including any profits or losses realized on each sale. Groupings of securities and the statistical characteristics of those groups can be included in useful comparative tabulations with similar statistics for the same Federal Reserve district or state, usually on a semiannual basis.

Transactions in Federal Funds Purchased or Sold: Activities in other money market instruments should also be detailed.

Loan Report: Because lending policies and procedures vary widely among banks, it is very difficult to generalize as to the recommended content for a loan report. Certainly new commitments of lines and loans of a certain predetermined amount and above should be reviewed, including the present total of indebtedness of the borrower, the interest rate, nature of security and/or guaranty, the history of the repayment capacity of the borrower, and other pertinent credit information. There should be similar reporting for renewals. Large loan payouts should be detailed on the report.

Past-Due Loans: Any past-due loans above a predetermined amount should be listed and detailed. Many banks include in such a report a description of the collateral or co-maker, an estimate of probable loss, brief comments as to actions being taken to collect the loan, and the name of the officer or committee which approved the loan or renewal. The report should also contain information on delinquency percentages on all loans, by type, in enough detail to indicate any trends which may be evident.

Loans Requiring and Receiving Special Attention: The increased levels of loan delinquencies and loan charge-offs experienced by the banking industry in recent months would indicate that this type of report—an "early warning system"—has not been as prevalent in banking as perhaps it might have been. Every bank should recognize its own potential problem loans long before they are discovered by the bank examiner. Accordingly, banks should create their own problem-loan list in addition to those loans criticized and/or classified by the examiners, review the list monthly, and determine what action has been taken to insure ultimate collection. Loans which might be candidates for inclusion in such a list would be those for which there has been a material variance from the original payment schedule, loans which have been renewed X number of times without reasonable principal reductions, loans currently classified by the bank examiners, loans that in the opinion of the lending officer or the loan committee bear a greater-than-normal risk, loans that are over Y days delinquent, and loans without satisfactory current financial information.

Review of Demand and/or Term Loans: Some banks review about a twelfth of these loans each month, thus cyclically spreading the review over the entire year and eliminating the need to spend an inordinate amount of time in such a review at any one meeting.

Loans Recommended for Charge-Off: The content of this report could vary, but it might include name of borrower, date of note, original amount, net amount recommended for charge-off, nature of collateral or co-maker, reason for loss, recovery possibility, name of officer or committee approving original loan, etc. In some banks authority for smaller charge-offs is delegated to certain officers or committees, and only larger charge-off recommendations are reported.

Auditor's Report: The auditor's report should be presented to the board of directors at the regular monthly meeting and can cover progress and details of the internal audit program, including any exceptions discovered. Many banks include in this report tellers' "over and short" acounts, cash items involving checks drawn against insufficient funds, etc. Other banks separate these latter items from the auditor's report.

Officers' and Directors' Borrowings: A number of banks include somewhat detailed reports on these subjects among their monthly reports, and do not include them in the loan report.

Significant Overdrafts on the Books for Ten Days or More.

Some of the above reports might be utilized by certain banks on a quarterly rather than monthly basis. Among other reports which seem to lend themselves to quarterly presentation are:

Profit Plan Forecast and Performance: These quarterly reports show variances from the plan and detail brief explanations for such variations.

Trust Department Earnings, Expenses, New Business Activities.

Branch Report: Included might be expenses, income, earnings, and deposits, all compared with projections.

International Banking Department Activities.

Recapitulation of Dealer Loans Outstanding.

Loan Charge-Offs and Recoveries: This report would include a summary of charged-off loans by loan category, and would include an analysis of recovery activities, also by loan category. Recovery efforts on specific charged-off loans above a certain amount should be reported in detail, until such loans are determined to be absolutely irrecoverable.

Reconcilement of Capital Accounts: This statement should show credits to undivided profits for current earnings as well as dividends and miscellaneous charges and credits to the capital accounts.

Reconcilement of Reserve Accounts: This should show the details of entries to the reserve accounts so that directors may have complete knowledge of written-off assets and recoveries.

New Business Report: A reasonable amount of detail should be included showing significant new and closed accounts, public funds activity, and other pertinent new business information. A section might be included describing in appropriate detail the extent of officers' business development calls and results achieved thereby.

Status of Expansion Plans, Including Bank Building and/or Branching Plans.

The following reports seem to lend themselves best to semiannual presentation:

A Review of Various Expenditures for Civic and Charitable Contributions, and Their Relation to Budget.

Reports on the Bank's Advertising and Public Relations Programs; Expenditures Incurred in Connection therewith, and Their Relation to Budget.

Market Share Report, Including Deposit Growth.

Report on Economic Conditions, Local and National.

Important Operating Changes Made and/or Suggested, Actions Taken in Connection with These, and Results Achieved.

The following reports appear to lend themselves best to annual presentation:

Annual Budget and Annual Capital Budget.

Annual Marketing Plan, with New Business and Marketing Goals for the Coming Year.

Report on Bank's Insurance Coverage: This report would include description of fidelity coverages, insurance of premises and fixtures, liability policies, extra expense coverage, progress in packaging various coverages, and a report on the most recent appraisals of buildings and contents for insurance purposes.

Personnel Activities: This report could be prepared by operating personnel of the bank, or might be a by-product of the activities of the directors' compensation committee, if the board has such a committee. In either case, the report would include a review of the adequacy of pension, profit sharing, group insurance, and other fringe benefit plans, on a continuing basis. It might include a personnel inventory for both officers and employees, and describe the current personnel development activities of the bank. Compensation levels within the bank could be compared with banking industry levels, as well as with those of other local employers. The bank's recruiting and hiring programs and policies should be reported, as well as their current status.

A Discussion of National and State Trends in Bank Services, Banking Structure, and Bank-Related Legislative Proposals Which if Enacted into Law Might Affect the Bank and Its Programs and Policies.

There are also a number of intermittent reports, which would be submitted at irregular intervals, such as at the regular board meeting following a particular occurrence, or when board approval is necessary, or when the matter should be brought in timely fashion to the board's attention:

Affirmative Action Programs, Requirements, or Problems.

Communications of Importance from State or Federal Agencies, Bank or Nonbank.

Crimes and Defalcations against the Bank.

Directors' Compensation Committee: This might take the form of a report or might be the minutes of this committee's most recent meeting. The committee could report on a number of subjects, including its approvals or recommendations with respect to all salaries over a given amount and all others in aggregate; could report on the status of the bank's pension plan and its portfolio; and could present its recommendations or observations with respect to the bank's management training or succession programs.

Directors' Examining or Audit Committee: This also could take the form of either the minutes of this committee's most recent meeting or a special report prepared by that committee.

Directors' Trust Audit Committee.

Report of the Bank's Independent Auditors.

Legislation or Court Decisions Affecting Banks, Federal and/or State.

Litigation, for or against the Bank, if Material.

Changes in the Bank's Lending Policy and Investment Policy.

Reports of Examination and Related Correspondence, for the Bank Itself, for the Trust Department, or for Its Electronic Data Processing Activities: Presumably, additional management reports would be promptly prepared to accompany the Reports of Examination, such that a review of the criticisms and suggestions contained in the Reports of Examination and the actions taken by management pursuant thereto could be considered by the board at its earliest opportunity. In a number of banks, Reports of Examination are evaluated by the Directors' Examining or Audit Committee and form the basis for a specific report by that committee to the board.

At first glance, the foregoing list of possible reports seems long enough so that were all of them to be utilized by a bank's board of directors, the directors would be approaching full-time employment status in that bank. In that regard, I should like to make a few suggestions which, if implemented by management, might contribute to greater efficiency in directors' meetings:

1. Have an agenda prepared for all board and committee meetings and follow each of them strictly.

2. Have all written directors' reports available well before the board meeting, and encourage each director to spend some time before each meeting studying those reports. To encourage such a practice, one banker I know provides an informal lunch for his directors preceding his 2 P.M. board meetings. Almost without exception, the directors go from lunch to the boardroom and read the reports prior to the meeting.

3. Make certain that each director knows that board meetings will last at least two hours (or whatever length of meeting is necessary in the particular bank), and be certain that he is generously compensated for that time so spent.

4. Plan and implement a calendar of special subjects for the board's agenda which will provide a systematic manner of presenting those special topics to be considered on an irregular basis, thus eliminating the occasional excessively long meeting.

5. Assign inside operating officers to present various reports, limiting each of them to a specific period of time for their presentations. There are certain ancillary benefits to be gained by so utilizing these officers: it helps to further the development of their own banking and expository skills and gives them a greater sense of participation in the management function; it enables the board to evaluate them better as it observes them in action; and it often results in better presentations of reports, for the presentations are being made by persons specializing in the activities described by the reports.

6. Use visual aids for presenting reports; a number of photocopy-

ing machines can easily make transparencies for overhead projectors, and there are good opaque projectors available. It is well established that presentations which are both visual and oral are more meaningful and can result in a savings in time as compared with a discussion of the same report presented only in written form.

Some banks send minutes and certain reports to directors prior to directors' meetings, in the belief that this practice can shorten the time required in the meeting itself. Most banks, however, do not do this; they also insist that no documents or material supplied directors for use at meetings are to be taken from the bank's premises.

Many banks provide loose-leaf books, one copy for each director, with updated contents for each meeting. The books are usually made available in the directors' room at least an hour before each meeting, so that board members can study them prior to the meeting and prepare questions.

In some cases, directors' books include some pertinent current reference material, such as a copy of the bank's current Articles of Incorporation, a copy of the bank's current Bylaws or Code of Regulations, an up-to-date organization chart, an updated copy of the bank's Lending Policy, an updated copy of the bank's Investment Policy, a roster of the bank's officers, showing their functional responsibilities, a list of the board's and the bank's standing committees, a copy of the bank's Codes of Conduct for Officers and Employees, and a schedule of future board and committee meetings.

No discussion of management reports to directors can be complete without some comment upon how the director himself can utilize and respond to such reports. Here are a few suggestions which I hope are germane to that subject:

1. Be willing to expend sufficient time to be a really effective bank director. It is inherent in this suggestion that a director should allocate a meaningful amount of directorial time in addition to that required for attending meetings.

2. Become as well informed about banking subjects and techniques as possible. You might ask the bank's chief executive officer to provide you with subscriptions to one or two banking magazines and/or newsletters, and to be on the lookout for articles on special banking subjects in which you are interested.

3. Do enough homework to feel comfortable in asking meaningful questions at board meetings.

4. Promote and participate in the policy of rotating assignments among the various standing committees of the board so that every director can broaden his experience.

5. Insist that follow-up reports with respect to action programs or projects presented to the board be made available on a definite schedule or on a definite suspense date.

6. Encourage the inclusion and utilization for purposes of comparison in various reports of minimum levels of performance or condition considered acceptable or desirable by banking regulatory agencies and/or the banking industry as a whole.

7. Know the extent of your legal and public liabilities and responsibilities as a director of a commercial bank.

8. Insist that the board be provided with current and pertinent bases of comparison of the bank's performance. Examples of this type of information would include:

Selected balance sheet and income and expense data for your bank, as compared with other banks in your state and in your trade area: These are available on a semiannual basis from the Federal Deposit Insurance Corporation at no charge.

Specific reports of condition and income reports of any and/or all insured banks in your market area: If you are especially concerned as to why one or more of your competitors seems to be outstripping you, you can obtain these reports for any insured bank from the Federal Deposit Insurance Corporation.

Delinquency rates on bank installment loans, as well as a report of the number of repossessions of automobiles and mobile homes: These are reported on a state-by-state basis, and they are available from the American Bankers Association.

Functional analyses of bank costs: These are available to banks which are members of the Federal Reserve System, if they participate in the Functional Cost Analysis Program of their local Federal Reserve Bank. You should be cautioned, however, that participation in this program is somewhat time-consuming, and the data derived from it must be very carefully interpreted.

Operating ratios: Federal Reserve Banks provide their member banks with operating ratios annually, for that district as a whole, and for the member banks in each state in the district. Various of the operating ratios of the bank, which were mentioned earlier as a monthly or quarterly report, can usefully be tabulated on a continuing comparative basis with local competitive banks, as well as with banks in the same region and state.

Finally, through various trade association sources, bank stock analysts, or bank regulators, the management of your bank can obtain, on a continuing basis, a variety of statistics against which various functions or operating results of your bank can be compared or measured. Special circumstances in a given bank may indicate that seeking such statistics would be appropriate.

9. Encourage your fellow directors to follow these same suggestions, so that they too can best utilize and best respond to the reports they are receiving.

The director of a commercial bank today serves in a dichotomous role. On the one hand he is faced with mounting directorial liability and responsibility, arising out of his role as a director of a quasi-public, highly regulated institution. On the other hand, he serves on the board of directors of a company which is engaged in a dynamic, sophisticated, and challenging industry, which in recent years has been experiencing decreasing operating margins and declining capital ratios and liquidity.

What kind of contribution, then, can directors make to banks whose important functions are directed by executives who by and large are more talented, better trained, and more highly motivated than they used to be, and who at the same time face more challenges than ever from without? This question confronts us with a paradox: The increasing competence of management appears to make the board of directors both more of an anachronism and potentially more useful and more necessary than ever before.

As I see it, the board is in a position, by insisting upon a reasonable array of meaningful and timely reports, to strengthen the bank in successfully accomplishing all of its operational activities; and by comprehending and utilizing those reports to their fullest potential, to make an ever increasing contribution to the bank's achievement of its goals.

C. C. CAMERON

Marketing and the Bank Director

A UNIVERSAL RESPONSIBILITY everyone has as a director is to help his or her bank in its marketing effort. Those of you who serve on the community bank advisory boards may not have legal or policy-making responsibilities, but you do have marketing responsibilities; and your devotion and commitment to the fulfillment of the latter are critical to the future growth and strength of your bank.

That the banking industry is experiencing change as never before is undisputed, and with that change your responsibilities are growing in magnitude. It is more evident than ever before that for your bank to realize its fair share of the market it must be more effective in the area of new business development, community involvement, and image development—with all its audiences.

To achieve these objectives, your bank must have your full support and a lot of your valuable time. Your bank management, if it is working with you effectively, should view your role as that of ambassador representing the bank to the public.

To help us better appreciate this role, the Bank Marketing Association has produced an audio-film strip. Its purpose is to help focus on the importance of an effective board of director's new business development program and to suggest how you might set up and operate a New Business Development Council, if you do not already have one. Perhaps the major point of this filmed presentation is the one made by the director who said, "Formation of the council is the best thing that has happened to our bank. It incorporates sales as a regular function of our roles as directors." We were told that to form the council and have it function effectively, you should:

1. Secure the cooperation of all the board members, management, and personnel of your bank—even shareholders.

2. Spend a lot of up-front time setting goals for the council by getting market share reports from the chief executive officer and marketing officer, and by determining what your bank's image is and what you want it to be.

3. Set your objectives so that they are achievable, yet of the highest standards.

4. Involve yourselves in consultative selling by working with your bank's chief executive officer and call officers and learning all there is to know about prospective customers.

5. Bring your awareness of your community to your service for the bank by being alert to community relations opportunities and new business prospects.

Perhaps this presentation will inspire some new ideas for those of you now serving on boards without new business development plans. And for those of you with such plans, I hope it may provide some understanding of ways to improve what you are already doing. It is helping First Union management in organizing an effort that will be introduced soon to our many distinguished community boards of directors throughout North Carolina.

Obviously, the success of a New Business Development Council depends almost solely on the degree of enthusiasm, personal commitment, and input that each director gives. If you, as a director, make these personal contributions, then there is no doubt about the benefits that will accrue to your bank. After all, you have been asked to serve because you are a leader with influence, business and social acumen, and an awareness of your community and what it needs and wants. You, in effect, are the image of your business and your bank in your community. A bank's image is fast becoming a strong marketing influence in our economic and social environment—its image not just with customers, but with all audiences: shareholders, employees, the media, government, community, and the public in general. The efforts of the boards of directors and management must now more than ever be directed toward dealing with the perception all these audiences have of a company as a place to work, to invest money, to do business—a place that is concerned about the quality of life of all the people in the community and the society. We can no longer expect public acceptance if we are comfortable with providing good products or services at a profit for the benefit of shareholders.

A bank director's marketing responsibility becomes a communications responsibility to help management reach all its audiences with the best possible image, and to carry that responsibility to public forums when necessary, to provide the facts and information necessary to show the public—be it a congressman, consumer advocate, or potential bank customer—that your bank is a business enterprise representing quality and value for the community and society in general.

This is asking a lot more than just your participation in the marketing effort to develop new business. It is asking you to represent your bank openly and proudly to all audiences. To be able to do this, you must examine your own attitude toward your bank and your personal and business relationships with it. Ask yourself these questions: (1) Do you do all your personal banking at your bank? (2) Does your business enterprise do the major portion of its banking with your bank? (3) Are you personally familiar with all the consumer and corporate services of your bank? (4) Do you encourage personal friends, clubs, churches, organizations, and business peers to use your bank's services? (5) Do you stay abreast of your corporation's affairs so that you can answer questions about it when asked? (6) Are you an owner of your bank's stock?

If you answer no to a majority of these questions I would suggest you ask yourself why. Maybe you should reevaluate your personal commitment as a director. In that evaluation perhaps you will determine those changes your bank needs to make in order for you to respond affirmatively to all those questions, and subsequently have your bank, through its board and management, make those changes. If you do this, you will be making changes for a lot of other customers and potential customers who probably have the same attitude you had. If you do, you will proudly represent your bank in your community to all those audiences it needs to reach to remain a vital, growing business enterprise that contributes to the economic and social well-being of the people.

TERRY E. RENAUD

The Marketing Function and the Bank Director

OVER THE PAST twelve to eighteen months (1974-75), as our country's economic position gyrated between recession and recovery, all bank directors have been questioned or have heard somewhat disparaging remarks about the state of banks and banking in the economic environment of 1975. Certain spokesmen have suggested that to some degree banking's heavy merchandising of their services has contributed to their economic woes and has detrimentally affected banking's public image. In light of these attitudes, there are two main points to cover: (1) a brief history of bank marketing, particularly as to how it reached its point of prominence in the industry; and (2) what bank directors should expect from their bank's marketing function, how marketing can best serve the interests of directors and of their banks.

Bank directors are a part of an enterprise that is unique among financial industries throughout the world. In our country, almost fourteen thousand individual banks and many more associates and branch offices strive to serve the financial needs of separate and individual communities. These institutions have, of course, only that singular purpose: to serve, on a mutually profitable basis, their respective communities, from small municipalities to metropolitan areas throughout the world. Each bank's image is not contrived; rather, it is the result of the success the bank realizes in achieving its basic purpose. In other words, the image of a bank as a successful organization depends primarily on an understanding of what the community served wants from its bank. If these needs are met—and the needs may encompass strength, solidarity, aggressiveness, friendliness, imagination, and innovation—then our banks are viewed as successful and important to the community. If they are not, then our communities will express their dissatisfaction ultimately to the point of seeking out or creating a financial institution that will satisfy their needs.

While on the surface this premise seems rather basic, it is important to remember that the needs of our communities are not constant. As changes occur in the financial environment, people's expectations of their banks and their bankers also change. Many of us can look back and recall the time when demand deposits far exceeded savings and time deposits, when installment-type loans were considered a novelty, and when personal lines of credit were virtually unheard of. The bank with strong structural features and an air of complete security typified the image held by the community. Bank personnel were, of course, selected and trained to complement this overall public view. Bank operations were customer-oriented, with tailored and individually produced statements and controls. Advertising and promotion were largely limited to the publication of the bank's statement of condition.

With the emergence of a mass market for financial services—a market of younger, better-educated, more affluent people, who were more demanding of business in general—bankers recognized the change occurring in their community and began to introduce services to fill the new needs. To do so banks were required to be considerably more innovative, imaginative, and marketing- and production-oriented than before. The introduction of negotiable certificates of deposit, low-cost checking accounts, market-oriented savings accounts, and a myriad of personal credit programs brought about the need for expanded and better methods of account maintenance and retention. As bank technological competence and marketing expertise grew, new markets for financial services grew also, and banks found themselves reaching farther and farther both geographically and internally. This effort required a vast insertion of both operating funds and professional competence, demanding from our banks the most difficult of all tasks: the ability to change their public image at the rate of change demanded by the public. Early endeavors to meet this challenge included the usual superficial and eventually aborted attempts at image alteration. This development phase was best illustrated by a national TV comedian's remark: "If all banks are as friendly as they say they are, then why do they chain the fountain pens to the desks?" Ultimately, banks did change and generally provided their communities with the services and facilities they wanted.

Viewed as a total organizational function, marketing is obviously not a new facet of banking. It has, however, gained more prominence over the past fifteen to twenty years, and for good reason. Since the end of World War II, our changing national economy has forced a gradual, persistent change in banking's management posture. Prior to this time, management's emphasis was predominately on the asset side of our organizational structure. Our raw material deposits were in adequate supply and, in the eyes of the owners, not of great value as an income producer. Capital was also in adequate supply, with little thought of its leveraging possibilities. In other words, in the banking system there was an excess of liquidity that had been increasing since the late 1930s. It was in the area of loans and investments that banking's greatest professional and managerial efforts were required, and it was here that the marketing effort as it then existed was concentrated. With the pressures created by the gradual decrease in demand funds, the emergence of an affluent middle class, greater technological ability, advanced communication networks, a growing understanding of spendable income as an income producer, and the proliferation of consumer credit, the need for effective liability management emerged. With this emphasis on liability management came the need for an expanded and more sophisticated marketing function.

The marketing practitioner himself evolved, of course, during these times. It was in advertising that the bank marketer was originally involved. The need for bank services for the so-called mass market was obvious. The job was simply one of communicating the services banking offered to fill those needs while informing the market of banking's interest. This latter point plus the growing image problem banking was experiencing because of the further tightening of the money supply proved to be a substantial challenge. The bank marketer, consequently, added the public relations responsibility to his job.

During this same period, the market itself was changing. The mass market was segmenting itself into a myriad separate and distinct markets more difficult to understand and harder to reach. Bank costs were skyrocketing; pricing and profit became the watchwords of banking. Competitive situations were altered radically with the advent of the holding company movement and the emergence of specialized financial intermediaries. In each instance bank marketers added to their responsibilities. Market research entered the spotlight. Sales training became a necessity, as did product development, product management, pricing, and legislative involvement.

At this point, several things occurred almost simultaneously. First, large banks, aware of their newly developed marketing muscle and with the added impetus provided by registered bank holding company legislation and a major increase in technological abilities, then began to reach out into new fields of endeavor and into new territories. Second, small banks were increasingly feeling the pressures of the sophisticated marketing techniques of their big city brothers and of the inroads into their markets being made by other financial institutions. As a result, small banks, too, moved toward greater marketing sophistication. Third, all banks became aware of a major concentration of a basic line responsibility—marketing—in a staff department. Fourth, the bank marketer found his function more complex as services became more intricate, as legislation on methods of communication became more restrictive, as the markets to be served became more diverse and segmented, and as line management became more demanding of professionals.

This then is bank marketing's history. It was born of competitive necessity in the framework of our society's free enterprise system. In 1975 the bank marketer is more concerned than ever with the day-to-day operations of the bank. He is more involved in planning. He is more concerned with profits and losses than ever before, and he is vitally involved with the customer or the consumer.

There is no question that marketing programs and events affect the bottom line, and in most cases bottom line performance is top management's responsibility. As a consequence, I sense an increasing understanding and appreciation of marketing techniques among bank-line officers, which leads to a fundamental point: bank marketing is often described as a function or a role or a title rather than a corporate philosophy. And when that happens the bank is confronted with the argument between line and staff, top management and middle management. Who is responsible; who is accountable? I suggest that marketing is both a philosophy and a function that starts at the top and works its way down. The ultimate marketing decisions must be made by the executive officers of the board, for the scope of these decisions will determine the future of the bank.

What then should the bank director look for in a marketing function, and what should marketing expect from its director? It sometimes seems ironic that bank directors appear to counsel and guide in those banking areas that are outside their field of expertise. As successful businessmen in their own right, largely because of their ability to understand their markets and products and the many facets of consumer motivation, bank directors have an insight into marketing problems; their counsel and guidance can be of great value to the bank they serve. Yet, in board meeting after board meeting, the bank's marketing activities receive short shrift while loans and investments, the field of the banker's greatest expertise, at times receives inordinate amounts of attention.

From the director's point of view, the marketing function in banking warrants close scrutiny for a number of reasons, not the least of which is the expense involved. It is estimated that our industry will spend over $659 million in 1975. Some of the obvious questions each director should ponder are: Are our advertising dollars being spent in a professional and disciplined manner? Do they effectively sell our bank's services? If our bank's name were replaced by that of our competitors, would the ads still have the same meaning to the reader? Do the ads enhance or detract from the bank's image? Are they aimed at a specific market, or do they try to be all things to all people?

A leading advertising specialist once stated that most bank advertising is ineffective because bankers all try to be "nice guys" in their advertising. I think this is a valid observation, but it is a result rather than a cause. The cause is that bank advertising men have nothing to fight about. Since the total marketing function does not really exist in many banks, the advertising manager is provided little basic data on what Rosser Reaves in his book *Reality in Advertising* calls USP— Unique Selling Proposition. He therefore must resort to the nice approach. When our advertising personnel are given basic data on potential markets, information on who the people are, how they live, and where they are, a different picture emerges. The profitable use of this merchandising function, advertising, rests therefore on how well the total marketing operation, including basic market research and product analysis, functions in the bank.

This factor raises another question for the bank director to consider. Is the bank allocating a reasonable part of its marketing budget to market and product research? Regardless of the size of the bank, basic market research capabilities are available to assist in market segmentation and market and product analysis. Some banks have recourse to in-house research specialists; others, to professional research firms, local businesses, the bank's correspondents, and other state universities or national banking associations. In addition, a director should not overlook his bank's executive officers' intuitive understanding of the makeup of their markets. Market analysis can never take the place of management judgment. It merely provides the basis for making better management decisions in market situations. The bank's chief executive officer is not where he is because he was a good credit man, or operations man, or comptroller. He is there because he understood the needs of his markets and the ability of his bank to fill these needs better than anyone else. Without this attribute, no matter how specialized he may be otherwise, a chief executive officer could not long satisfy the needs of his directors, stockholders, customers, or employees.

Finally, there is one other reason why a bank director should carefully and consistently monitor his bank's marketing efforts and programs. From a purely selfish point of view, a paramount benefit a director should receive from his position on the bank's board is the enhancement of his own image and that of his business in the community he serves. The bank's image therefore should be of genuine interest to a director, and it is the overall bank marketing program that establishes and maintains the way in which the public views your bank. While protecting his own self-interest, a director can also serve the bank in a most important and timely manner. Needless to say, banking is a highly competitive industry and promises to become even more competitive. While competition is basic to our free enterprise system, intense competition in any industry breeds overextension in merchandising efforts and ultimately presents the potential for image erosion.

In this regard, every director should pursue a basic thesis: It is better for the bank to advocate what is right, even though its stance may be unpopular, than to tell people what they want to hear, even though it is not in their best interest. Now it is natural to reply that banks have always followed this premise. Have they really? Have bankers spoken up on the economic affairs of their country or their municipality? What outward position have they taken on the thinking among some segments of our society that profits are immoral? There are many directors who say that this is an impossible situation, that there is not much a banker can do or say to change public attitudes on matters such as these. But take a look at what happened to the great gold rush of 1975.

On December 31, 1974, it became legal for individuals in the United States to buy and keep gold. The public seemed to become obsessed with gold fever, or so the press wanted us to believe. *Newsweek* magazine, for example, blew the whole issue into a cover story, leaving the impression that Americans were likely to stampede their local banks, brokerage houses, jewelers, and other retail outlets in what would become the great gold rush of 1975. What did the bankers do? First of all, most bankers were cautious, adopting a wait-and-see attitude before they launched any promotional efforts. While a few did choose to compete through advertising for the gold market, they did so almost in the manner of offering a public service to their customers. Many of the ads explained both the pros and cons of gold ownership, the cost involved, the risks which might be taken. As it turned out, the great gold rush went down in history as the great gold bust. What is important, however, is that the kind of advertising banks engaged in is the kind of public service information which will do a lot to improve the image of banks. In many cases, the pitch was, "You may not want gold; it may be a bad investment for you for these reasons. . . . But if you want to buy it, come and see your banker, and we'll do our best to advise and counsel as well as sell it to you." In my opinion, this kind of promotion lends credibility to the banking industry and will do more toward creating an interest in banking's basic services than most of the ads that are now run daily.

The view that banks should be the spokesmen, promoters, and interpreters in their own field can carry over to regulation as well. Rather than waiting, as many have done in the past, for criticism to come and regulatory measures to be proposed, our bankers should take the lead in proposing appropriate regulations, based on what they know about their customers. Truth in lending, for example, found banking taking a purely defensive position and, consequently, becoming saddled with a cumbersome law which failed to offer any real alternative. Why didn't banks anticipate that agitation for truth in savings would not be far around the corner? There seems to be little question that all bankers could do a lot more than they are doing to acquaint the public with the real issues behind some contemporary mutual concerns.

An even better approach to consumer complaints is to take the initiative in the first place to insure that government regulations will not be imposed. The Bank Marketing Association, for example, is doing just that by developing a code of ethics to help curb abuses in bad bank advertising before any real outcry from the public develops. The abuses are evident, though perhaps unintentional, and perhaps have escaped the raft of consumer advocates largely because bank advertising is primarily local in nature. The beneficial publicity which could result from such a move could go a long way toward strengthening the image of the banking industry in communities which are becoming increasingly aware of being "taken in" by someone.

It is, of course, obvious that we are now in the midst of a new era of change for financial services, and that all banks will once again be required to alter their current way of doing business. Despite the outcries of banking's critics and the prognostications of many, the need for banking today is not for retrogression, not for a return to the banking of the last few decades. Rather, all banks should apply the increased technological and marketing expertise they now possess in finding new and more innovative ways to meet changing public needs. Doing so consistently, regardless—though not unmindful—of changing national and global economic conditions, will provide the means to keep the banking industry a central, vital, and viable part of the communities each bank serves. The strength of each bank rests primarily on the strength of its directors, its officers, and its staff. How adaptable we are to the needs of the customers we serve, how sensitive we become to the changing ways in which our communities view us, and how adaptable we can become to the changes that, as a result, will constantly occur within the bank itself will in the future, as in the past, determine the commensurate rewards for banks and bankers. Our banking system, like our individual banks, provides the opportunity for both success and failure. There will always be some of both. The success or failure of our individual banks will be determined by the effort each of us consistently makes to maintain and enhance banking's image as a strong, professional, and ethical industry.

JOHN H. PERKINS

The Changing Financial Structure

IN THE TEN YEARS (1966-76) that I have served as a bank director, the job and the responsibilities have grown in seemingly geometric proportions. Whether bank directors are associated with a small bank or a large unit bank, with a branch or a holding company, whether they are located in an agricultural area, a suburban district, or the central city, the days are past when they can merely go to a board meeting, listen to management, have lunch, and then return to their own businesses. The challenge of a bank director is greater than ever in this era of rapid and escalating change. If nothing else, directors are all beginning to appreciate the legal responsibilities that have come to be more and more significant in recent years; and these growing responsibilities must be emphasized as the expectations of society and the courts make each of our jobs more challenging and demanding.

In reviewing recent banking history, it seems to me that we have done an outstanding job of fulfilling our economic and social roles in an extremely volatile environment. Probably all generations of managers have felt that they have operated in unusually difficult times, but I think it is fair to say that in recent years the demands of society in general and of our customers in particular have undergone major changes in an environment of significant legal and legislative changes affecting banking. And added to this there has been a virtual revolution in the technology for the delivery of financial services.

Affected by this rising pace of change are three key areas that deserve special attention. These are the holding company and related changes in banking structure, technological change—generally included under the heading of Electronic Funds Transfer—and the closely intertwined legislative and regulatory areas which have created change as well as responded to change in significantly determining how banking can or cannot respond. I have been fortunate indeed to have been able to observe developments in these key areas as chairman of the Government Relations Council of the American Bankers Association, which is especially concerned with federal legislative and regulatory developments, and the equally important developments at the state level which affect or are affected by federal actions.

Change in these key areas is here. It is not a matter of whether, but rather of when, how, and how much things will change. Broad changes in banking structure really got underway in the holding company and branching and merger legislation of the late 1960s. While the feverish pace of change has slackened a bit at the moment, it continues in 1976 and it will in the future. Technological developments in the delivery of banking services have been rapid; legislative and regulatory changes seem to proceed at an ever increasing tempo. At various levels of government there has been a growing belief, strongly shared by all kinds of special groups, that almost all kinds of social ills—either real or imagined—can be cured by legislation or by regulations directing the banks to do one thing or another. Proposals are dropped into the legislative hoppers daily with what often appears to be extreme naïveté (to be charitable); and all too often there is no objective examination of the economic or social costs to us, or of the long-run effects they may have on our system. There does not seem to be a willingness to look at the record. It is discouraging for us to draw attention to what appears to be a convincing record of a proposal which has failed in the past but which is being offered again by some regulatory agency, only to find that the proposer is really not interested in hearing the facts. He is terribly sure he could succeed where others, for pretty valid reasons, have clearly failed.

These broad trends affect all of us; none will escape their impact, although the degree, timing, and ultimate direction will vary widely in each case. Naturally, we are all more concerned and involved with our immediate affairs. It is frequently hard to relate our own situation to some development in a larger bank or in a bank far away from us. Indeed, we may not have a real awareness that a change has taken place for the very obvious reason that we are busy and can only be expected to handle so much. Many of these developments have a way of appearing on our doorstep eventually, however, and then it may be too late to take effective action or, at least, to respond in a timely and competitive fashion. There are very few of these major trends that will not affect all banks sooner or later. Some of us have been radically affected by the holding company legislation of the 1960s and 1970s. Some of us have seen holding company or branch systems go regional or statewide; others of us are from states which retain unit banking. Some banks, such as Continental Illinois, have been in the forefront of the vast movement of U.S. banks following our customers into worldwide operations, while the majority of banks have remained essentially tied to one area or region. Regardless of which category we might consider ourselves to be in, it is fair to say, although sometimes difficult to see, that these broad trends do affect us all, and as bank directors we need to consider their implications for the future of our banks.

In looking back on the "go-go" era of the late 1960s and early 1970s when bank holding companies were expanding, bank diversification was the fashion, if not the fad, and within the same structure many banks pushed in a major way into relatively new areas, we will recall that American industry was doing the same thing. On hindsight, the lesson is clear once again that we must either move with the times or watch the parade go by our institution. But at the same time we must do this in a reasonable way, keeping our basic business healthy and in focus. There were excesses in banking as there were in industry, yet the period of correction is moving along nicely and, in spite of a few highly publicized and perhaps overpublicized situations, banking has come through in a strong and statesmanlike way. While there have been other periods when excesses, particularly in the real estate field, have led to a major correction at a time of a major recession in the economy, this time economic history will show that the cooperation of bankers and their customers combined with an understanding approach, in general, by the regulators has enabled us to get through this period in a relatively strong fashion.

Most bank directors are familiar with the broad outlines of development which have changed the structure for delivering financial services. As trends increased rapidly over many years, branching and the movement of holding company banking to larger multiple office operations took place at all levels. Local banks expanded into detached facilities, or perhaps into local chain banks or branch systems. Bank branches and holding company operations moved countywide, sometimes appearing in several counties and states. At the same time, many new unit banks were chartered and have since prospered.

There was also the emergence of various holding company subsidiaries, which, in specified areas, crossed geographical lines. For example, real estate, consumer loan, mortgage, data processing, and other subsidiaries have developed to begin performing services similar to those offered by a bank, but they have done so in areas outside the boundaries set aside for the bank. Subsidiaries have proliferated in varying degrees, ranging from local to statewide operations; some of the consumer finance subsidiaries of bank holding companies cover many states throughout the country. There are also the Edge Act subsidiaries for international banking which we and others have throughout the United States. Foreign bank offices have also arrived in this country. This type of expansion continues today on a substantial basis, although the pace has slowed markedly because of the shake-out in the real estate field, poor experience in some other areas, and the inclination of bank managements and regulators to go slow. But this is a pause, not a change.

Closely related to the expansion in banking are the technological changes taking place. Machines can now be located almost anywhere, and, under proper conditions, can handle the great majority of individual transactions with speed, ease, and economy. Less noticeable but equally breathtaking are the technological advancements which have provided efficient tools for management, accounting, record keeping, and the processing of bank transactions of all kinds.

Bank directors should be concerned with the broader implications of using machines for bank management. For example, at Continental Illinois we have terminals, tied to a network that is shared with other banks and savings and loans, in grocery stores and around our own facilities. This type of shared network, as opposed to a proprietary market, is going to be the trend. An advantage, of course, is that equivalent facilities will be made available to banks that would like to have them but cannot afford the development cost. On the other hand, this type of facility is not used only as a part of a network; many banks employ the machines for specific needs in a limited operation.

Will the consumer do banking through machines in shopping centers, retail stores, and other heavily traveled locations? Will he do it on a twenty-four-hours-a-day, seven-days-a-week basis? We do not know where this trend will end; we do know that it has major implications for each of our banks. We do know that the machines are spreading rapidly, perhaps too rapidly to be economical. We do know that some consumers get used to the machines faster than many of us thought they would; some people seem to prefer the convenience of the machine. Others, of course, prefer the check stub and traditional banking methods.

We know, too, that there is much legal and legislative sorting out still ahead of us. While the Supreme Court declined to review lower-court electronic funds transfer decisions that were unfavorable to banking, the National Electronic Funds Transfer Systems Study Commission, Congress, and several state legislatures continue to look at implications and potential applications of EFT. There is great uncertainty, but we know the technology is moving fast and we must consider what this means for our banks. In branch and holding company areas, and even in unit banking areas, the planning of new facilities and the need for brick and mortar must be reconsidered in light of the new technology.

Another major consideration we sometimes lose sight of is the spread of nonbank institutions into the field of banking services. While bankers and legislators argue about what banks should or should not be permitted to do, nonbank organizations are moving rapidly into banking areas. There are many types of financial transactions taking place in huge volume outside the banking system: cashing checks at the grocery store, using credit cards for all kinds of purchases, obtaining personal credit at retail stores or other nonbank financial institutions. In focusing on our own affairs, we may lose sight of just how far this has gone and what a major business it has become. Then consider what the adaptation of these operations to the new machines could mean for the future of banking. As I have noted, the EFT commission is looking into these questions right now, and Congress and several state legislatures are also interested. Where this will end remains to be seen, but the issue is by no means settled as to who will ultimately have the franchise on these new methods. Certainly, the Congress and many of the courts seem to have a clear predilection for spreading these powers beyond banking.

We must also be aware of the increasing number of services being offered by the savings and loan industry and that fastest growing financial institution, the credit union. In one of the housing acts a number of years ago, Congress gave the Federal Home Loan Bank Board—the regulatory agency for federal savings and loan associations—the power to permit federal savings and loan associations to offer third-party payment arrangements. In banking language, this is simply the power to offer a checking account under another name. For some special reasons, this authority has only been used aggressively in the past couple of years with Negotiable Order of Withdrawal (NOW) accounts, primarily in the northeastern states. After much legal and legislative wrangling, the mutual savings banks in these states acquired the same authority. So now the federal savings and loan associations are in the checking account business, and they can generally handle this type of transaction all over the country. These accounts are expanding and, on legal advice, most of the new automated clearing houses in national and regional money centers are permitting these institutions to enter the payments system directly through the bank clearing house.

In addition to this new power, the Federal Home Loan Bank Board, under existing authority in certain housing legislation, is permitting federal savings and loan associations to branch throughout their states. This is happening rapidly, even in Illinois, traditionally a strict unit banking state, where they are moving into the attractive growing neighborhoods served primarily by local banks. This trend is a matter of concern for bankers, since the NOW accounts in many states pay interest, so already there are existing accounts that pay interest on demand deposits, the equivalent of checking accounts. (The economics of paying interest on checking accounts is dubious under present practices.)

Expanded powers are also being given to the credit unions, always a group especially favored in the Congress. (Incidentally, there are 27,000 credit unions in the United States as compared with about 15,000 banks, although many of the former are very small.) The important point is that the result of these trends is that financial institutions are becoming more and more alike; thrift institutions are acquiring more of the powers traditionally associated with banks. How far this will go and what the economy and the market will accept remain to be seen.

These are not new developments. Quite the contrary, they are specific developments that have been underway for some time under existing legislation and resulting regulation. They came about primarily as part of broader efforts by Congress to encourage housing, to solve special problems of the housing industry and the thrift institutions when money is tight during periods of heavy demand and high inflation. Or perhaps Congress wished to encourage certain institutions that it believes were socially desirable for one reason or another (such as the credit union). Often the motivation may be to help certain institutions compete with what are perceived to be the stronger commercial banks. This explains, for example, the regulation and legislation giving thrift institutions the right to pay savers a higher rate of interest than banks, even though both institutions are competing for the same savings dollar.

In 1975 there was the furor and resulting battle over the Financial Institutions Act which would have made major additional changes in the banking system and its regulation. Some years ago, a presidential commission was appointed to take a broad look at the financial structure and come up with a package of recommendations for further major changes. This was called the Hunt Commission Report. The Treasury Department later took the report and modified it into what came to be known as the Financial Institutions Act.

The American Bankers Association worked with and supported the concept of a package approach to financial legislation. We at ABA judge legislation by applying certain standards to determine whether it is in the public interest, whether it is fair, enabling all institutions, large and small, to compete fairly, etc. For years, legislative and regulatory proposals on a piecemeal basis penalized the banks by seeking or giving new powers to other financial institutions. The aim of the ABA was to take a package approach requiring a quid pro quo on powers. It was a fact that thrift institutions either had or were getting additional powers under a specific authority that had existed for some time. It was reasoned that the sensible approach would be to work with these trends, but only if banking received equal treatment. This would involve requiring other depository institutions to assume equal responsibilities and burdens, particularly in the key areas of taxes assessed, cash reserves maintained, equal regulatory responsibilities, and competition for the savers' dollar. In the end, the Senate came up with a bill with certain unacceptable features, including interest on demand deposits. Then the House came up with a truly one-sided, antibank bill with radical and unfair changes, indirect allocation of credit, and an undesirable major restructuring of bank regulation. Banking went all out to defeat this bill, as did a number of other organizations and important regulatory agencies. Although it was resoundingly defeated, our problems were not completely solved. Many of the recent trends in banking are not needed; many are very uncomfortable. Some are undesirable and clearly not in the public interest at present, or, in the long run, in the interest of a healthy economy. Organized banking will be working diligently to help promote desirable and even inevitable change in a constructive manner. I just hope our record in the years immediately ahead will be one that we can be as proud of as we are of our record in the immediate past.

Meanwhile, we can look ahead to a continued, if not a more deliberately paced, evolution of the banking structure. Clearly, the technological revolution will roll along, although it will be significantly influenced by legislative decisions and by court decisions. New regulations and more reports in greater detail will come daily, and many will be unjustified. Certainly Congress will be active and full of proposals in a number of key areas, such as the payment of interest on deposits. But financial institutions at home and abroad will continue to fulfill their obligations and exercise their powers.

The most encouraging aspect of all of this is that it does offer many opportunities that we must not lose sight of as we look at the present problems. I sense in bankers from all over the country the growing interest in and appreciation of the need to address these problems. In our great and growing banking system there is opportunity and room for all kinds of diverse institutions. Rather than expending our energies in narrow areas working for short-range advantages against each other, we in banking must maintain this interest and work together to meet these needs in a changing world.

PHILIP E. COLDWELL

Appraisal and Planning

THE DIRECTORS OF ANY ORGANIZATION—whether a commercial bank, a nonbank financial institution, or a nonfinancial institution—have a responsibility to their organization to insure that the management is doing a proper job of planning ahead and appraising all the relevant factors affecting each of the planning problems. This is not to say that the directors should be involved at a level which infringes upon management's prerogatives; but, in addition to dealing with other facets of directors' work, they should keep themselves well informed of the progress of management, making certain that management is in fact doing the job of planning, not only for short- and intermediate-term projects, but also for long-range situations. More specifically, a director's responsibility includes seeing that management is devoting appropriate time and personnel toward long-range planning, is keeping the directors adequately informed, and is availing itself of the expertise of those on the board of directors to help solve long-range problems.

There are a number of problems which your banks should be considering now. For example, is your bank management thinking of the future and planning for changes in the structure of banking in your state? Structural changes include the new holding company law and its impact, potential changes in branch regulations, effects of the holding company structure upon branching and unit bank operations, and the potentials (both favorable and unfavorable) for organizing a bank holding company.

Similarly, is your bank management planning ahead to consider new competition, since it is apparent that in a longer-range context some of the present nonbank financial institutions may obtain banking authority and could become strong and vital competitors on the local banking scene?

Of course, there is a wide range of forward planning necessary in management succession, personnel assignments, potential unionization and personnel responses to such unionization, and in the continuing job of keeping the bank employees abreast of both salary and fringe-benefit positions of the community as a whole.

Let us focus our attention, however, primarily upon what the directors should be considering in the field of economic and financial planning, and upon some of the things directors can do to assist their managements in the better forward planning of loan commitments, revenue and deposit sources, shifting economic bases of communities, and banking responses thereto. And, in a much broader sense, directors should consider economic planning to adjust to the changing circumstances and conditions reflected in the national financial markets and the effects these have upon bank profitability.

As directors you have outside contacts in your own businesses, and through your own associations, with information and attitudes which should be of immense help to the officers of your banks in developing their own ideas about the changing environment of the nation and the shifting markets for financial instruments. Perhaps more important, you as directors should be having monthly discussions with your bank's management on the way in which the financial environment is developing, any new trends which seem to be on the horizon, and how your own personal appraisal of these trends might affect your bank's operations. You should be counseling with the management of your bank on all aspects of future economic planning, making sure that your bank's officers have the data which are regularly published and available in the public arena; that they maintain a continuing awareness and interest in the status of the financial and economic markets of their primary customers; and that they reach toward consultant help through your correspondents, through the services of the Federal Reserve and other regulatory agencies, and, of course, through regular newsletters of financial consultants.

Probably of equal importance, though, is the application of common sense. Despite the broad changes in banking and financial affairs of the nation, there are certain repetitive patterns which develop over the business cycle and over the financial cycle response to changes in the growth rate of the nation. It is important that your managements recognize these repetitive patterns, learning that a change in the objective targets of monetary policy toward a restraining policy can forecast a reduced availability of credit, a slower rate of deposit growth, an eventual problem of liquidity, and certainly a rising pattern of interest rates. I would caution you, though, to modify your judgments to account for some of the new elements in the situation, particularly the availability of nondeposit sources of funds, basing your modifications on your own bank's situation, not merely following the judgments of your correspondents or the trends of the national money market banks. While it may be appropriate for a large city bank to participate in some of these nondeposit sources, it might be wholly inappropriate for your own bank. As I review the developments from 1972 to 1975, and my contacts with boards of directors, I find that too few have spent time with the managements of their banks in trying to forecast the coming changes in financial markets, even though some changes were clearly predicted in the trends of Federal Reserve monetary policies, the nation's fiscal policies, and the published economic and financial data.

It is, of course, not only desirable from a citizenship standpoint, but almost a requirement for a bank director to know something of the workings of the nation's central bank. The Federal Reserve System is charged with responsibility for developing monetary policy. Its objective is to provide a supply of credit compatible with the demand which will support a high-level utilization of resources at reasonable price stability. The Federal Reserve is also involved in a number of other matters, but its monetary policy work is the prime mission of the system. The Federal Reserve Board and the Federal Reserve Banks use discount rates, reserve requirements, and Open Market operations to accomplish their policy requirements, with the latter being most heavily used in both a day-to-day and an overall implementation basis.

The central feature of any responsibility for monetary policy is the creation of credit. It is this single source of power which makes any central bank of prime importance in the economic stabilization of the nation. For example, if the Open Market Committee decides that additional reserves must be created to improve the supply of credit in the nation, it instructs the manager of the Open Market Account in New York to purchase government securities. After a brief go-round with the dealers in government securities, the Open Market desk decides upon the best price available and decides to purchase, say, $100 million of such securities. It places the order with a dealer and, assuming regular delivery, receives those securities the next day, paying for them by check. The dealer, of course, is not interested in holding the check, so he quickly deposits it with his commercial bank. That bank in turn, deciding to obtain the funds represented by the check, takes it back to the Federal Reserve Bank of New York, which then credits the reserve account of the commercial bank. At this point in the procedure, the Federal Reserve has purchased $100 million of government securities and has paid for them by check. Now, where did the money come from? Well, obviously, it came by creation of credit by the Federal Reserve. Its final step was to credit the reserve account of the commercial bank.

For those of you who wish to keep track of Federal Reserve changes in policy, there are data published every week indicating the level of reserves, the changes in those reserves, and the Open Market operations as reflected in the books of the Federal Reserve Banks. You should, of course, be extremely careful in making judgments from short-run data. Take a longer look over a quarter or several months, and I believe you can discern the trend of Federal Reserve policy. The policy, of course, is not as precise as the data, but for your purposes in guiding and directing a commercial bank the trend of policy is the important factor.

It appears that some banks customarily hold one-hour directors' meetings once a month in which management reviews the conditions of the bank and some of its important credit lines but seldom gets into a thorough discussion of the planning and forward thinking of the management. While we can blame management for not doing its job, I submit that it is also at least partly the fault of the directors of the bank in failing to encourage management to take a longer view, and failing to participate in committee work or board action to insure the careful appraisal of longer-term and even short-run economic and financial trends.

Even in states such as Texas where the banking structure is oriented toward a unit banking law, the growth of chain and group banking is such that virtually every bank in the state should be carefully appraising the impact of the developing structural shifts, the value of group versus chain banking, and the impact of these two upon the viability of a unit banking law. Thus, as directors and owners of the banks, you should be appraising your position, deciding whether it is desirable to join such a group and what your competitive reaction would be if your competitor down the street should make such a move.

Another intermediate- to long-range problem is the pattern of community or national economic and business development. The basic sources of economic growth seldom shift rapidly in a single community. The more usual pattern is a one- to five-year cycle of the development of a new industry and the growth of that industry's credit needs which will have to be accommodated by a financial institution. It took a number of years for the cattle feedlot industry in West Texas to develop, but the financial institutions of that area needed to look carefully at both the capital and operating requirements of that industry to determine what part their banks could play in supplying this credit and what part others in the financial arena might absorb.

To maintain the competitive position of banks among all financial institutions it is highly desirable and almost imperative that banks anticipate the development of new economic growth patterns and appraise their own responsibility and response to new business developments. Many banks are involved in credit card operations, but those which are not so involved need to appraise carefully the operational, credit, and lendable fund impact of this new credit device. For the somewhat larger banks, planning horizons should now include preauthorized payment plans, as it seems likely that from 1978 to 1988 there will be a major movement toward limiting the number of checks being passed through the financial community. And it appears that preauthorized payment plans offer one viable means of at least partially accomplishing this end. Among the variety of things a bank must consider are costs, returns, volatility of deposits generated (if any), and the volatility and lack of control over loan demand in the credit card area, as well as the operational needs in such departments as computer and personnel, and the legal and corporate requirements which may be necessary in the establishment of preauthorized payment plans.

The following check list should be useful to you as directors in evaluating your bank management and your bank in the overall financial community.

1. Is your bank planning ahead, and do you have a directors' committee or a board of directors' mandate both to contribute to and to appraise the results of your management's planning efforts?

2. Are you participating in the future planning of your bank and

contributing your knowledge of the developing trends in local industry, both present and potential, as well as contributing your personal appraisal of the longer-range economic and financial developments?

3. Do you personally try to stay ahead of the published data to judge the next turn in financial affairs?

4. Do you have a regular discussion with your bank management on the forward trends of the economy and your bank management response?

5. Is there a time in your board meetings when bank management will report the results of its forward planning and lay out its policy moves to adjust your bank's operations to the anticipated conditions?

6. Do you encourage your management to participate in analyses of costs, such as the Federal Reserve Functional Cost Program?

7. Do you as directors participate in the planning of the bank for financial structure changes and for major changes in service to customers?

If your answers to these questions are in the affirmative, and if you aid your bank management in solving its long-range problems, I think you will find that your bank is moving ahead of your competitor. Too few banks in the nation are doing sufficient forward planning.

JAMES S. HALL

Capital Needs and Planning

ALTHOUGH IN THE PAST I have served on the boards of six banks that were, when I began serving, under $7 million in deposits, my discussion of capital needs and planning will apply to any size bank, unless it is less than $5 million in total assets at the present time and has no chance of being in excess of $5 million in the next five years.

Capital is going to be hard to come by in the foreseeable future. It is essential for any board of directors of a bank to evaluate the bank's capital needs and, in conjunction with management, to develop a plan as well as a policy for future capital needs.

Our lead bank has 267 correspondent bank relationships. Not a month passes that a banker doesn't come in and say, "The regulatory authorities won't let me continue my present dividend policy until we bring into line our capital-to-deposit ratio." Or, "The bank commissioner won't let me build a main office or a new branch until we get more equity. What do I do?" Or, "People are a lot more sophisticated than they used to be in my town. They do not buy stock in the bank just for conversation at the country club any more. They want to know what our growth in profits has been in the last few years. Then they told me after reviewing the record it was not consistent enough. What should it be? What can I do?" *You should not wait until you have a crisis such as these bankers had to plan ahead.*

To be honest, banks and bank holding companies do not have the image they once had in the marketplace. Selling equity is tough and could get much tougher. Your capital plan should definitely be the joint responsibility of the board of directors and management. Your plan is a vital priority of your institution. Capital needs and capital planning are important to stockholders, boards of directors, management, employees, depositors, and the community.

We will have accelerated future needs for capital and difficulty in obtaining capital because of a worldwide capital shortage, more selective investors, a market interested only in top performers, capital controls leverage, rapidly changing technology, increased security costs, more competition from without the banking community, and greater demands from the consumer.

In defining the functions of capital, Mr. Leavitt of the staff of the Federal Reserve Board of Governors has stressed four functions of bank capital:

1. To protect the uninsured depositor in the event of insolvency and liquidation;
2. To absorb unanticipated losses with enough margin to inspire continuing confidence, to enable the bank, when under stress, to continue as a going concern;
3. To acquire the physical plant and basic necessities needed to render banking services; and
4. To serve as a regulatory restraint on unjustified asset expansion.

Then there's Hall's function: (5) to maintain the confidence of the bank's various publics—the uninsured depositors, borrowers, regulatory supervisors, stockholders, employees, and board of directors.

I think Mr. Leavitt would agree with me that poor management, not lack of capital, has caused the failure and near failure of many banks in recent years. Let's not think about capital so intently that we forget the most important ingredient of bank solvency—the management of the bank.

It is important to be informed on the basic elements of a capital plan. Management and the board of any bank should have a capital structure policy. This policy should specify the appropriate equity ratio and the permissible degree of departure from this ratio that the bank's individual characteristics dictate. The regulatory authorities and sophisticated investors look at a bank's capital-to-deposit ratio, or in other words, how many dollars in capital the bank has in relationship to each million dollars in total deposits. They like to see a capital-to-total-deposits ratio of 8 percent. When it drops below 8 percent they start talking to management and the board. When it drops under 7.5 percent they start telling you that you must come up with a capital plan and they would like to know what it is. Then, if it drops under 7 percent, they really start screaming.

If your bank has excellent management—and the regulatory authorities are looking more and more to the quality of management—if it has an excellent earnings record over the years, if it has a good liquidity position, if it has a formalized plan showing ways to bring and maintain ratios in line with what is normally expected, if you have a loss record on loans and securities that is entirely acceptable, and if you have very few classified loans, then you can bend the rules of the regulatory authorities. They will allow you anywhere from 1 to 1.5 percent deviation from what I indicated earlier, but never under 6 percent. On the other hand, if you have had bad loss records, poor profit performance, marginal liquidity, weak management or no management succession, or the management and the board show a disregard for future capital planning with these items, you are in trouble at 7 percent.

There are other factors that can help or hurt you. Regulatory officials prefer:

1. A low percentage of fixed assets, bank buildings, etc., in your asset mix; stable deposits as opposed to fluctuating deposits and a high percentage of savings—especially passbook savings, but all savings as opposed to demand; and excellent credit file and record keeping in the bank.

2. A dividend policy designated to maximize access to the equity or debt market. Needless to say, if an excess amount in dividends is paid out, it might help to attract equity from an investor who needs income. However, it could very well hurt from the regulatory standpoint and from the standpoint of issuing debt to shore up capital structure.

3. A forecast of capital base—equity and capital notes in relation to one another geared to achieve your bank's future objectives. The amount of equity you have pretty much determines how much debt you can issue. Therefore this very important element should definitely be included in your overall capital plan.

4. A financing plan designated to meet the requirements for capital base consistent with the capital structure and dividend policies.

You need creative planned response with *alternatives*; you just cannot put *one* plan down and say, "This is what we are going to do in the future," because you don't know what the interest rates are going to be on debt, and you do not know exactly when it would be appropriate to issue equity. Therefore, you need alternatives; and when markets indicate in either area that you have an opportunity to move, your bank is ready. The point is, when your ratios and forecasted needs to meet your planned objectives are within your three-year planning range, move when you can. The proper time is then; do not wait for lower cost on debt issued or better price on your stock if equity is indicated and you can afford the current rates and/or price of your stock.

Unless your bank is highly overcapitalized, which creates a problem in itself, or unless your bank is in a very stable environment and is not expected to grow in total assets in the three- to five-year range, you need to develop your market now, not a year before your bank indicates capital needs. The ways in which you can develop your market now for future issues of debt or equity are manyfold and are dictated to some degree by the market that you are going to enter. Since most of your banks are not capable of issuing capital notes or equity in the national market, a local market is developed.

There are many ways to develop a local market. Take for example a bank in Arkansas in a town of two thousand people. In 1961 the bank had $3 million in total assets. In 1976 the bank had $30 million in total assets and the town's population had increased by about four hundred people. The president did several things to bring about this growth. He encouraged his directors to give him the names of anyone who might be interested in either debt or equity, whether it was today or in the future. In addition to his regular board of directors, he appointed an advisory board of directors, who served a maximum term of two years, principally outside of his community—in his trade territory, which included the three competitive banks within a twenty-mile range of his bank. He kept his stockholders and note holders constantly informed of the current status of the bank by means of a regular letter from management, he had luncheons and picnics for them, and he held very informative stockholders' meetings. He kept them excited about the progress of the bank. He also did something that I picked up and used myself, something which might be of interest to you when you issue capital notes or equity. He kept an excellent prospect list even though he might not want to issue notes for a three-year period. This list included people who bought government bonds through his bank, people who had major savings and loan deposits and those who had accounts with competitive banks, and potential organizers of a competitive new bank—young comers in his trade territory. Not only were they good prospects because they had money, but they were better prospects because they generated new money. One of the problems that you have when you issue notes and sell equity is that funds are shifted from savings and demand accounts into notes; therefore, no new money is brought into your bank. The bank president was working on those people who had funds outside his bank. When he issued notes, money was not simply moved from one department in his bank to another. This approach has been highly successful for him, and highly successful for the institutions I have been involved with. Again, the point is not to wait until you have such immediate capital needs that you must rush your community to sell equity or debt. Develop now an interest in your bank, develop now a prospect list for equity and debt issues. And particularly, get people now from outside your bank who are interested in these issues so that you can hit the market when your needs fit the economic environment.

Our philosophy is to go for capital any time we can get equity—at a price we can afford to pay. Your CPA or your correspondent bank controller can determine what would be a realistic selling price for equity at any given time. The same is true if you are seeking debt. You should know the price you can afford to pay.

In making a capital injection into a bank, various avenues are available. Potential forms for raising capital are subordinated debt, which includes long term debentures, convertible debt, and capital notes; prefered stock; and common stock—new equity issues and retained earnings. Subordinated debt means that the debt issues are not insured by the FDIC and take a secondary position in liquidation to the regular deposits of the bank. They are, of course, in a preferred position in liquidation over the common stockholders of the bank. Of banks listing debt in their capital accounts in 1975, more than three-fourths are banks under $100 million in deposits.

In the 1960s and early 1970s long-term debentures were very popular in the capital acquisition plans of banks and bank holding companies. The sales of the debentures were made to institutional buyers; i.e., insurance companies, retirement and profit sharing plans, etc. This market has essentially dried up in 1976, although it might open up in the future. The reason it is no longer viable is primarily the investment community's loss of confidence in the banks and bank holding companies in the United States, due to the recent experience of some banks and bank holding companies in their asset management and profitability. The main thing that triggered the withdrawal of institutional investors for bank debt was the lack of communication the holders of debt experienced in the liquidation of the Franklin, as well as their loss of the principal they had invested.

There was another means of selling debentures in the sixties and early seventies that is fast disappearing: the sale of debentures to large correspondent banks. This was popular because it was easy. It also proved to be very costly to the smaller bank in that normally the correspondent required compensating balances for the purchases of the debentures, materially increasing the cost to the small banks. The small bank not only had to pay the interest on the debentures but suffered loss of investment income on dormant compensating balances. This means of selling debentures also proved unpopular for the correspondent bank in that many banks got too many bank debentures in their investment portfolios. It proved most unpopular with the regulatory authorities, and they are becoming more and more stringent in this area. The reason the regulatory authorities do not desire this as a means of raising capital is simply that it does not provide any new capital funds for the banking system as a whole. Their view, and they are correct in their view, is that the banking system as a whole needs new capital infusion. Since this method does not generate any new capital, but only shifts funds from one bank to another, they are putting more and more pressure on the large banks not to purchase the long-term debentures of a small bank. My conclusion is that debentures are very difficult to sell at this time unless you have a small insurance company and are on its board of directors and hold 30 percent of the insurance company's stock.

Another source of subordinated debt is the issuance of convertible debt, convertible to common stock at given prices in the future. This has been of some value to some larger banks with active trading in their stock, but I would venture to say that it would be effective to less than 1 percent of banks represented at this 1976 assembly for directors. The recent history of the stock market has not indicated to investors that convertible debt issues are worth the loss of income they would have received had they bought straight debt, which normally sells at a higher price than convertible debt.

I personally feel that capital notes are the most viable form of subordinated debt for banks in the $5 million to $750 million area. These notes can be sold locally in denominations as small as $500. I would suggest nothing under $1,000. They can be sold in any maturities, but they are not included in the capital structure as far as regulatory authorities or investment analysts are concerned unless they have a maturity of seven years or longer. They could be issued with or without sinking fund requirements. They have a disadvantage, as does all subordinated debt, in that they do have a maturity, and the refinancing of the debt, or the retirement of the debt, must be faced. My suggestion would be to issue notes of varying maturities from seven years to twenty years. There should be, in my opinion, a limit on the amount that you would sell in any one given year. This limit should normally be a maximum one-half of the projected earnings of the bank after tax each year your notes mature. The reason for this is that in any given year, if because of market conditions you could not refinance the maturing notes, you could use one-half of your profits and retire the notes.

Properly planned and properly marketed, capital notes are thus a viable part of most banks' capital planning. You must recognize that in a national bank you can only issue in any form of subordinated debt the dollar amount that is up to 100 percent of your paid-in capital and 50 percent of unimpaired surplus, which includes surplus, undivided profits, and the tax-paid portion of reserve for loan losses. In no instance will the comptroller or the FDIC allow the issuance of amounts in excess of 33⅓ percent of your total capital in subordinated debts. State banking laws may differ.

Of course, there is an overall advantage in subordinated debt; the interest paid is tax deductible, whereas dividends on common stock are not. There is also some advantage in the fact that the present stockholders do not have to put up more equity if there is a situation where everyone wants to "sort of" retain their present percentage of stock ownership in the bank. Debt creates leverage and if properly invested can yield more earnings per share.

Preferred stock, except in some very unusual situations, is not a viable source of capital. This is because during the Depression the Reconstruction Finance Corporation bought preferred stock in those banks that were considered weak at the time. That throws an unfavorable image upon any bank showing preferred stock in its capital structure. Over the years, however, this could change, since it is a viable part of the capital structure of utility companies.

As for raising capital through common stock, equity can be developed in two ways: by the issuance of new shares to be sold in the marketplace or to existing stockholders, or by the retention of earnings. Equity is the most important element of a capital plan. It allows you the flexibility of moving into subordinated debt issues, if you so desire. Without the equity, you can get yourself into the position, as many banks did, of leveraging with subordinated debt to the point where you could sell no more subordinated debt and the bank stock market was so depressed that you could not sell equity either. You must have an adequate equity base in your capital structure. It is best to broaden the base of your stockholders if at all possible by asking your stockholders to waive their rights, their privileges to any stock issue, and then selling your stock in your community to create new depositors and new friends. Remember also that in equity you don't have to worry about refinancing. It has no maturity. There is also no required payout. You can adjust your dividend rate, whereas you cannot adjust the rate that you must pay on subordinated debt.

The retained earnings approach is the best and cheapest method of creating equity, particularly if your stockholders are amenable to a major retention of profits; i.e., a dividend rate of, say, 20 percent of net earnings, realizing that they will have capital appreciation on their stock and realizing that when they sell, capital gains rather than ordinary income will be incurred. Both in creating equity and in the sale of equity, and in the sale of subordinated debt, recognize that an excellent consistent profit performance is *always* the key.

In order to assure consistently excellent profit performance, the board and management should watch at least these important keys to performance in your bank: (1) net income on assets; (2) return of equity; (3) loan loss experience; (4) reserve for loan loss adequacy; (5) leverage position; (6) capital adequacy; (7) liquidity position; (8) deposit mix; (9) employee utilization; and (10) utilization of funds.

Stock dividends are a viable substitute for cash dividends in smaller banks that are highly profitable and growing. Stock dividends can be an effective alternative to cash dividends in banks where the asset growth and profit growth is *excellent* and where there is an active local market for the stock. Stock dividends that result in dilution and/or force the decline of stock prices are of little value.

As directors interested in your bank's long-range needs, the first thing you should do is encourage management to develop a capital plan for the approval of your board. The overall plan should normally include a finite plan for three years with a reasonably detailed five-year plan and a very loose but basic ten-year plan—one with more philosophy and policy than detail. If you and your management do not feel that you have the expertise to plan, hire a consultant or a correspondent banker to assist you. I emphasize that you *hire* them and pay a fee, even to a correspondent, because you will get a better job. You should have major outside assistance the first year, less assistance the second year, monitoring the third year; the fourth year you should be on your own. I am convinced that you should plan in areas other than capital. If you are going into planning, go into it at all levels, and a $5 million bank can plan just as well as a $500 million bank.

In my association with many bank boards in the past I have found that they were inclined to attune themselves to problems that management should take care of; for example, the making of small loans or deciding whether Susie gets a raise. They seem to be fighting the gnats around their head and losing sight of the rattlesnake at their feet.

The board of directors should pay particular attention to (1) capital and debt planning; (2) large past dues and large loans; (3) actual results as compared to plan; (4) major deviations from plan and the strategies to correct deviations; (5) quality of assets; (6) management as well as management succession; (7) the hiring of outside auditors and consultants; (8) the mission, the philosophy, and the major policies of the bank; and (9) the market share.

Of course, there are audit and legal responsibilities of directors. Just remember, do not fight the gnats and let the rattlesnake bite you. Spend the funds and the time to have an overall bank plan, and particularly a capital plan. You as a board member hold an awesome responsibility. On the other hand, you have a great opportunity to help your publics, whether they be stockholders, other board members, employees, depositors, or your community. You cannot serve on any other board that can have a more positive effect on your publics.

WILLIAM H. DOUGHERTY, JR.

Capital Adequacy, Access to Capital Markets, and Financial Planning

THE ONLY THING which may be said about the issue of capital adequacy with any certainty is that nothing is static. The past several years have seen a continuing dialogue on this topic—with regulators decrying the erosion of capital ratios and bankers protesting that the decline in capital ratios was necessary to maintain attractive returns on equity and to support the credit demands of the economy. During the course of 1974, a third distinctive voice—the market—began to be heard. The market was—and is today—expressing concerns over asset quality (ergo capital adequacy) and liquidity. The market's message, in terms of bank stock prices and long-term debt rates, is that it will not be possible in the near term to obtain those capital funds necessary to meet simultaneously the regulators' capital requirements and the economy's expected credit demands.

There is a consensus within the industry about this dilemma. To continue to grow, our economy will require continued credit expansion, at a rate in excess of the rate at which the banking system retains earnings. Bank managements are unwilling to sell equity at prices below book values and at historically low P/E multiples. With the increased disclosure being required by the SEC—much of which tends to increase investor uncertainty about the banking industry—the market is certainly not going to bid up our stock prices to enable the economical sales of equity which would resolve the impasse. Unless the regulatory bodies are to allow further slippage in capital ratios, the dilemma will persist.

What is adequate capital? No one knows for sure whether a bank needs X or Y dollars of capital for each hundred dollars of loans, or whether capital is needed for support of loans only, or loans and securities, or total assets. The parties cannot agree on whether capital is equity alone, or can include prudent amounts of long-term subordinated debt. Yet they do not have much trouble in agreeing that—aside from the current capital market—"capital should get no lower."

There are three basic points which, I feel, affect an institution's capital needs. First, the need for capital in a bank is less important to the more profitable bank—a bank which has the earnings and earnings potential to cover loan losses, inflationary cost increases, etc., out of current earnings.

Second, the market, the regulators, and bank managements should stress liquidity. I am not saying that capital is unimportant—I could never take such a position. Capital and liquidity are aspects of the same issue. A highly liquid bank needs less capital than its less liquid competitor—for the likelihood of its having to absorb losses during a "fire sale" asset liquidation is infinitely lessened. The real test of liquidity in the bank-related area is the proper matching of assets and liabilities, plus bank line coverage of commercial paper. For a bank, the test is more complex because of the variety of its sources of funds. Assuming the bank has an acceptable level of purchased funds outstanding, the first line of defense in the liquidity issue comes from diversity of its funding sources.

Third, in the future we must rely more heavily upon asset quality measures in comparing individual banks with the average for the industry.

As an aside, loan losses this year may be very heavy by historical standards, but they will not be catastrophic. Even the much-maligned exposure of many large banks to the REIT industry immensely overstates the true risk. Real estate has value, and even if every REIT in the country were to go bankrupt, losses to banks and other lenders would not be staggering—provided the underlying projects could be "worked out" by a financial intermediary with enough staying power to see it through.

What I believe is that the analysis of a bank's overall quality must stress capital and three other equally important factors—profitability, liquidity, and asset quality. Implicit in each factor is the underlying quality of management, which will to a very large degree determine the success of any bank.

Is the apparent conflict between the regulators and banks in the current environment real? I believe this used to be the case, for we once had many banks in this country striving for growth in earnings through asset expansion in an environment of thinning margins and growing credit demands of the economy. This resulted in erosion of capital ratios, and virtually all regulators were simultaneously saying that capital considerations were paramount, and that concerns for shareholders had only secondary importance, because of a slowdown in the economy. This situation has improved. The consensus among bank managements is that there can be no further erosion of capital ratios; and the regulator posture is much more flexible, particularly with regard to the status of debt capital as a means to increase shareholder returns while minimizing depositors' risk.

Even though there may have evolved a tacit agreement among bankers and regulators, the environment posed by the market is most difficult. Briefly, these market-related problems are:

First, until the uncertainty surrounding today's economy is resolved, our price/earnings multiples will remain low—both absolutely and relative to other companies. The price/earnings multiple is clearly the best indicator of a firm's ability to attract external equity funds on economical terms—that is, at a price which will avoid significant earnings-per-share dilution while providing the basis for asset growth in future years which could not be obtained from internal sources. In the first quarter of 1965, the average price/earnings multiple for the banks in a sample of 35 larger banks maintained by Salomon Brothers was 15.5. Even aside from the very depressed state of the stock market in 1974 (the recent rebound notwithstanding), we have been in a downward trend ever since. Only in 1972 did there occur a significant reversal of this trend, and that reversal was, as we all now know, destined to be short-lived. It is also interesting to note that this bank sample's average multiple has always been below the S&P 425 industrials' multiple—never having been closer than 88 percent of it, and moving farther away from the S&P multiple when the economy worsened (1967 and 1971 being good examples). This indicates that the banking system will probably have poorer than normal access to the equity market so long as our current recession continues.

Second, our long-term debt instruments will likely continue at wider-than-normal spreads from similarly rated industrial instruments. This is the direct result of liquidity and loan loss concerns and of our large capital needs.

It is believed that the Securities and Exchange Commission's efforts to obtain quantitative disclosures relating to asset quality will continue to have significant impact on the ability of the banks to market both debt and equity securities. The Securities and Exchange Commission has been increasing its disclosure efforts in this area. Concurrently bank and bank holding company assets have shown a deterioration. There is presently a wide disparity in definition of standards or measures used. Among the regulators there is a high degree of subjectivity in the application of such standards. While asset quality is expected to improve by the end of the year, such improvement will not be significant enough to allay investor uncertainties. In addition, educating the investor on credit classifications and their significance will take a good deal of time. For the year 1975, $305 million of bank and bank holding company debentures have been underwritten to date—not a large amount when measured against the industry's need. There is no doubt that the increased disclosure requirements will keep many banks from the capital markets; and for some of those which do go to market they will result in higher money costs.

Third, it appears that for the near term funds will be less expensive to a bank than to its holding company. This too is related to recent bank failures, in which the Fed has shown that in almost all circumstances the bank's depositors will be made whole, while the holding company's creditors have no such support.

Fourth, with the increased usage of purchased funds in banking have come higher and more variable interest costs, a "tiered market" in which size is frequently equated with quality, and restrictions as to the maturity and quality of assets which may be funded with such short-term funds. This is particularly true in the case of commercial paper, with the SEC possibly requiring its registration under the 1933 Securities Act.

Fifth, I would expect that we will feel increased inflationary pressure on the non-balance-sheet factors which affect our income statements. For example, operating expenses as a percent of earning assets have risen from 2.1 percent to 3.0 percent since 1955. With the likelihood of sizable increases in personnel and occupancy expenses in the next several years, together with the diminished availability of productivity increases, this trend will continue unless management takes positive action to reverse it.

The environment I have just described will clearly present a challenge to every bank or bank holding company—large or small. To prosper in this environment, the financial or capital planning process of each bank or bank holding company must be very refined. Asset growth must be constrained to that level which can be supported by the internal generation of equity, supplemented to some degree by whatever debt financings the market will provide. Bank managements must examine closely all funds-using services to make certain that all lines of business meet the profitability objectives of management.

There will be tremendous competition for capital. Simply to maintain capitalization ratios at the present levels, in the next five years the banking system would have to attract $30 billion to $35 billion of external funds over and above the internal generation of equity to support earning asset growth at rates approaching historical trends. It is naïve even to think of the banking system as being able to raise an average of $7 billion in the capital market annually, when we have only raised between $2 billion and $3 billion in the best of recent years.

Capital planning is essential in an environment such as this. The planning must be reasonably accurate, must be flexible, and above all must be in tune with the capital markets. We at NCNB use the "building block approach" in our capital planning and structure the capital funds of each funds-using unit as if it were "free-standing." Our bank has that capital level appropriate for, and in effect required by, its regulator. In our case, that is the comptroller of the currency, and we therefore maintain capital at least equal to one-eighth of loans. We employ up to 30 percent debt funds in this capital base, since it is our strong feeling that subordinated capital debentures are an appropriate supplement to equity. They are a viable means to lower—to the virtual minimum—depositors' risk and at the same time enable us to maintain a return on equity equal to or better than those offered by other nonfinancial enterprises.

Each of our nonbanking subsidiaries is capitalized as if it were a free-standing company in that same business. For example, our consumer finance company has a leverage of about 6 to 1 on equity, with relatively high levels of long-term debt layered on top of that. This long-term debt is typical in the consumer finance industry and reflects the fixed rate, long-term nature of that business.

We have recently reduced drastically many of the longer-term assets (such as mobile home loans) of this company. This was done in recognition of the fact that our ability to capitalize this unit properly was limited by the present capital market—and being unwilling to raise capital in that market, we decided to shorten the maturity structure of its assets.

Putting these individual subsidiary pieces together to come up with a capital structure for the consolidated holding company is a simple exercise in arithmetic. Simply stated, the company should have that capital structure called for by each component, weighted by relative usage of funds in each unit.

The fundamental issue regarding any company's structure must center around the degree of financing risks which leverage has introduced. If each component part, be it a bank, a finance company, a mortgage banker, a factor, or a leasing company, is adequately capitalized relative to the credit and maturity risk of its individual portfolio, then almost by definition the whole must also be adequately capitalized. While this concept seems sound, it is not always accepted within the capital markets.

The traditional form for an indenture of a publicly offered issue of bank holding company debt contains a clause which prohibits the bank holding company from having senior-term debt greater than 50 percent of senior debt plus equity. There is, however, an effective limit imposed by the market of 40 to 45 percent. This limitation is both real and significant, because this one-to-one relationship of debt to equity imposes a limit upon the degree to which any holding company can increase the relative size of its nonbanking assets. Taking the indenture definition of capital as being senior-term debt and equity, it is obvious that banking requires much lower levels of capital funds than do nonbanking assets, particularly where consumer finance or commercial finance is concerned. Thus, by combining banking activities with a relatively low ratio of term debt to equity—in the order of one to two—with nonbanking activities where both the absolute level of capital funds as defined above and the ratio between term debt and equity as defined above are much higher than is the case in a bank, it is fairly easy to see that unlimited expansion into nonbanking assets cannot take place. This problem, a fundamental one, is due, more than anything else, to the market's general unwillingness to make qualitative distinctions about the relative mix of assets types between debt issuers. Given this limitation, it is inevitable that many companies will be placed in the situation where some subsidiaries, particularly those requiring more term debt than equity, may be better funded on a decentralized or independent basis.

CAPITAL ADEQUACY 153

Despite the means of funding subsidiaries, the real challenge is in balancing the capital funds and the investment opportunities available while maintaining the margin. Our approach at NCNB involves three stages. The first is a long-range planning process, in which key units' proposed plans for future expansion are weighed against one another as competitors for loanable funds and as consumers of a limited amount of capital funds projected to be available, based upon some expected earnings growth rates. A key element in the long-range planning process is an economic forecast of the future credit demands of various sectors in our trade area, and/or our future ability to raise external capital. Thus in this process we allocate capital funds to those asset generating functions which meet our target returns and serve the economic and credit needs of our region, and we limit the total growth to that amount supportable by forecast capital levels.

The second stage is a profit planning process, which operates on a much shorter time frame to make specific plans by asset and liability category for each of our profit centers. As in the long-range plan, the profit plan is analyzed to evaluate its impact upon the interest sensitivity balance of the company.

The third stage is a continual monitoring process, a function performed by monthly profit plan review sessions conducted by top management. The purpose of these meetings is of course to determine our progress in meeting the plan, to isolate any trends away from the interest sensitivity balance, and to correct any deviation from course.

The first two processes are relatively simple. The complexities arise in the third process—management of the spread while meeting the profit plan. This is a very difficult subject, and one on which most bank managements are actively working.

To summarize, banking has evolved into a capital-scarce industry. At least for the near-term, the market's willingness to provide most of our industry with external capital has apparently lessened. We must therefore place maximum emphasis upon the internal generation of capital—through improved profitability and through reducing dividend payouts over time. The banking system must learn to control its destiny better; more sophisticated financial planning approaches are essential if we are to operate profitably within the complexities of our future economic environment.

It is our belief that the equity market will reward with high multiples those banks having the most steady and predictable earnings growth and adequate capital ratios. In view of the competition for capital among banks in future years, it is highly likely that only those banks meeting this high standard will be able to raise significant amounts of external capital. Therefore, above average growth can be attained only by those banks able to demonstrate over a sustained period that they possess the management and the planning techniques to achieve these results.

FREDERICK DEANE, JR.

Capital Needs in Banking

IN TAKING A HARD LOOK at the future, the banking industry is faced with the essential problem that its needs for capital may well exceed supply, a situation which will weaken its ability to grow and expand. Most affected by this short-fall will be the smaller-sized and least profitable banking organizations; i.e., the larger money center banks and the best performers among the regionals will probably get their share at someone else's expense. Bridging this potential gap should be a primary concern of bank directors and management.

As a rapidly changing, more complex, and increasingly competitive financial environment unfolds, the banking industry's capital planning procedures must emphasize (1) innovation, looking beyond traditional ways of doing things; (2) less dependence on customary markets for debt and equity; (3) more disclosure to satisfy regulators and prospective investors; and (4) an activist role in pushing for legislative-regulatory changes to facilitate innovation.

It is of primary importance to treat the investment community with the same systematic, marketing-oriented approaches that we employ in dealing with other sectors of the marketplace. Debt and equity are a product, just like loans or deposits, which must be priced, promoted, and merchandised effectively.

Banking's capital needs must be placed in broader perspective. The considerable talk about a national capital shortage appears exaggerated. To the extent that there is a problem, it is related to the ability of existing suppliers of business capital to allocate funds efficiently, and to the relative severity of existing tax structures applicable to investment. There should be a fundamental reform that goes beyond the issue of capital needs in banking. The President of the United States has pledged attention to this matter, and as bankers and businessmen we must advocate that the pledge be kept—we hope, in a beneficial way (for example, a tax deduction for preferred stock dividends).

Nonetheless, it is not an exaggeration to talk of a capital shortage for our industry. In a paper—"The Growth of Commercial Bank Equity Capital"—prepared in late 1974 by former FRB official Samuel Chase, it was projected that by 1980 commercial banking assets would total between $1.6 trillion and $1.8 trillion, based on an average annual growth rate of 9-11 percent. Equity capital and reserves would total between $104 billion and $116 billion, and would continue to approximate 6.5 percent of total assets.

Through 1975, Chase's projections were on target, with assets growing at about a 10 percent annual rate. Capital and reserves amounted to $74 billion; however, the growth in capital was on the low side of Chase's growth rate projections, while asset increases tended toward the high side. This gap, moreover, was being widened implicitly by regulatory insistence that capital ratios be greater than 6.5 percent.

According to these projections, by 1980 banking will need to increase capital by between $30 billion and $42 billion and supply an overage to satisfy capital adequacy demands. How much of an overage is still uncertain, but a 7 percent ratio would mean an extra $8-10 billion.

Presuming that retained earnings would supply 75 percent of equity capital, banking would need to find new funds of between $8 billion and $10 billion, plus the capital adequacy overage. Putting aside this overage, we would require new funds in the amount of over $2 billion annually. Between 1970 and 1975, new capital formation—funds from investors—averaged less than $2 billion annually. Here is our shortfall: about $500 million to $1 billion a year or slower rates of growth.

The Chase data agree with Booz, Allen & Hamilton estimates, except that the latter study shows a lower asset growth rate and a higher capital ratio. Both, moreover, apply only to the banking side of our business, not to a holding company's bank-related activities. Thus, in addition to banking's basic capital needs, we must find debt and equity for our bank-related units. We have no data on how much will be needed, but an extra 15-20 percent does not appear farfetched as an estimate.

The Need for Capital

To keep pace with projected rising demand for business capital and business credit, banks must be both suppliers and users. There is a stronger demand now than there has been in the past for federal, state, or local government debt financing of many social programs—particularly housing. We are competing for capital—chiefly equity—to finance our own continued geographic and product diversification and to maintain acceptable levels of asset growth. Continued diversification recognizes that the Federal Reserve will encourage 4-C-8 expansion, especially on a de novo basis; the permissible list is not engraved in stone, as indicated by the Federal Reserve's savings and loan acquisition attitude and its decisions broadening the management consulting market. There are discernible trends toward trade area (regional) banking (for the immediate future this is an uncertainty, not an improbability) and multinational banking.

Perceived capital adequacy is also needed. This well-articulated public policy requirement stemming from our industry's 1973-75 debacle has led to demands for higher capital ratios—faster capital than asset growth—and reduced leverage of debt to equity, a faster capital growth with a markedly higher proportion of equity. It is the larger banking organizations which seem to have the lower capital ratios and which will be most active (and best positioned) in shoring them up. From a regulator and consumer view, as revealed by our 1973-75 operations, banking in 1976 is generally a riskier business and one which has moved away from traditional operations. Like it or not, we will have to satisfy these public perceptions while operating in "The Age of the People."

Finally, we need capital to handle our immediate refinancing of maturing bank and bank holding company debt. This is replacement capital, not new capital. Due in 1978 will be $345 million in maturing intermediate long-term debt, $975 million in 1979, and $800 million in 1980—a total of some $2 billion. These amounts are in addition to the short-term debt we roll over each day. This maturities bulge is also a supply problem. This burden was acquired when holding company movement was a market favorite. At the present time we are not a favorite, and, while there may be exceptions in individual institutions, the chances are that we will not be for some time.

The Supply Side of the Equation

It is most evident that the organized capital markets, particularly the institutional investors, are cold to banking. The current atmosphere is improving somewhat, but banking, especially in the areas of regional holding companies, is not likely to be as attractive again as it was in the 1968-72 era.

The overall capital pool—dollars available for investment—appears to be growing at a slower pace than the combined needs of business, government, banking, and other financial institutions. We need reform to increase the flow of capital into the market. If the relative supply remains constant for financial institutions, more banking organizations will be seeking these dollars. Also, nonbanks, especially thrifts, will most likely be forming holding-company-type organizations—or converting to stock charter—and thereby will begin to compete for these dollars. In the emerging new competitive environment, more competitors will be chasing the same relative amount of capital.

Finally, there is evidence that we are moving toward an era of purchased funds, the cost of which will be determined more by free market forces than regulation. Will this trend impact the price and availability of equity and debt? And assuming we pay higher prices for debt, will we be able to maintain an adequate spread in passing it on to customers?

In summary, these trends in banking suggest (1) that our projected capital needs probably will exceed our ability to attract funds from our traditional supply sources; and (2) that these traditional sources cannot be counted on to deliver the same proportion of capital as that provided in the past.

The Supply-Demand Equation: Solutions to a Dilemma

There are several ways of attacking our dilemma. One way is to clean up our image. This chiefly involves insuring that banks have adequate disclosure practices and, most important, good earnings and overall management performance. Increased profitability will allow us to build up retained earnings and pay better dividends. The former adds to capital; the latter is helpful in attracting a larger share of investment capital. The staggering expenses associated with our entry into the world of electronic banking could pose a major challenge to increased profitability and our earnings retention programs. We do not have a good handle on what EFT and its components will cost; nor do we even know what the rewards will ultimately be.

Stress planning is another way to help alleviate problems. We must do a better job of identifying needs and assigning priorities to them.

We must focus on what is vital and most profitable; we can no longer do everything we want to do. Some regional holding companies have made recent decisions to concentrate on the commercial side of the business and minimize their retail banking activity. Focusing on what will bring in the best and surest profits involves our industry's special need to get a better handle on costs. Poor cost-pricing is a weakness we must overcome if we are to enhance profitability.

Innovation, however, appears to be the key solution in meeting bank capital needs. We must not rule out alternatives that have not been used before; we must be open-minded. Remember, stigmas (for example, best-effort offerings) tend to disappear with success.

Programs to Consider

Many of the following suggestions will require changes in law and regulations. Our job is to make change happen. We must be active, not reactive. The retail sale of equity and short-term debt within your distinct market is one program to consider. Bank of Virginia Company has done it both ways—self-sales and sales through local brokers on a best-efforts basis—with identically structured issues.

Sales on balance, which is the best approach, depend on at least these key variables:

1. The structure of your market, the level of education and sophistication, the levels of disposable income, etc.
2. The effectiveness of personnel as a sales force.
3. Most important, an aggressive corporate attitude supporting the marketing techniques employed; e.g., Bank of Virginia Company's 9 percent price-oriented advertising.

Another approach is the selling of forward contracts in low-denomination multiples to consumer investors on the installment plan. When paid, convert the contracts to either common or preferred stock.

As AT&T has been doing, offer—indeed stress—dividend reinvestment programs (possibly at a discount) for additional shares. Alternatively, dividends might be reinvested to purchase short-term debt instruments.

In connection with the dividend reinvestment program, offer equity as interest on longer-term investment-type thrift accounts. This could be a logical addition to an IRA program or a Keogh plan for the self-employed. Incidentally, a number of banks are prepaying interest on longer-term consumer certificates. In some cases, interest has been in the form of consumer goods (TV sets in Hartford). Why not offer equity or debt?

Link our own equity and debt instruments to "money desk" portfolios; seek to sell our product along with savings plans, IRA accounts, governments and municipals, and selected common stocks.

Critical to the foregoing concepts is a sense of market. Without question, these ideas are not oriented toward the institutional investor, but toward savings customers and trust customers, in particular, as well as toward individuals and brokerage firms who know the bank and its reputation, and toward that very vital market, the bank's employee base.

At Bank of Virginia Company we have an Employee Stock Purchase Plan. As of September 30, 1975, 18 percent (567) of our employees participated. The average monthly deduction was $60. Against an average January-September market price of $13.81 per share, employees paid 15 percent less, or $11.74. Given our current annual dividend of $.88 per share, this reflects a 7 percent yield. Through September, employees purchased more than 21,000 shares. At market rates, this is about $300,000 in new equity, which we believe will yield $500,000-$1 million a year, given time and explanation.

Another type of innovation is the Corporate Bond Fund managed by Merrill Lynch, whereby a holding company arranges a private placement with this investment banking firm. It then combines the long-term debt obligation with securities of other banking organizations into the corporate bond fund, which is then sold to the public—chiefly to individuals. In time, this concept may well take hold and grow.

Lastly, it is quite apparent that we must consider foreign sources of capital; and, of course, *foreign* very specifically means the oil-rich nations. The dollars are there; so is the demand for high-grade debt and equity investments. Moreover, as Samuel Chase has noted, one reason for American banking's capital problem can be traced to the sharp rate of asset-deposit growth in our foreign offices. Why not seek out the supporting capital, too? Bank of America just did that with a worldwide stock offering.

But be forewarned of the problems. There is American antipathy to foreign ownership (indeed, there is traditional isolationism). There are volatile foreigner attitudes, made more volatile, incidentally, by political as much as by economic events. Thus, there is always the question of whether they will stay with you. There is also the foreigners' predilection for being "big chunk" oriented. Will they want too large a slice of your pie?

Much can and will be added to this brief listing of capital-building programs. Doing so is our requisite task, as is the creation of a positive, receptive environment. If innovation is a must, so is militant advocacy.

I recommend the Virginia Bankers Association–commissioned study on *Capital Requirements of Virginia Banks.* Projecting from 1975 through 1980, this study shows that assets will grow on a CAGR of 14 percent, or slightly more than the 13 percent for the preceding six years. It concludes, moreover, that retained earnings will be insufficient to meet future capital requirements, that long-term debt will be a less important source of capital because many holding companies already are heavily leveraged, and that new stock issues will be expensive and difficult to sell in a generally depressed market for bank equities. Accordingly, the study argues that banking organizations in Virginia must become increasingly selective in their loan and investment policies in order to avoid capital-asset ratios below the regulatory limits. *We must, in effect, slow our growth.*

I find this unacceptable. Perhaps most of you feel the same way. This is the reason why we must find solutions to banking's capital needs and the prospect that demand will exceed supply. It is why we must be willing to innovate, willing to disclose more about our operations, and willing to adopt a more aggressive posture in pushing for needed legislative and regulatory changes to facilitate innovation and experimentation in the area of capital acquisition.

HAROLD R. HOLLISTER

Managing Bank Investments

IT IS TIME for positive decisions. It is time to act and not to react, for no one remembers the second man who flew the Atlantic. Management must manage. If there was ever a time and a need for management, it is now. So many changes took place in the banking industry over the past decade (1966-76) that if you had not moved in tune with the bulk of them, you would now find your bank 90 percent obsolete. And as Captain Andy used to say on the Showboat: "This is only the beginning folks, only the beginning." The changes which are taking place now, and those that will be taking place over the next few years, will once again completely change the face of this industry as we know it. You will continue to see more regulation and centralization of control over the banks. You will see continued efforts to place all financial institutions under closer Federal Reserve control. You will see a centralization of bank examination and reporting under one major authority.

We are now seeing the entry of the grocery chains and other establishments into the banking business through the emergence of EFTS and the checkless society. It makes us angry, but it is all part of the change. We, of course, have been in the merchandising business ourselves for some time in our efforts to gain deposits through the sale of kitchenware, blankets, popcorn poppers, and what have you. We have also excelled in the travel agency business. Much depends, I suppose, on whose foot is being stepped on.

You, as bank directors, are really the football coaches watching the game films from last Sunday's game. You must be able to spot the weakness in your line and the ineffectiveness of your own team's offense. You must be able to add your judgment and expertise to your banking team. In these times of the new, the untried, and the different, it is essential that you be your own best man, doing your job on an informed, best effort basis. Too much has already been lost in this country as a result of the blind leading the blind.

Since this is an election year, the struggles and the infighting going on tend to distort and cloud the true picture of the economy and the money markets. The investment markets, both debt and equity, are moving along on a day-to-day basis in a rather dynamic state of flux and confusion, and they will no doubt continue to do so until the election in November, 1976, is behind us. The markets have become very emotional, and emotional markets are always dangerous, tending to over-correct in one direction or the other on the basis of small bits of plus or minus news.

In this environment it is little wonder that today's banker is confused and uncertain about what he wants to do or what he should be doing. Like all other businessmen, he is being very selective and cautious with the employment of his reserves. His loan demand is down in many cases because of the recessed economy, and he is being very selective with the loan demand that he does have, well remembering the blunders of the past. It is no fun getting your turkeys before Thanksgiving. His need for tax-exempt income is down because of poorer earnings in some cases—more specifically, in the case of the smaller banks because of the change in tax law boosting the lower tax base to $50,000 from its normal $25,000 base rate. The banker has also lost a good deal of faith in municipal bonds in general as a result of the credit problems of the major cities, such as New York. He has also been fearful of overcommitting reserves to the government market too soon because of the glut of deficit financing that has been and is yet to be channeled through the Treasury market. And he must not forget that Dr. Burns's main concern is to prevent the inflationary overstimulation of the economy by holding the monetary aggregates in check, even with higher interest rates if necessary.

The banker is confused. If he has investment profits, should he take them now; and if he does, where does he reinvest the proceeds? If he has losses, should he take them or keep hugging the losers until the markets are better? If he has excesses in federal funds that are costing him precious income, should he get them invested in something better or continue to call the markets and wait for better rates? It is the inability to see clearly and to measure the accuracy of what we are seeing in today's markets that is creating the problem.

We must start with two basic premises:

First, you are the commercial banking industry for your respective communities, and all of your interactions control the reserves that create loans and investments which in turn create money supply in the banking system. You are responsible for the creation of roughly 80 percent of the narrowly defined money supply (M-1) that Dr. Burns is so concerned about. The key to the operational levels of both the debt and equity markets is pretty much determined by the availability of credit, or, more simply stated, by the availability of money supply. You then are the major factor in determining the course and the level of interest rates in this country. That fact alone should give you a pretty good leg-up in portfolio planning.

Second, you must keep foremost in your mind that everything a commercial bank decides to do with its deposits is going to wind up being a loan in one form or another. The bank will loan this money to its customers on an individual or a corporate basis. It will loan it to the federal government and its various agencies through the purchase of their taxable debt instruments. It will loan it to the various municipal governmental units through the purchase of their tax-exempt debt instruments. Or finally, it will loan it to its correspondent bank in the form of secured or unsecured federal funds, or as free correspondent balances. It is the successful mix and management of these assets that will determine whether or not a bank has good solid earnings with which to build capital base to support future growth.

The bank's hardcore deposit base must be allocated to cover the bank's cash, loan, and investment needs in that three-part package. If a bank continually attempts to carry more in loans and in investments than its hardcore base will support, it must then turn to the marketplace to attract new deposits in the form of bank CDs or federal funds borrowed. Since these are both very expensive deposits, the bank is placing the cart before the horse. It is managing liabilities rather than assets; and when it can no longer attract interest in its bank CDs, or borrow effectively in the funds market, school is going to be out. We have had several banks point this up quite clearly over the past year or so.

Proper asset management, not liability management, is now, always was, and always will be the real key to successful bank management. I have heard the other side of this scenario played, and my comment is "baloney."

Another problem area is in the cost of doing business, which has become a tremendous factor influencing bottom line figures. Banks must get a better handle on their costs. I doubt that many bankers know what their actual costs really are. We want size, we want to be larger than our competitor, and we take chances in our desire to expand. Bankers are still giving their banks away in the name of competition, and this is dumb. Bankers plead guilty of doing a good job before they are even accused of it. If someone so much as questions their policies, they immediately volunteer to cut the price of their services; or worse, they simply give them away. Many bankers get into trouble by taking undue risks for additional yield in an attempt to squeeze too much out of their loan and investment dollars. Closer surveillance on the cost side, through budget, might prove more beneficial. Many of us may be watching the wrong side of the ledger.

The bank investment account must be required to perform two basic functions: (1) it must store liquidity on an earning basis, creating a pool to cover expected, or, even more important, unexpected loan demand and deposit drain; and (2) it must be a residual account for the employment of funds that cannot or, in all probability, will not be loaned.

Bankers have a tendency to operate their investment account on a stop-and-go basis, like a stepchild or a poor relation. This is because the banker is primarily loan oriented, looking only to his investment account for help when loans and bank earnings are down. The real irony here is that when loan and bank earnings are down, so are the yields in the investment area. The investment account must be run on a continuing basis as an extension of the loan account, which it actually is. It will then be properly structured to carry the bank through some of the leaner years in bank earnings.

When reserves are tight, banks will place any and all deposit growth on the loan side, even stealing from the investment account through liquidation, or maturity, for additional funds for the loan commitment. This is a rather common basic error, for if bank investments do not keep their proper perspective in bank growth, the asset mix moves into poor balance, and the day will come when the bank finds it has left itself open-ended.

Bank investments are anything but a crap-shoot, as so many bankers tend to treat them. They are, or at least should be, high grade loans, purchased on quality, to complement and pick up the slack in the bank's loan demand and to provide secondary reserves to meet deposit drain and loan buildup.

It is therefore of the utmost importance that a bank have an overall investment policy and operate its investment account within the framework of policy, as set forth. Policy should be flexible and subjected to periodic review to determine goal achievement. To accomplish this properly a bank must first break down its present loan position as to commercial, installment, and real estate loans to determine the liquidity, or illiquidity, in the loan position itself. Obviously, a bank with heavy installment volume has built-in liquidity from run-off alone, where a bank largely tied to real estate commitments does not.

Once the loan account has been broken down and classified by type, the bank must compare the dollar volume of loans to deposits to arrive at an optimum level of loans that would be desirable to carry, if available. It is no longer prudent or fashionable to lend just for the sake of making a loan. The weight of the percentage of loans and the amount of liquidity found in these totals is an excellent guideline to the point at which the maturity of the investment account must be centered. The heavier the percentage and the more illiquid the loan portfolio, the shorter the investment account must obviously be.

Once we have the loan picture pretty much in mind, we must take a hard look at the deposit structure of the bank. How much in demand as opposed to time? How much of the time is passbook as opposed to CDs and certificates? This analysis gives us both a liquidity and a cost factor. Normally, the heavier a bank is in demand deposits, the greater the deposit fluctuation will be and the greater the need to gear the investment account to compensate for these swings. Time deposits are normally more stable, especially in the passbook area, and the heaviness of the passbook area will dictate any maturity extension that might be considered in the investment account. If the bulk of the time is in the form of CDs and certificates, however, I would consider these to be most unstable, and would want it well covered in the investment area. The loyalty found in CDs and certificates is just not the same as in good old passbook savings.

Once the loan and deposit areas have been broken down and classified, we must take a look at the trade area in which the bank operates. From this, we can normally project and time the seasonal swings in both loans and deposits. Surprising as it may seem, some banks operate in areas that cannot generate adequate loan demand, while others fall under the influence of one or two large depositors that can create dramatic short-term deposit fluctuation.

These are just some of the basic elements that must be known before one can even attempt to build the framework of investment policy for any given bank. Too many bankers have built their investment accounts on a hit-and-miss basis, and when they finally decide that they should have a stated investment policy, they find there is no way to get there from where they are.

Building a workable investment philosophy must begin with setting goals for the bank on both an annual and a longer-term basis. From the bank's present position in loan and deposit mix, goals should be set for the coming year. From the bank's existing balance sheets and projections for the end of the current period or calendar year, taking into consideration the trend in interest rates, a projected income goal for the next period should be set. The bank already knows its average loan yields, potential loan demand, and seasonal needs. It already knows the average yields in both its taxable and tax-exempt investment portfolio, together with the possible trend in interest rates on maturity roll-over and replacement. From this known position the bank should project where it wants to be in the following year or at any given point in the future. It may not get there, but it certainly will not arrive without a plan.

The time to formulate goals is in January, not as the year comes to a close when you find that you have too much taxable income or, even worse, too little; or that you have been crippled all year by illiquidity that has weighed heavily on bank earnings in borrowing costs; or through loss liquidation of assets; or that you have had undue excesses of federal funds for which you have been unable to find a home.

The bank's investment account must be structured and managed under the following policy guidelines: (1) maximum safety of funds— 90 percent borrowed capital; (2) provision of adequate liquidity; and (3) maximum return on fund employment.

As bank reserves accumulate, the taxable side of the investment portfolio is one that tends to get overbuilt, simply because of the ease of investment, the standardization of security, and the vast availability of offerings. However, I do not especially want to hold more taxable securities than are necessary to hold the top (48 percent) tax bracket, to handle by liquidity requirements, and to satisfy pledge requirements where collateral restrictions are invoked. Normally, a bank will not be well enough compensated after taxes for the assumption of market risk that has been built into this area over the past few years, stemming in part from the Fed's adoption of the money supply concept through aggregate control. As a backlash to policy enforcement, moving into the control range for money supply and federal fund target ranges has necessitated wide swings in shorter term interest rates. Over the longer term this is a healthy approach, as it would eventually create stability in longer-term market rates, if policy is adhered to.

I can foresee little chance of limiting the volume of government and agency obligations that will come to market to finance a continuing federal deficit. This continued heavy volume will place a steady floor under any dramatic fall in interest rates in the taxable sector. When Dr. Burns decides to pick up his marbles and go home, the game is going to be over. While the Federal Reserve can take money supply out of the system through the reserve route, there is no way of taking the federal deficit out of the treasury markets. It just rolls around there, first being funded and then continually refunded. The only way to get the federal deficit out of the system is to run budgetary surpluses, and I cannot think of a way known to man to accomplish that hat trick.

I prefer to hold the maturity range of the taxable sector in the one-to-five-year range or one-to-seven-year range, with the heaviest weighting on the shorter side. Since it is the bank's poorest earning asset, it should be relegated to a secondary reserve position, which is its chief function. I would relent, however, and go to the new ten-year limit on notes, where coupon limitation sets in, but only under certain market conditions, where high coupon warranted (8 percent notes of 86). While I can see no romance in longer-term government obligations, there may be exceptions to the rule, as there are to all rules. Needless to say, a commercial bank should not speculate with depositors' funds, but there may be a time when an account might want to lengthen maturities beyond the longer limits of its prescribed program to take advantage of market swings. But in such cases the bank must realize that it is out of its prescribed position and must return to it by some preset date, by either taking its profits or taking its losses, if it has guessed wrong. It is the marriage to the losers that creates the real problem.

I would make use of the federal agency issues in the taxable sector within the same maturity restriction, but only when the yield spread justified such a move. When yields narrow, as they have in 1976 markets, because of the heavy volume of treasury deficit financing, I would hold to the full treasury issues; they have a better market floor due to difference in guarantee.

We all like to think we are experts in the investment areas. We all like to call and predict markets. Unfortunately, there are no experts in the investment area, there are only the lucky and the unwashed. When you can purchase governments and agencies at near 8 percent or better in the one-to-ten-year range, and tax-exempt securities at a 5.00 basis or better, which is a 9.61 percent taxable in the one-to-ten-year range, you are going to come out rather well over the longer term and you should not try to call the markets. I do not like to chase markets, and that is why I will remain flexible in my invested position, shifting from the longer to the shorter term, or back again, in certain types of markets. It it rather like running your bond account in a neutral position, so that you are not committed to going forward or to backing up all of the time.

I do not like governments much below the 7.5 percent number or municipals below 5 percent, but I will stay invested at some level on the shorter side during periods of depressed interest rates. At the moment, when I cannot secure 8 percent taxable or 5 percent tax free in the ranges that I am shooting for, I am hiding on a tax-free basis in 1977. If I can secure a 3.50 percent tax-free yield, I am hiding at a 6.73 percent taxable equivalent yield, and still have mad money at hand to get home with next year when rates, I hope, will be more to my liking. I do not particularly like federal funds as a semipermanent investment vehicle. In this area it becomes too easy to overcommit in what we call lazy fed funds; and there is inherent credit risk involved, whether funds are secured or unsecured.

The municipal, or tax-exempt, portion of the bank's investment portfolio should share with the bank's loans as the prime income producers. It has become paramount that we exercise sound credit judgment and analysis in the selection of the risk we will be willing to accept in acquiring this type of loan. Creditability has become a real problem in the tax-exempt area. The rating services have become most suspect over the past few years, and I do not believe we can rely solely on their letter designations for our quality control. While the fault has not been basically theirs, because there has been poor disclosure on the part of the issuer, it is going to take our own credit analysis of each individual issue to give us that control.

We cannot, however, put our heads in the sand either; we will continue to purchase general market names on quality. On this basis, I would limit acquisitions to the top four Moody ratings—Aaa, Aa, A-1, and A—and I would be very selective in purchasing the lower limit of this scale. In the local market, where a good many credits trade on an unrated basis, the financial statement and the banker's general knowledge of the credit must prevail.

Revenue bonds, if used in portfolio, should be classified as higher risk loans because of the method of repayment, and quality restrictions should be imposed by policy. Industrial Revenue bonds, if used in portfolio, should be subjected to discount committee review and approval prior to purchase. This is an area that has been troublesome, and extensive surveillance should be maintained by discount committee review to ascertain ongoing quality. I would limit such acquisitions to large, national companies where the credit speaks for itself, or to those companies residing in your industrial park where the company shows solid promise and you are providing a community service. A good question to ask yourself is whether you would personally purchase common stock of this company if it were available. If the answer is no, the rest should be quite obvious.

I have no basic argument with corporate bonds in portfolio, but I can't really see that there is too much to be gained, on a net basis, over and above the taxable governments and agencies over the longer term, especially when you stir up the creditability mud puddle.

Municipal credits that trade under the protection of an insurance contract do not intrigue me. If they are not strong enough to trade on their own merit, there are too many other good credits available to me. I do not want a piece of the rock.

As to the maturity structuring of the tax-exempt account, this will naturally vary from bank to bank depending upon the analysis of internal factors, but generally either a one-to-fifteen-year range or a five-to-fifteen-year range should fit most portfolio planning. I can appreciate that some banks prefer to hold their tax-exempt purchases in the one-to-five-year range; however, if your taxable side is properly structured, you will be double-teaming liquidity at the expense of solid income lock down.

As for the overall maturity structuring of the investment account, the following distribution is a pretty good guideline: 75 percent of all securities maturing in one to five years; 15 percent of all securities maturing in six to ten years; 10 percent of all securities maturing beyond ten years. If we include federal funds, 50 percent of all securities should mature within two years. The greatest problem in the tax-exempt area is creditability.

We are now making the flight to quality, away from the unknown risk. All of a sudden we have found religion. You know the good Lord helps the needy, not the greedy, and we have been in the wrong camp for a long time. We blame New York City for all our problems, and while it is true that the problem surfaced there and has been penalizing all municipal credits as far as financing costs are concerned, there are a good many similar situations existing today, some local in nature. New York City's problems have accomplished one positive thing in that they have put the fear of God into many other communities and municipal governments, making them take a much broader stance in fiscal responsibility. We see a lot more bonds being voted down and a lot less supply coming into the markets. It has been mainly the stronger names that have been able to market their securities. The poorer, marginal names have had poor market acceptance.

It is evident that municipal governments have had a very difficult time attempting to provide the essential services in the face of inflation. Property taxes have certainly not kept pace with the inflation rate, and many communities are reaching their taxing limits, as are their taxpayers. Many do not have too many avenues open to them to attract the needed additional revenues. In addition, the problem becomes compounded by both the federal government and the states, which continue to impose new programs and mandates on the cities for such things as health, education, welfare, ecology, etc., without providing the funds with which to carry them out. Many municipalities have also misused their borrowing ability in an effort to help private business placement and expansion, thus wasting part of their firepower needed for more important projects.

The area of revenue sharing, which in reality is deficit sharing, is also a dangerous trap for many communities. This federal deficit that is passed along to the cities as a bonus to make possible special projects has been built right into the budget by many. This is a classic error, and will one day haunt them. It is time to make the flight to quality. It is time to upgrade your portfolios. It is time to bring your bond accounts home if they have been in foreign fields. It is time to ask yourself not where can you get a better yield, but where can you get the most credit for your money.

We are about to see the emergence of the taxable municipal bond. The legislation is presently in the Congress, and it should be only a matter of time and final form. It will allow issuing municipal bodies to have the option of continuing to sell tax-exempt bonds, or to sell taxable bonds, with the federal government subsidizing a minimum of 35 percent of the differential in cost. It would broaden the marketing base for municipals, it would reattract the large and small bank investor who no longer has need for tax-exemption, and it would attract the now tax-free institutions. But most of all, it would get rid of tax-exemption once and for all, consummating a long-range objective at the federal level—at the expense of the American taxpayer.

While all of us care about interest rates, we are most concerned about where they are headed and when they will move. Since you are the ones who will determine interest rates that lie ahead, you had better start watching each other closely. I quite agree that interest rates are very easy to misjudge, because while all interest rates are on the tail of the same dog, they do move at different speeds in one direction or another, and for different reasons. When we look at short-term interest rates, we are basically looking at the results of Federal Reserve policy with regard to the easing or the tightening of commercial bank reserves. When we look at longer-term interest rates, we are looking at the near term expectations as to the course and the level of inflation. Most banks, through lack of proper program planning, will normally buy losses in portfolio because they buy and space maturities in a backward fashion. When interest rates are extremely high it is because banks have all their available reserves committed, and mostly to their loan portfolios. They turn away from the securities markets, driving interest rates to inordinately high levels. At this point, the banker is only liquidity conscious, and if he invests at all, which is doubtful, it will be to get the highest yield possible with a maturity of about fifteen minutes. In low-yielding markets, when loans and rates are down, the same banker now becomes very income conscious, and will buy longer-term bonds at lower rates to get additional income, thus locking down losses for the next turnaround.

Bankers must never feel locked into their portfolios, for as long as they have taxable income they can correct their errors through loss-taking and replacement in current markets. *Never be married to anything in your portfolio.* If bankers would stop to analyze why they have losses in portfolio, the pieces would fall quickly into place:

1. They have losses in portfolio because interest rates have gone up, and interest rates have gone up because bank loans are very high and reserves are scarce. If loans are high at the high interest rates, their income should be excellent and provide them with the vehicle to lower taxes by loss-taking to correct market mistakes, while letting the government pick up 48 percent of the tab for improving their invested positions.

2. Conversely, when the bank has profits in its portfolio it is because interest rates are down, and interest rates are down because reserves are more plentiful and loans are down. If loans and rates are both down, bank earnings will be down, and, once again, bankers have the vehicle to take profits to bolster sagging earnings.

Too many bankers report high taxable earnings and pay out 48 percent of them to the federal government. Once they write the check, the funds are gone forever—funds that could have been better employed by improving the bank's investment portfolio.

I can't urge you enough to be your own man, to make judgments and decisions that will help the team. Be the same professional in your investment portfolio that you are in all of your other bank functions.

"The day of buying two blues, a red and a green are gone forever."

RICHARD L. KATTEL

Real Estate Problem Loans and the Future

WHOEVER HEARD of a bad real estate loan? As late as 1973 there were very few of us in the banking industry who had. As a matter of fact, those of us who have been in banking for only the last fifteen to twenty years had not, with a few exceptions, seen bad loans of virtually any sort. In many cases, our people and systems were simply not prepared to deal with the experiences we have had during the last four years (1972-76), and this applies to the handling of problem loans generally, not just real estate loans.

Now many of us are having to deal with some problems and we are saying to ourselves: How did we get in this situation, and where do we go from here? Good times compensate for or overcome a lot of mistakes and inexperience in the banking business. That is what we had in the years following World War II, on up to our recent economic downturn; and the last fifteen years or so of that period were especially good. It has taken the downturn to help us really see what we are doing wrong and where we need to restructure our training and procedures in loan administration.

One of the fundamental assumptions that we bankers made for years and years was that a loan secured by real estate was one of the best loans we could make. If we kept a relatively safe loan-to-value ratio, we would always be able to come out. "After all," we reasoned, "they aren't making any more land." There are a number of problems with that assumption, and in many cases these have been translated into loan losses. It's just not that simple.

The appearance of the real estate industry's first troubles was simultaneous with the development of serious inflationary problems in the economy. And whether the inflationary spiral is to be attributed to the energy crisis or to the easy money period of 1971-72, the effect was still the same. When prices of raw construction materials such as steel, cement, and lumber began rising at historically high rates, while at the same time shortages of these same materials were occurring, developers began to experience tremendous cost overruns. In some cases, construction was actually forced to a halt. Both of these conditions impaired the ability of developers to repay their construction and development loans.

At the same time, as unemployment increased sharply, consumer confidence declined and individuals became wary of making new commitments for major purchases, particularly homes. Companies began to look harder at expansion of offices or development of regional offices. They pulled in their operations, cut expenses, and thereby absolutely destroyed the demand that had been anticipated for new office space in some parts of the country. Similarly, with increasing building and development costs, apartment developers were unable to structure rental charges which would cover the overhead of a new project. It simply became financially unfeasible for the homeowner to trade up, or for the company to expand; and projects under construction became economically unwieldy because the cost and revenue estimates on which they were based became miserably outdated overnight.

Inflation, tight money, and the collapse of the housing and building industry are all obvious, but there were other underlying causes for the real estate problems our industry has today. A lot of these problems were brought about because we as commercial bankers simply overlooked many fundamentals of lending and all but one—collateral—of the "five Cs" of credit.

In 1975 I made an analysis of our real estate loan losses, and in virtually all of them one or more of the following problems existed:

1. In many cases, we relied too heavily on collateral to bail us out. Also, we valued it incorrectly, failed to assess its marketability under adverse conditions, or failed to control it when necessary.

2. We either failed to appraise management quality properly—for example, we might let an inexperienced subcontractor get in over his head—or assumed that good management could overcome some pretty obvious deficiencies on the balance sheet or elsewhere.

3. We loaned far too much to highly leveraged borrowers or to borrowers who had no personal equity in a deal.

4. We forgot the importance of "character."

5. We used poor documentation procedures.

6. We simply did not take into account the market's ability to absorb the projects that were coming on stream at the same time. We were lending on the basis of anticipated demand for real estate as though our projects alone would be available to fill that demand. For example, we might have been financing a new hundred-unit apartment development, after a market feasibility study showed such a development made sense, only to look across the street and see another such development, financed by a competitor, coming out of the ground at the same time.

7. In many cases we failed to take into account the specialized nature of real estate lending, and therefore did not match the experience level of our bank officers with the requirements of the customer. The result was that, instead of *our* banking the *customer*, the customer ended up calling all the shots.

8. In our hurry to take advantage of some very attractive yields on construction and development lending, we neglected to examine each deal carefully.

In other words, we found ourselves caught up in the same speculative mania that had taken over much of the real estate industry.

The same kinds of basic lending mistakes were made in many good solid banks, both large and small, in many parts of the country. If we had not had in the early 1970s the most severe economic downturn since the depression, it is probable that many of these shortcomings in our lending decisions would never have amounted to much. But we got caught. The fallout from these mistakes was that many banks totally rejected real estate lending, and many of us are left holding workouts, nonaccruals, and foreclosed real estate.

In light of all this, there are really two basic questions we now have to ask. First, do we as bankers have a place in real estate lending? In other words, is this a business where we can provide a real service on a sound banking basis and provide it profitably? And second, what is the outlook for those real-estate-related problem loans that are presently on the books?

On the first point: the easiest thing in the world for us to do would be to back away from the real estate industry, at least the construction and development side of it. I think this would be a mistake. For one thing, we are chartered to provide services to our certain markets; and if real estate development is an integral part of that market, we miss some major opportunities to serve our communities as well as to generate earnings for our shareholders. The key point for each of us is to avoid any undue concentration of these or any other types of loans in our portfolio. We need to set well-conceived limits on real estate loans and live within those limits.

And why throw out all those expensively developed resources we have acquired over the past few years? We have more banking *professionals* lending money to the real estate industry than ever before. For the last three years, our lenders have gotten a Ph.D. in what *not* to do by having to work out of bad situations. Our procedures are better, and in general we are better equipped to do real estate lending than at any time in the past. We have learned to be more conservative, looking for hard equity from the real estate developer going into a deal; and this means cash, not "appraised value" of real estate. And we are better able to assess the demand for a real estate project.

We are, in general, dealing with more sophisticated management and getting more sophisticated financial information from real estate developers. The fly-by-night operators are long gone. Most of the developers now in the trade have a good track record of performance and a better understanding of cost control and pricing. With all this in mind, I say let's hang in there. We are now equipped to lend the industry *properly*, and thus *profitably*.

Now, what do we do with those problem loans we have on the books? First, it is awfully important that we make our directors aware of our real estate problem loan situations and that we seek their assistance in dealing with them. We have found our own directors to be most helpful, particularly in dealing with our customers and prospects. I am sure that each of you is given a list of the types of properties presently in your bank's portfolio, or that at least you have some idea of what the totals of these loan categories are. The more you know about specific situations, the more you can help.

Regardless of how diligently we all work together, however, we know we are not magicians. The workouts of these loans are simply going to take time. How long it will take will depend on the absorption rates for real estate in your market. Based on present absorption rates in the metropolitan American area, for example, we anticipate that it will take about three years to fill up existing suburban office space, approximately three to five years to fill up the downtown office space, and approximately one to one and one-half years to fill existing apartment vacancies. In the case of industrial property, we believe there is about a six-month supply of space available. We think it will take about three and one-half years to use the existing supply of developed residential lots; and it will likely take about three years for the market to absorb the existing condominium projects. These figures are based on current absorption rates. Clearly, if the economy picks up, this time could shorten proportionately. In that case we could also look for an earlier recovery in new construction and development.

Having analyzed thoroughly what we have in the way of properties, either on nonaccrual or foreclosure, and having looked at the rates of absorption, we have a good idea of what our outside exposure is. Where we can, however, we try to cut that by getting our properties through the pipeline early in the game. And there are some effective things we can do. For example, we have had good success in moving residential lots by carefully selecting builders to go in and construct homes on these properties. Here, we look for builders who can put together an attractive product of competitive value at a price that may be $500 to $1,000 lower than the competition. We have found that $500 to $1,000 difference in price for a comparable product can make a great deal of difference to the homebuyer.

In the case of income-producing property generally, and office space particularly, we are looking for ways to attract permanent investors. Obviously, the best way to do that is to get it leased up. Here, a case could be made for cutting rental rates on the front end in anticipation of raising them later. But we do not believe this is the whole answer. If it takes putting in a few more dollars to make the project more attractive, then we try to do this. Unless it is a very unusual situation, we will completely finish the project, except for tenant finish, for two reasons: first, if we put it off it is simply going to cost us more when we get around to it; and second, it is awfully difficult to lease a property if it has an unfinished appearance.

But perhaps the most important factor in disposing of these properties is their management. We have found that superior property management, that is, the leasing company or the leasing agent that is working with us, makes the real difference in how fast a building is occupied. Here is where you as directors can make a real contribution. If you are familiar with the marketplace and know who the good folks are, you can help identify them and put them together with bank officers. Beyond this, it becomes a matter of identifying permanent investors and interesting them in the property.

Each area of the country is different, but there are some public relations activities we have undertaken in Atlanta which I believe have been effective. For example, about once a year we invite all the major investors who have properties in Atlanta to a meeting with all the business and financial leaders in the city and the state. We want to let them know what is happening here; we want to talk about the marketplace, and in some cases give them some reassurance. The response to this has been overwhelmingly favorable. This is another example of the kind of activity in which you, as directors, can play a very important role.

To those of you who are in the mortgage-origination business and are working regularly with permanent investors, I say, stay close to them. Keep them up-to-date on your market and give them everything you can find in the way of information about what you think your market will do over the next few years. Then, work directly with them in placing your specific projects. If you do not have existing ties with permanent investors, seek out brokers or folks in the industry who have experience in putting buyer and seller together. There are some very good ones around the country, and they can offer you a great deal of help.

As I see it, permanent investors are more interested in looking at deals right now than they have been in some time. We have seen long rates softening a bit and sort of bumping downward over the last year. Some of the larger investors, such as the large insurance companies, are still a bit picky, but they are more receptive than they have been. Also, you might see what your local savings and loans would be interested in doing with small income properties. By and large, the S&Ls are flush with cash, and we have found in many cases that they are interested in looking at the $100,000 to $500,000 deals.

The bottom line in dealing with these problem loans, in my view, is simply this: it is going to take time to work out the inventory of real estate loans we presently have in the banking system, but there are some specific things that can be done to improve that time frame. It is important that each of you look for ways you can help in your own banks.

Finally, there is one major uncertainty which has particular significance in the handling of problem real estate loans, and that is the unresolved issue of accounting for restructured debt, including foreclosed properties. This issue has been up in the air for about a year, and it surfaced last fall when the Financial Accounting Standards Board issued a proposed statement on accounting for troubled loans. In the face of a number of serious questions about their proposed statement, the board later withdrew it and broadened the scope of their discussion.

Last May the FASB issued a discussion memorandum on these points which pretty well stirred up the banking industry and has been called the most significant proposed accounting change ever to hit us. Basically, the discussion memorandum touches two major issues: (1) whether the restructuring of a loan with one of your borrowers must be recognized as a transaction requiring reconsideration of the value of the loan—and the possible write-down of that loan, if the value has declined; and (2) in reconsidering this value, whether it must be discounted to reflect certain related costs or other factors in addition to the market value of the collateral. For example, the value of a restructured loan or foreclosed property might have to be written down by the difference between what the loan will earn as restructured and what it could have earned originally, or that loan might be written down by an amount equal to the interest expense necessary to carry it on your books, or it might be written down to reflect a number of other factors.

Both of these major issues have a tremendous impact on a bank's operating statement—to the tune of billions of dollars, industrywide—in that they would result in immediate charges to earnings. Furthermore, such write-downs would tend to penalize current bank earnings—and the banking industry's access to capital and money markets—while potentially creating the basis for future gains/profits as the real estate markets recover.

Since there has been no exact definition of what a restructured loan is, this proposal, if adopted, could be applied to anything from renewals to changes in interest rates, to foreclosures, to placing a loan on nonaccrual.

We are waiting for the FASB to come out with an exposure draft on the topic which will give us some hint as to which way they are leaning. Right now, we have no idea when any such changes, if adopted, might be effective, although the FASB previously indicated it would have both the exposure draft and final rules available by the end of 1976. This looks doubtful as time slips by.

Of the big eight accounting firms, four think we should use some discounting similar to the changes being proposed; and four of these firms are equally persuaded that we should not do so, which indicates the split in the accounting industry. As far as the bankers are concerned, you can bet that our industry views were almost unanimous in opposition to these suggested changes.

In any case, the resolution of these accounting proposals could have a devastating impact on how the banking industry determines its posture in real estate lending in the future. I believe we will be well able to ride out the economic cycle and see property values recover. The banking industry has proved over the last four years that it is quite resilient and able to deal with these situations. If these accounting changes do not knock us off our feet, I believe workouts can be handled, and in time real estate lending can contribute a healthy amount of bank earnings.

LEONARD W. HUCK

Trust Business

IF, AS BANK DIRECTORS, you have not paid close attention to your bank's trust department recently, perhaps this is the time to become well acquainted with it, particularly in view of the staff report of the House Domestic Finance Subcommittee, which includes such evaluations as:

1. "Bank dominance of the financial market place must be halted if the competitive character of our economy is to be sustained."

2. Trust departments are concentrating their investments in the stocks of relatively few large companies—the fifty largest for the most part. Thus, the market for the securities of hundreds of small corporations has been reduced, "diminishing the strength of the free enterprise system."

3. Enormous conflict of interest problems are created by the coexistence of commercial and trust departments within the same banking institution.

4. Trust department portfolio activities can be coordinated to benefit trust accounts at the expense of the banks' shareholders and depositors.

5. Trust department investments can be used to help "bail out" an ailing corporation heavily indebted to the commercial department of the bank.

6. Loans can be withheld from competitors of corporations heavily represented in the investment portfolios of trust accounts, thereby diminishing ability to compete.

This report was bound to have an impact on the hearings before the full House Banking Committee chaired by Representative Wright Patman, and when it concluded with "there is no effective way of preventing the exchange of such information between the commercial bank and the trust bank when the will and the temptation are both present," it leaves banking in a rather suspect position.

I do not know how many of your banks have trust departments and how many do not. I would be afraid to ask how many have them, but wish they did not! In the interest of semantics, it might be said that no bank has a trust department, but rather that it has a fiduciary department. Our banks serve in fiduciary capacities for our customers. Fiduciary means having trust or confidence, and this "service for the benefit of another person" is evident in every capacity in which banks serve—as trustee, executor, administrator, guardian, agent, or registrar of stocks and bonds.

If this is our capacity, then, how did we become known as trust departments? Well, trust is a creature of English common law. It has no civil law counterpart. In the conduct of their businesses, trust institutions are governed by the cardinal principle that is common to all fiduciary relationships—namely, fidelity. Policies predicated upon this principle have as their objectives safety, good management, and the ultimate in personal service. Many years ago it was established that when a bank—or a person, for that matter—acts in a fiduciary capacity, the very existence of that relationship of trust and confidence absolutely prohibits any transaction by the fiduciary which involves self-dealing or conflict of interest. These are the suspects of certain extensive trust department studies.

Unless you have actually lived in the environment of a trust department, it probably is difficult to appreciate the respect with which trust officers hold the basic trust principles. The courts have deliberately made loyalty to the interests of a beneficiary, at the expense of the fiduciary's personal interest, the overriding concern. Further, the court has said it is the duty of the fiduciary to use all the ability he has; and if the fiduciary does a poor job, i.e., fails to use all his ability, he can be surcharged for the resulting loss.

How did this highly respected corporate fiduciary concept develop? It seems to have paralleled the growth of the corporate organization, free enterprise, and the acquisition of individual capital in America. As individual fortunes were amassed as a result of the industrial revolution, the strong human desire to preserve one's family wealth brought about a need for the immortality and stability of a professional corporate fiduciary. The other ingredient which could best be supplied by a corporate fiduciary was expertise. Only professionals could provide the highly technical skills required in fiduciary relationships. There was no doubt that the need existed for some entity to deal with the increasing complexity of assets, and also to cope with the mobility of beneficiaries which began to typify affluent America in the 1800s.

First, insurance companies created annuities in trust, and soon they were administering estates and inter vivos trusts. With the increased growth of industry and the corporate structure, there developed a need for such corporate trust services as bond indenture trustees, transfer agents, and registrars. As the trust business became profitable, some of these insurance companies phased out of their conventional insurance activities and became trust companies. Their creativity resulted in variations of their annuities in trusts, referred to as annuity contracts and deposits in trust. Eventually, the trust companies found themselves in deposit banking.

With the enactment of the free banking laws, deposit banks began to look at trust business, and by the end of the nineteenth century trust companies were well established in banking, and state banks were well established in the trust business. National banks did not gain trust powers until the passage of the Federal Reserve Act in 1913. This act became the reference point for all banks in the operation of trust departments because of the regulatory powers applied by the Fed affecting state member banks as well as national banks.

Just four years after the Federal Reserve Act became effective in 1913, there was an amendment to the act which stipulated that separate books and records must be kept for the trust department. This resulted in the complete physical separation of the trust department in some of our banks. Recognizing this moral partition between the commercial and trust banks makes it all the harder to acknowledge the value in some of the research projects that are under way through government commissions.

Securities, of course, must be pledged as collateral for trust funds on deposit in the commercial side of banks. The loan of trust funds to directors, officers, and employees of the trustee bank has been a criminal offense since the 1913 Federal Reserve Act. Allocating brokerage commissions resulting from transactions in trust accounts on the basis of the deposit balances maintained by your broker customers is a "no-no." These and other strong regulations act as a wedge in separating the commercial bank from the trust bank.

Comprehensive and scholarly addresses have been made on the advantages and disadvantages of structurally segregating the trust bank and the commercial bank, so the depth of that subject calls for more than just a comment. I hope this will not become another case of throwing out the baby with the bath water. There are so many advantages in having the same institution offer trust services and commercial banking services that we should not let a very few abuses spoil a good thing for our customers. Applications by national banks for permits to exercise fiduciary powers are looked at from many angles, not the least of which is the consideration of the adequacy of the bank's capital to stand behind the discretionary acts of the trust departments. Even in a business where integrity is the compelling discipline, it is reassuring to the customers to know that the bank's total capital and surplus are at risk if improper exercise of fiduciary powers should be proved. In the event of mandatory separation, one of the first problems would be arriving at a capital figure small enough to enable the trust business to provide an attractive return on invested capital, yet large enough to inspire public confidence. Today, bank capital is used for dual purposes, supporting both bank and trust activities. Separation would drain the bank capital and potentially affect lending limits, stock prices, debt rating, dividend policies, and acquisition plans. The rule of thumb most often referred to in estimating the capital requirement of an individual trust operation is two times the five-year average of gross trust revenue.

Regulation 9 of the *Comptroller's Manual for National Banks* is quite specific in setting forth the trust duties which are the responsibility of bank directors.

1. The board of directors is responsible for the proper exercise of fiduciary powers by the bank. This includes the determination of policies, the investment and disposition of property held in a fiduciary capacity, and the direction and review of the action of all officers, employees, and committees utilized by the bank in exercising its fiduciary powers.

Fortunately, the regulation goes on to say: "In discharging this responsibility, the Board of Directors may assign, by action duly entered in the minutes, the administration of such of the bank's fiduciary powers as it may consider proper to assign to such directors, officers, employees or committees as it may designate."

2. No fiduciary account shall be accepted without the prior ap-

proval of the board or the officers or committees to whom the board may have designated the performance of that responsibility.

3. The board also shall insure that at least once during every calendar year, and within fifteen months of the last review, all assets held in each fiduciary account where the bank has investment responsibilities are reviewed to determine the advisability of retaining or disposing of such assets.

4. All officers and employees taking part in the operation of the trust department shall be adequately bonded.

5. Every national bank exercising fiduciary powers must have competent legal counsel.

6. Every national bank shall maintain a record of all pending litigation to which it is a party in connection with its exercise of fiduciary powers.

7. A committee of directors, exclusive of any active officers of the bank, shall at least once during each calendar year, and within fifteen months of the last such audit, make or cause to be made suitable audits of the trust department.

Despite these specific and rather burdensome responsibilities, Regulation 9 has given more freedom to the boards of directors in carrying out their authority than did its forerunner, Fed Regulation F. The common trust funds regulations were liberalized, the establishment of the trust investment committee was reduced from a requirement of the board to a delegated responsibility, and the acceptance and closing of trusts realistically became a committee function rather than a direct board responsibility. The comptroller recognized the merits of issuing a manual of instructions, *Representatives in Trusts*, which is an authoritative interpretation of Regulation 9 as well as the instruction book for the federal trust examiners. It sets forth many regulatory requirements and guidelines, and reproduces all of the questions in the National Bank Trust Department Report of Examination. In other words, this manual shows what the examiner is looking for, and there is no reason why every trust department should not have the manual readily available to assure proper trust administration. As a matter of fact, I think every national bank does have one; as I remember, we were required to buy one.

At one of the first Assemblies for Bank Directors, Dean Miller, deputy comptroller for trusts, said, "Most breakdowns in trust departments result from the failure of the directors to acquaint themselves with the basic fiduciary principles. Decisions in a trust department must be completely divorced from the considerations of the commercial side of the bank, with the sole reference point being the purpose of the individual account and the well-being of its beneficiaries."

What do these responsibilities which have been placed upon directors really mean? First, the acceptance of trusts suggests that you should have someone scrutinize very closely the new business that is offered to your trust department before it is actually accepted. You can weed out some unprofitable business and perhaps avoid potential lawsuits at this point in the procedure. Prior approval on all accounts is an absolute must.

Next, be certain that your investment function is specifically assigned to competent trust investment officers and that investment reviews of the accounts are held in a timely fashion. Be certain that an annual audit is held by a committee of the directors or by competent auditors whom you may direct to make such an audit. Be sure that initial reviews are held just as soon as possible after acceptance of the account to assure that all account assets have been obtained and that they have been set up properly on your books. This would include the registration of the assets in the bank's name as fiduciary. Be sure that all cash is invested promptly and that substandard assets are converted to quality assets. Be sure that real estate is appraised regularly, and that adequate insurance is maintained. Watch for improper investment in stock of the fiduciary bank. Specific authority in the governing instrument, or a court order, is required for this kind of investment.

Be concerned about the voting of stock of the fiduciary bank. In national banks a provision of the national banking act prevents voting of stock held in trust in the election of directors, except in certain situations. In other words, the bank, in its fiduciary capacity, must vote the stock of the fiduciary bank solely with reference to the purposes of the account and the interests of the beneficiary. Be alert for transactions which could be considered self-dealing, such as purchases or sales to the trust department which appear to serve the interests of the bank, and where the trust department might possibly come out second best. Pension and profit sharing trusts should be mentioned, as these frequently are the targets of examiners. Remember that employers cannot use pension or profit sharing trusts as another source of capital. Sometimes an effort to accomplish this manifests itself in broad authorities and exculpatory clauses in the governing instrument, but from all that I can learn, this is an invitation for trouble. Pension and profit sharing trusts must be administered for the exclusive benefit of the employees.

What about the profitability of trust departments? The Federal Reserve Bank of New York's annual survey of trust department earnings and expenses for 1972 shows that ten large New York City bank trust departments earned aggregate net operating profits of $5.2 million compared with a net operating deficit of $18.3 million in 1971. The operating profit was the first since 1968 when it totaled $6.8 million.

After the addition of allowed credits for deposits, trust departments' net earnings for these ten New York City banks totaled $111 million. Good news, you say; trust departments have finally shrugged off the image of being a burden on the bank's profit objectives. Unfortunately, this war has not been completely won, but we do have a battle or two to our credit.

In the same survey, 108 trust departments, excluding the 10 large New York City banks, showed their aggregate expenses exceeded their total fees and commissions by 1.5 percent. Here again, credit for deposits brought final trust department net earnings to 26.8 percent. Exactly half of the 108 reporting departments showed net operating losses before allowed credits for deposits. Even after the credits, 23 departments continued to show a loss.

If profitability is a problem even in the large metropolitan banks, why are we in the trust business? Well, going back to the Federal Reserve Act, among the criteria listed for banks qualified to exercise fiduciary powers was the need of the community for a corporate fiduciary. At this point in time, almost one-third of the commercial banks of the nation, or about 4,200 banks, are operating trust departments. Of these 4,200, 2,500, or about 60 percent, have trust assets with book values of $10 million or less and are troubled by chronic department unprofitability. Quite naturally, this results in the management and the boards of directors of these banks relegating the trust functions to a status where they are grudgingly tolerated but not promoted.

As a bank director it is important that you not only understand the problems blocking profitability in your trust department, but also recognize its strengths in order to help promote it into profitability. First of all, you should examine your own situation. Have you named your bank as executor of your estate? Do you have, or have you made plans to have, a living trust or an agency account managed in your bank's trust department? If you are in business, is your bank serving as trustee for your employee profit sharing plan or pension plan? If your business has the need for corporate trust services, such as stock transfer agency, registrar, dividend paying agency, bond trustee, and related services, is your bank providing these services?

If by chance you have not been able to answer yes to each of these questions, it would be best to examine the possible reasons. Do you perhaps lack confidence in the people who are performing the trust functions in your bank? Is this because you have not made it a point to get acquainted with them, and to learn of their areas of specialization? Or, is it a result of your knowledge of the salary structure in your trust department, which might bring you to the conclusion that attorneys, investment officers, property managers, and tax specialists working at these salaries could not possibly represent the very best in their respective fields? Trust is a highly specialized service and requires real experts if we are to deserve the confidence of the people in our respective communities who could benefit from the trust services.

If you represent one of the ten thousand commercial banks without a trust department, please give careful consideration to the man you select to start it. He must be a salesman to bring in trust business, an investment man to know how to manage the assets held in trust, an operations man to keep accurate records and see that errorless reports are rendered, a tax man for obvious reasons; he must either be a lawyer or be very familiar with law applying to trusts and estates, and, of course, he should have a working knowledge of accounting. Please don't try to get him for a salary of $12,000 per year.

I submit that it will continue to be difficult for your trust departments to acquire the volume of new accounts that they need to become profitable if they cannot command attention and commitment from their board members.

Perhaps another of the reasons that crossed your mind when you answered no to some of the questions posed earlier had to do with the quality of reports or the sophistication of some of the services offered in your trust department. Encourage your management to review with your trust department manager the methods, procedures, and equipment your trust officers use. Although expense controls are as critical in bringing about profitability in the trust department as they are in any other department of the bank, too frequently bank managers are not aware of the modern operational techniques which could result in increased business, increased efficiency, and increased profits. Although trust is an extremely personal service, a large volume of items must be handled on a low unit-cost basis. An optimum staff productivity is mandatory if profitable operations are to be achieved.

Then there is the possibility that your negative answer was predicated on the fee structure that may have been quoted to you. As a converted commercial banker having a pretty good idea of the commercial banking services, I can say unequivocally that the trust services in most banks are the best bargains in your total inventory. In fact, it is very possible that your fee schedules are inadequate! In some cases, this is because of statutory legislation; but in many others, it is due to the competition having set these prices, rather than the costs of the services being known and an appropriate markup added into the price tag for the customers. Think of the plight of your trust department in trying to reach profitability when management and directors too often ask for concessions on fees for the commercial bank customers who have valued commercial bank relationships. How many services does your trust department provide the commercial bank without compensation? How does this affect the profitability potential in your trust department? Very often, trust departments are asked to help with tax returns, escrows, securities safekeeping, investment transactions, stock transfer service, preparation of the bank's own dividend checks, and many other services without compensation.

I encourage you to have your trust department personnel implement some kind of cost system so that you may learn the actual costs of administering each type of trust account. When you know what it costs to administer each individual account, then reexamine your bank's fee schedule to see if it is consistent with management's objective for trust department profitability. Some have said that a trust department cannot possibly reach profitability until the assets under management aggregate $5 million up to $20 million, depending on the formula used. Others say profitability will not come until after annual income has hit $75 thousand. Others use the size of the community as the measuring device and suggest that a trust department cannot be profitable unless the community it services numbers at least twenty-five thousand people. These are considerations if your bank does not have a trust department, but believe me, it is harder to get out of the trust business than to get in it, so if you are exercising trust powers, learn the costs incident thereto.

If profitability is not the motivation for a trust department, what do we have to recommend the services we perform? Consider the following as just a few:

1. A trust department makes a bank a completely integrated financial institution and broadens the potential sources of business for the bank as a whole.

2. Your trust department, if performing its job competently, retains business in all departments of the bank by creating and strengthening customer relationships.

3. It is an important source of deposits in your bank because normal trust administration creates a large number of small trust balances, and their concentration in one fund very likely identifies the trust department as being the largest depositor in your bank.

4. Your trust department brings prestige and good will to your bank, and should generate confidence and respect in the eyes of your bank's customers as well as in the eyes of the general public.

5. It may very likely have the opportunity to perpetuate existing businesses that are bank customers by providing continuity of management during changes of ownership or in passing the business from generation to generation.

6. Finally, it does have the potential of being the source of worthwhile earnings in your bank.

Since a sizable number of unprofitable trust departments do exist, this in itself may be ample evidence that many directors feel there is adequate justification for a chronically unprofitable trust operation. This can become self-perpetuating, however, as management may become increasingly parsimonious in budgeting funds for competent trust personnel, modern equipment, and adequate supplies. Under these circumstances, it is inevitable that the quality of trust administration, as well as the business development trust, would become diluted, and there would be no way for the department to improve its performance. With the gradual loss of effectiveness, it becomes less attractive to trust prospects, and when the quality of trust service becomes marginal, this in itself could impair the reputation of your entire bank. No bank can afford a cheap trust department; unless a bank can afford to pay salaries commensurate with the quality of work and the degree of responsibility expected of trust officers, it simply should not engage in trust business.

Going back to the statement adopted in 1955 of principles of trust institutions, it is written,

> A trust institution is entitled to reasonable compensation for its services. Compensation should be determined on the basis of the cost of the service rendered and the responsibility assumed. Minimum fees for trust services should be applied uniformly and impartially to all of its customers alike. A trust institution is under no obligation, either moral or legal, to accept all business that is offered.

In summary:

1. Everyone is looking at trust department activities. A congressional staff has recommended a Federal Trust Management Commission to regulate and supervise the management of all foundations, charitable trusts, and pension funds. It has been suggested that investment advisory corporations be licensed to manage all pension, foundation, and charitable trust investments. With these functions removed from bank trust departments as we know them, the next recommendation is to separate completely from the commercial bank those trust departments holding $200 million or more in assets.

A Federal Reserve governor, a former trust officer himself, recommended that trust operations be spun off to separate bank subsidy units to forestall more drastic remedies. Holding companies may be the answer to growing public doubt about bank-operated trust departments.

A chairman of the Securities and Exchange Commission has gone before Congress to read a carefully worded statement depicting his increasing apprehension about the growing power of banks in the securities market.

The Securities Industry Association and the Investment Company Institute have pleaded with a comptroller of the currency to rescind a predecessor's ruling that automatic stock purchase plans are appropriate and legal activities for national bank trust departments.

Deputy Comptroller of the Currency for Trusts Dean E. Miller has reemphasized the prohibition in Regulation 9 against advertisement of common trust funds, including reports of trust department holdings. A president of the trust division of the American Bankers Association has reminded us that confidence is required to get individuals into the stock market. If disclosure will help build consumer confidence in our securities markets, he believes it is worth the administrative and economic costs to institutional investors so long as disclosure is limited to significant data.

The Uniform Probate Code now in effect in Idaho and Alaska has been enacted in Arizona, Colorado, and North Dakota. Bills incorporating the code have been introduced in at least fifteen other states.

Pension legislation affecting vesting, funding, portability, plan termination insurance, and fiduciary standards seems headed for enactment this year.

2. Fiduciary responsibilities are awesome and your trust personnel are as dedicated to sound trust principles as they are formally trained to perform their specialities. Understand and respect them for that commitment.

3. The corporate fiduciary developed out of a need for immortality, stability, and expertise through a relationship of trust and confidence which absolutely prohibits any transaction involving self-dealing or conflict of interest.

4. Your bank directors are specifically charged with responsibility to see that your bank properly exercises its fiduciary powers.

5. Trust departments do have other virtues to recommend them besides profitability, but properly organized and operated they can be a significant source of bank earnings.

6. It will be very difficult for your trust department to acquire the volume and quality of new accounts needed to become profitable if it cannot command attention and commitment from its own bank directors.

RICHARD B. JOHNSON

The Trust Department and The Board of Directors

Board Responsibilities

THE PERFORMANCE OF MANAGEMENT determines the success of a bank. The board, which should select and direct the bank's executives and which is the management's source of authority, should be informed, vigilant, and committed to the successful operation of the bank in all of its functions. The board is specifically responsible for formulation of sound policies and selection of appropriate objectives, and is charged with promotion of the bank's welfare and supervision of its affairs, including conformity to law, regulation, and the spirit of public service which the bank's charter implies.[1]

A bank's directors are assigned broader public responsibilities and accountability than are directors of most other corporations, for they are responsible for the safety of the assets of others and for provision of services to the community as well as to the stockholders who elect them. The board may and should assign responsibility for administration, but it does not thereby escape responsibility for performance.

The bank's capital accounts are exposed to decisions for which directors are responsible. In the bank's commercial business the vigilant director can rely upon his good business judgment to protect the bank from unusual losses and himself from personal liability. Trust services, however, require technical understanding which the average director does not command, and fiduciary responsibilities may in the future expose the bank to losses greater than those encountered in normal credit administration and other commercial banking operations. Under present regulations banks cannot expense for tax purposes contributions to reserves for substantial trust losses. For these reasons the trust services of a bank demand of the board and the officers of the bank more meticulous administrative and supervisory procedures than usually are imposed on the bank's commercial division. The board's oversight of the trust department also requires a somewhat different orientation than its review of the commercial division of the bank, because the procedures which the department's responsibilities require must be directed as much toward preservation of capital and the propriety of distributions as toward the production of income.

Delegation of Authority

The total board of directors is responsible for the policy and supervision of the trust functions of the bank, as it is of all of the bank's operations, but it may and normally does delegate the authority for supervising the trust department to a committee which may include nondirector officers of the bank, usually trust officers, as well as directors. Outside directors serving on the trust committee assume special duties and responsibilities involving legal and accounting issues more complex than they typically encounter in their other responsibilities to the bank. In fulfilling their responsibilities on the trust committee, such directors necessarily will rely upon officers of the bank to supply information and propose and apply policies. It is particularly important, therefore, that they have confidence in the abilities and integrity of the officers who administer the trust department.

Definition of Responsibility

The duties of directors in their exercise of trust responsibilities are defined by statutes, by court decisions, and by federal and state regulatory agencies, and beyond these by ethical principles.

The common law and statutes relative to trust departments deal principally with fiduciary responsibilities and problems arising in their performance, including avoidance of conflicts of interest, self-dealing, use of privileged information, preservation of confidentiality, and prudent administration.

Regulation 9 and Other Directives

Regulation 9 of the comptroller of the currency[2] provides the governing rules of administrative law for trust departments of national banks and is generally accepted by state banks and state bank regulatory agencies as their guide in trust administration. Trust acts of the states and regulations promulgated in their jurisdictions also define trust authorities. Section 9.7 of the comptroller's regulation and interpretations of it prescribe the following conditions to govern administration of fiduciary powers:

1. All matters pertinent to the exercise of fiduciary powers by the bank are the responsibility of the board, including (a) determination of policies; (b) investment and disposition of property held in a fiduciary capacity; and (c) supervision and review of all officers, employees, and committees utilized by the bank in exercise of its fiduciary powers.

2. Administration of fiduciary powers may be assigned, but responsibility is nondelegable.

3. No fiduciary account shall be accepted without prior approval of the board or its designated representative.

4. A written record shall be made of acceptances and relinquishment of accounts in the trust committee minutes or by equivalent record of the department.

5. Upon acceptance of an account a prompt review of the assets shall be made and acknowledged in minutes of the committee or in equivalent records of the department.

6. The board shall assure that at least once during every calendar year and within fifteen months of the last review, all the assets held in or for each fiduciary account where the bank has investment responsibilities are reviewed to determine the advisability of retaining or disposing of such assets.

7. All officers and employees taking part in the operation of the trust department shall be adequately bonded. If the director does not have access to trust assets he need not be bonded.

8. The bank shall designate, employ, or retain legal counsel who shall be readily available to pass upon fiduciary matters and to advise its trust department.

9. The trust department may use personnel and facilities of other departments of the bank only to the extent not prohibited by law, and similar constraints apply to use of trust department personnel and facilities in other functions of the bank. The prohibitions relate only to sale or purchase of assets. The trust department may use the commercial department of the bank to execute purchase and sale of securities, but sales between the trust and commercial departments are prohibited. Similar constraints are imposed on mortgage loan transactions.

Other sections of the regulation specify that fiduciary records shall be kept separate and distinct from other records of the bank, and that a committee of directors exclusive of any active officers of the bank shall at least once during each calendar year and within fifteen months of the last such audit make suitable audits of the trust department or cause suitable audits to be made by auditors responsible only to the board. The board may elect in lieu of periodic audits to adopt an adequate continuous audit system. The board in coordination with the audit shall ascertain whether the department has been administered in accordance with law, regulations, and fiduciary responsibilities.

Regulations also prescribe conditions and policies governing protection and investment of trust funds, distribution of funds, compensation of the bank for trust services, administration of collective investments, prevention of self-dealing, disclosure, and reporting procedures. All directors of a bank with trust powers should be familiar with regulations governing the trust department, and the board should provide that all officers of the bank who are involved directly or indirectly in the trust functions of the bank be aware of the regulations' prescriptions and their implications for bank officer performance.

The Securities Reform Act of 1975[3] created areas of joint supervision for the banking agencies and the Securities Exchange Commission, including stock transfers, the purchase of research and other services from or through brokerage firms, and policies and practices with respect to commissions paid for effecting securities transactions. Consumer protection laws and laws governing pension programs (ERISA) recently enacted also may be applicable to some trust department services. Directors should be conversant with their responsibilities which are implicit in these statutes and in implementing regulations.

Ethical Responsibilities

The ethical responsibilities implicit in fiduciary services go beyond the prescriptions of law and regulation. Each bank and its directors and officers should understand the ethical position which trust services require. A distinguished banker who has served banking as a trust officer and as a chief executive officer of his bank formulates the assignment as follows:

> [In trust services] the most important responsibility is to make certain that those administering trust accounts and handling relations be ever mindful of the sacred nature of their responsibility not only to handle the estate and trust assets in keeping with directions or related instruments and in a businesslike, effective

and prompt manner, but also to make sure that beneficiaries and others entitled to consideration and information receive counsel, reports and advice of such nature as to assure a comfortable and harmonious situation. [Directors should] monitor and encourage this wholesome beneficiary relationship by general observation . . . and evaluation of the service and reputation of the trust department for which they are responsible.[4]

Guidance as to principles which should govern trust departments is provided directors and officers in the statement of "Trust Principles and Policies" published by the Trust Division of the American Bankers Association.

Problems in Trust Administration

Problems of which directors should be informed associated with preservation of confidentiality, avoidance of conflicts of interest, and self-dealing have increased in recent years the complexity of trust department administration and have exposed banks to increased potential liability.

Regulation 9 and most state trust laws are detailed concerning self-dealing, but less so concerning conflicts of interest. Problems of confidentiality are dealt with only by inference or by general statements in the regulations. The board's responsibilities in these regards impose assignments which are difficult to define and perform, but which must be prescribed and fulfilled to protect the bank and the members of its board from onerous liability.

Dealing with Privileged Information

The *Comptroller's Handbook for National Trust Examiners*[5] specifies that "it is incumbent upon the directors . . . to establish policies designed to eschew self-serving practices and conflicts of interest. . . ." Such policies should cover matters involving the acquisition and disposition of fiduciary assets as well as the procurement of services for fiduciary accounts. Specific consideration should be given to those areas where the interests of the fiduciary customers might conflict with those of the commercial banking department.

Confidentiality is at the heart of the trust business and closely related to the problem of self-dealing. Obviously, confidentiality should be carefully preserved where personal aspects of accounts are given to directors; but in handling information that could influence purchase or sale of investments, what should and should not be communicated within the bank is often more difficult to define and should be dealt with very cautiously.

Section 10(b) of the Securities Exchange Act of 1934 and SEC Rule 10b-5 have been construed to require that anyone in possession of material inside information must either disclose it to the investing public, or, if he is disabled from disclosing it in order to protect a corporate confidence, or he chooses not to do so, must abstain from trading in or recommending the securities concerned while such inside information remains undisclosed.[6] This interpretation presents the director and bank officers with hard choices, for a trustee is expected to respond to all information reasonably available to him in managing fiduciary accounts. Officers engaged in the commercial departments of a bank and outside directors actively engaged in business and community affairs are likely to have privileged information which if available to a trustee must influence judgments as to whether assets should be acquired or retained. Whether such information should be exchanged within a bank or how it should be acted on thus confronts directors and officers with very difficult decisions. There are important benefits to trust beneficiaries and a bank's shareholders to be derived from free flow of information between directors and bank officers and between the departments of a bank, but despite those advantages informational barriers may be necessary to protect the bank from exposure to burdensome liability.

The chief executive officer of a bank in performance of his duties should have access to information which is not public and which may bear importantly on management of fiduciary accounts about which he also is informed, and lending officers of a bank may often encounter facts which would have significant implications if revealed to trust officers. For example, if a lending officer in reviewing a credit application discovers a situation which will greatly benefit a corporation and the value of its stock, should he inform the trust officers who may be considering acquisition or sale of the stock? Should he refuse to give information about the company if it is requested by the trust officer? Should he exclude the information in his report to the loan committee of the board because its representatives also supervise the trust activities of the bank? If, on the other hand, privileged information reveals to a commercial officer a development which may be disastrous to a corporation and the officer knows that its stock is owned in fiduciary accounts, should the information be disclosed to a trust officer?

The complex problems impliict in determining what is privileged and material and how such information should be dealt with in trust functions have not been resolved in law or in practice, and consequently a definitive statement of procedure cannot be prescribed. Many banks have chosen to create a "wall" which forbids internal communication of all information between the commercial banking and trust departments of the bank; others have sought to "screen" information, separating and dealing differently with "material" and "immaterial" information. An alternative approach is to provide that if any inside information which might affect trading in an asset becomes available, the bank will refrain from any trading in that asset until the information becomes public. Whatever choice is made, the remedies are likely to create impediments to operations and attendant costs or sacrifice of initiative. Clearly, in this troublesome area in which the board must be involved it is very important that the board be assured that persons engaged in trust functions, including the directors, be aware of the complexities which surround the problems of confidentiality, and responsive to them, and that the bank always comply with federal and state security laws.

Other Problem Areas

The bank director is ultimately responsible for the bank's proper performance of trust services. A trustee should "not deal with himself" or put himself in a position where his interests might conflict with his duties as a trustee. Transactions with trust funds resulting in indirect profit to the bank or the director are prohibited under that principle, including compensation as brokers or bankers or for professional or business services.[7]

Dealing with trust cash presents a special case in this regard. Fiduciary rules against self-dealing may be set aside in the case of trust cash, which may be retained in the trust bank, but the implicit conflict between the bank's benefit from holding such deposits and the trust's interest in minimizing cash holdings has led some trust officers to state that good practice may demand that necessary trust cash balances be kept elsewhere. Conflict of interest abuses in trust cash management which might occur include holding excessive balances in the trust bank, failure to credit trust accounts with benefits derived from holding trust cash, and retention by the bank of reciprocity gains for trust cash placed outside the bank.

It is important also to avoid improper accommodation of commercial customers through use of trust assets. Problems may arise in this regard in purchase or sale of real estate and securities, mergers and similar corporate arrangements, management of properties, and choices among brokers, dealers, and others in trust department activities.

The governing principle in such matters is that in any case of potential conflict the trust's interests rather than the bank's should be served. The responsibility of the trustee to handle trust assets prudently also requires careful definition and supervision of trust department performance in assembling information, analyzing alternatives, and responding to changing circumstances where management of trust assets is involved.

These exposures to liability demand of the directors careful fulfillment of their responsibility to oversee the trust department. They must rely in large part upon the trust officers whom they appoint to manage the trust department, but their total mission to oversee the performance can be accomplished only by an effective director's audit.

Audit of Trust Department

Regulations specify that directors should provide or arrange for suitable audits of the trust department, and fulfillment of director duties in their fiduciary responsibilities demands that the audit be carefully designed and meticulously conducted. The requirements for a suitable audit of national banks are contained in the *Comptroller's Handbook for National Trust Examiners* in the section entitled "Internal and External Audits."[3] The comptroller's office in its examinations also used a "Policies, Practices and Controls Questionnaire" which directors can use as a checklist in their auditing responsibilities.

Director's audits may be accomplished through internal audits conducted periodically or with a continual audit system using employees of the bank, by external auditors, or by a combination of internal and external audits. Whatever procedure is used, the directors should determine that those who conduct the audit are qualified to do so, that the scope and procedures of the audit permit the board adequately to fulfill its audit responsibilities, and that those who perform the audit are responsible directly to and only to the board.

Boards are urged to participate actively in the auditing process at least to the extent of appraising policies and reviewing the audit report with the auditors. In 1976 the comptroller of the currency made substantial changes in examining procedures which placed greater emphasis on appraisal of purposes and procedures and prescribed related changes in audit objectives. Now the emphasis of the comptroller in examinations is to determine the adequacy of bank policies and the effectiveness with which they are implemented, applied, controlled, and overseen, as well as to detect irregularities and to verify compliance with statutory and regulatory requirements. The comptroller specifies minimum requirements of independent verification procedures which the trust audit program must perform. The board should also ascertain through the audit or in conjunction with it that the personnel of the department are adequately informed concerning their assignments, properly assigned and supervised, and rewarded commensurately with their responsibilities and performance; that the continuity of efficient operations is assured; and that the cost of the department's operations relative to its income is reasonable, taking into consideration the benefits derived by the bank and the community which are not reflected by trust department income.

The director's audit committee should if possible be composed of directors exclusive of any active officers of the bank. If the board includes only active officers of the bank, the committee may be constituted of active officers other than trust department officers. The term "active officers" is considered to include directors who serve on trust department committees. The audit committee should: (1) ascertain whether the department is being administered in accordance with law, regulations, and sound fiduciary responsibilities; (2) evaluate the policies, practices, and controls employed to effect compliance and enforce correction of any violations, deficiencies, or weaknesses; (3) insure that the last report of examination and related directives to the department are considered by those responsible for the audit; and (4) confirm that exceptions, weaknesses, or deficiencies are corrected.

Regulations specify that the board shall review the report of examination of the trust department and that reports by the board concerning trust department activities shall be in writing and reflected in the minutes of the board. Current practice of the comptroller is to have trust committee members meet with the examiner and review the examination report.

Board Organization

Regulation 9 of the comptroller does not specify an organizational structure which a board should establish to direct a trust department. The FDIC's Statement of Principles of Trust Department Management, Form 114, specifies that a trust committee of at least three directors be responsible for and supervise the trust department and meet at least once every month. The organization of the board in relation to the trust department will depend on the magnitude and complexity of the department's functions. Smaller banks with small trust departments usually require less complex organizational structures than do large banks.

A director's trust committee is almost invariably utilized in national banks, although not required by the comptroller, and when the trust department is large, additional committees or subcommittees of the trust committee may be used. In most banks, however, the directors' trust responsibilities are supported by one committee of the board which reviews policy and performance in operations and investments and the general direction and progress of the department, including its response to opportunities, quality of service, conformity to regulation, control of costs, profitability, and any litigation, special assets, and unusual situations to which the trust department may find it necessary to respond. This committee should also review periodically operating policies and practices, and it may also review budgets and personnel performance. In these functions, the outside directors usually should rely on spadework done by trust officers and should confine their activities to verification and review.

PRESCRIPTION OF POLICIES

The manner of administration and the system of organization of the department should be prescribed in the bank's bylaws or by resolutions of the board, which each year should review the organization and administration to insure proper exercise of fiduciary powers. Policies should be written which provide a framework within which trust officers operate and which guide operation and administration of the department's actions. Policies should be provided which govern: (1) investments—setting standards which prohibit speculation, preserve principal and diversification of portfolios, optimize income without excessive risk, and sponsor execution of corporate and other responsibilities; (2) performance relative to self-dealing and conflicts of interest; (3) personnel—dealing with such matters as size of staff, qualifications of personnel, salary administration, and benefits; (4) ethical standards, including such issues as gratuities and bequests, disposition of fees earned for personnel services, and preservation of confidentiality; (5) responsibility of directors, in regard to provision of fiduciary services, business development, and extent of responsibilities to supervise, audit, and impose policy; and (6) fees—prescribing standards, relations to cost, and limitations on fee concessions.

The Board and Trust Department Survival

Many trust departments are reported to produce only modest returns or create losses, measured by conventional accounting standards. The providing of fiduciary services also imposes responsibilities upon a bank which may be considered difficult and onerous to fulfill, and in recent years exposures of the bank's capital created by the law's treatment of fiduciary matters have increased. Because of these circumstances the board, particularly in smaller banks, should be concerned with the character and magnitude of trust functions undertaken and perhaps with whether the bank should continue to offer trust services. In all banks the board should assure that trust functions undertaken are supported by qualified and adequately compensated officers and employees. Outside directors should be alert to avoid assumption of trust responsibilities greater than the department can effectively perform with its personnel. They should be adequately informed concerning the department's performance and problems, and should consider it their responsibility to assure work conditions within the department conducive to efficient professional performance of fiduciary responsibilities.

The trust department must be profitable in the long run to justify the facilities and the quality personnel required to render a superior trust service. It therefore is incumbent upon the board to prescribe the policies and provide the support which contribute to profitability of the trust department. Regulation 9 specifically recognizes the propriety and desirability of profit generation by trust services. The board's responsibility in this regard is to provide profit motivation and pricing policies for trust services whch permit adequate returns as well as quality performance.

The profitability of the trust department may depend to a considerable degree upon the contributions directors of the bank make to the generation of business. Directors should use their bank for their personal and business activities which involve fiduciary services and should strongly recommend those services to their family, friends, and associates. The measure of their confidence in the quality of the trust services for which they are responsible is the degree to which they utilize them and advise others to do so.

DIRECTORS' PERSONAL LIABILITY

Directors have only infrequently been called upon to defend themselves and their assets as a result of their service on a bank board, and even less frequently have suffered financial penalties therefrom. Trust departments have not endured losses through litigation which directors have been required to meet. Directors "who behave with reasonable caution and honesty and who consult their lawyers when in doubt"[9] probably still have little cause for fear.

The exposures exist, nonetheless, and the extent and magnitude of risk may be increasing. In banks with trust services all directors are probably exposed to the potential liabilities implicit in fiduciary responsibility, whether or not they serve on trust committees. Advisory directors also may be exposed. How should they respond?

1. Clearly, by being informed concerning the character of fiduciary responsibilities. Trust officers and legal counsel should see to it that the directors are adequately informed.

2. By being advised concerning statutes and regulations which govern trust department services and procedures. It should be the responsibility of trust officers to provide that guidance.

3. By assuring that policies governing the trust department are adequate and precise and that they are enforced.

4. By seeing to it that qualified and ethical officers serve the trust function.

5. By diligent performance as directors, keeping informed, attending meetings of the board and its committees on which memberships are held, questioning where uncertainties exist or where information is needed, and demanding of fellow directors and self scrupulous adherence to high principles.

The director who follows these precepts almost certainly has no exposure except to the harassment of providing a defense against unfounded charges, and that risk is probably small if members of the board have been prudent, honest, and diligent.

The director nonetheless deserves protection, which may be provided by the bank through indemnification provisions in the bylaws of the bank protecting against liability or threatened liability for mistakes in judgment, short of criminal or dishonest acts; and by insurance provided by the bank covering directors' liability not indemnifiable or not indemnified in the bylaws.

Notes

1. For discussion of board responsibilities see Richard B. Johnson, ed., *The Bank Director* (Dallas: Southern Methodist University Press, 1974); U.S. Treasury, Comptroller of the Currency, Administrator of National Banks, *Duties and Liabilities of Directors of National Banks*, 1972; *A Bank Director's Job*, 13th ed. (Washington, D.C.: American Bankers Association, 1970).

2. U.S., Treasury Department, Comptroller of the Currency, *Fiduciary Powers of National Banks, Collective Investment Funds and Disclosure of Trust Department Assets, Regulation 9, as Amended through August 5, 1974.*

3. Public Law 94-29.

4. From letter, Murray Kyger, Chairman of the Board (Retired), First National Bank of Fort Worth, to Richard B. Johnson.

5. U.S., Treasury Department, Comptroller of the Currency, *Comptroller's Handbook for National Trust Examiners*. Section 7 deals specifically with director duties and responsibilities.

6. 15 U.S.C., 78a-78aaa, 17 C.F.R. 240, 10b-5.

7. Problems which may arise in trust administration are reviewed in Edward S. Herman, *Conflicts of Interest* (New York: Twentieth Century Fund, 1975).

8. *Handbook*, Section 8.

9. Joseph Bishop, *Review of Securities Regulation* 28 (1969): 945.

Bibliography

Books

Bratter, Herbert. *A Bank Director's Job*. New York: American Bankers Association, 1970.

Hanson, Walter E. *The Changing Role of the Internal Auditor*. Dallas: Peat, Marwick, Mitchell & Co., 1976.

Herman, Edward S. *Conflicts of Interest: Commercial Bank Trust Departments*. New York: Twentieth Century Fund, 1975.

Johnson, Richard B., ed. *The Bank Director*. Dallas: Southern Methodist University Press, 1974.

Kennedy, Walter, and Searle, Philip F. *The Management of a Trust Department*. Boston: Bankers Publishing Co., 1967.

Koontz, Harold. *The Board of Directors and Effective Management*. New York: McGraw-Hill, 1967.

Lattin, Norman D. *Lattin on Corporations*. 2d ed. New York: Foundation Press, 1971.

McInnis, Edward. *Trust Functions and Services*. Washington, D.C.: American Institute of Banking, 1971.

Nicolson, Miklos S. *Duties and Liabilities of Corporate Officers*. Englewood Cliffs, N.J.: Prentice-Hall, 1972.

SAVAGE, JOHN H. *Bank Audits and Examinations.* Boston: Bankers Publishing Co., 1973.
STEPHENSON, GILBERT T., and WIGGINS, NORMAN A. *Estates and Trusts.* New York: Appleton-Century-Crofts, 1973.
TRUST DIVISION, AMERICAN BANKERS ASSOCIATION. *Trust Principles and Policies.* New York: American Bankers Association, 1968.
VAN HOUTTE, RAYMOND. *Responsibilities of Bank Directors.* St. Louis: Director Publications, 1974.

Pamphlets

President Profile, Bank and Holding Company. Heidrick & Struggles, 1974.
Profile of the Board of Directors. Heidrick & Struggles, 1971.

Speeches

MYERS, RAY F. "Trust Wall—Or, Stay Alive with 10b-5." Given before the 24th Southern Trust Conference, Pinehurst, N.C., 1976.

Government Publications

"FDIC Statement of Principles of Trust Department Management." FDIC Form 114, 5-1-59.
U.S., Treasury Department, Comptroller of the Currency, Administrator of National Banks. *Comptroller's Handbook for National Trust Examiners.*
U.S., Treasury Department, Comptroller of the Currency, Administrator of National Banks. *Duties and Liabilities of Directors of National Banks,* 1972.
U.S., Treasury Department, Comptroller of the Currency. *Fiduciary Powers of National Banks, Collective Investment Funds and Disclosure of Trust Department Assets, Regulation 9,* 1974.

J. D. SCHIERMEYER

EFTS and Its Implications

MANY TERMS have been associated with the letters EFTS, and many of us can easily be confused unless certain of these terms are defined. EFTS is an abbreviation that stands for Electronic Funds Transfer Systems. The three basic responsibilities of a banking institution are to accept deposits, to make payments, and to lend money. Funds transfer relates to the area of payments. Daily, goods and services are paid for with either cash or checks. This is in fact a funds transfer when we consider moving funds from one party to another. When the prefix *electronic* is tacked on to the concept of funds transfer, we immediately think that we have a new situation. The concept is not new, however, for we are now simply using modern technology to facilitate the movement of money from one party to another.

Movement of funds by electronic means has been utilized by the Federal Reserve System for quite some time in their Fed wire transfer system. Western Union, through the use of the telegraph, has been transferring money from one party to another much longer than the Federal Reserve System. In January, 1974, First Federal Savings and Loan of Lincoln, Nebraska, created chaos in the banking industry when it announced its Transmatic Money Service and the installation of two electronic terminals at two Hinky Dinky grocery stores in the city of Lincoln. First Federal was bringing electronic banking to the consumer at a point of convenience to that consumer. Since those days in January, 1974, many, many, many hours, days, weeks, and months have been spent by banking personnel throughout the United States studying the impact of EFTS and the implications for its consumer base.

What was the competitive stance of the savings and loan industry that could also be utilizing modern technology to increase the efficiency of funds transfer? In Nebraska, for example, the Nebraska Bankers Association formed study committees to determine how Nebraska banks should react to the competition of the savings and loans. As a result of these studies, the states of Iowa and Nebraska made a joint effort to determine standards, to make specifications for the issuance of plastic cards, and to establish electronic banking terminals. These studies attempted to develop a system that could be utilized by all banking institutions. While it is often said that EFTS is something only for the big bank, this is not necessarily true.

Electronic funds transfer encompasses more than one particular function. The general concepts can be described as basically a card-oriented system or a non-card-oriented system. Consider first the non-card-oriented system. Many of you are aware that the automated clearinghouse concept has been widely used across the nation in the development of functional ACHs, as they are called, throughout the larger banking centers in the United States. Currently (1976), there are in excess of twenty automated clearinghouses functioning. The movement of funds from one point to another has traditionally been handled by check or cash. In order to move the paper check, there has been a check collection system in operation. When a check is drawn on your bank, no matter where it is deposited it currently has to be returned to your own bank to be paid against the drawee's account. Now automation has been implemented and increased technology developed so that we can speed up this process of collecting payments of checks.

The automated clearinghouse is a vehicle for processing paperless entries. Such entries can come in the form of debits or credits, the latter being direct deposits of payroll, initiated either by an employer or, possibly, by the federal government. A good example of this form of paperless entry is the Social Security direct deposit.

The automated clearinghouse eliminates the pieces of paper, the checks, in the payment system. We are not by any means advocating in this movement that we eliminate the use of checks. However, when it comes to payments between the government and the individual, employers and the individual, and then, on the debit side, payments by consumers to businesses for goods and services, there is the possibility that the piece of paper can be eliminated, thus reducing the processing cost associated with the exchange of checks. Processing a check is very time-consuming and very labor-intensive, considering the number of steps that it must go through before the check finally ends up in the customer's bank statement. Currently (1976), volume is coming somewhat slowly through automated clearinghouse associations. Just like anything else, a new concept of this type requires a great deal of consumer education. As bankers, you and I bear this responsibility. Perhaps you have seen advertisements by the American Bankers Association and the publicity that the Social Security administration has given to the program encouraging people to sign up for direct deposit of Social Security. One thing is certain. In all the advertisements it is very important to assure the customer that in a direct deposit environment his funds are going to be available for his use. Confidence in the banking industry should not be decreased because of an electronic means of processing; rather, the consumer's confidence should be increased.

The state of Nebraska belongs to the Mid-America Automated Clearinghouse Association, better known as MACHA. My bank has worked from the beginning in the development of the ACH concept in Nebraska as well as in the four-state area covered by MACHA. Although volume has been coming through slowly, the statistics of MACHA transactions show that in April, 1976, we were running 67,220 transactions, but in May that figure had increased to 86,904. We have a long way to go in the promotion of direct deposit and preauthorized payment through a paperless environment, but the attention that has been given by all ACH associations to the marketing of this new service will continue to increase in following months. You, as directors of banks, should be aware of what is taking place in banking and how we as bankers are trying to reduce the increasing processing costs without reducing services to our customers.

The card-oriented EFT system has been more publicized than the non-card-oriented operation. It was First Federal Savings and Loan of Lincoln, Nebraska, and their Transmatic Money Service card that really alerted many bankers across the United States to the fact that a plastic card, such as Master Charge and BankAmericard, could be used for more than traditional credit transactions. Using a piece of plastic to gain access to and communicate with a bank in an on-line to the computer electronic environment has facilitated customer activity without depriving the individual of privacy in his bank relations. The term *on-line to the computer* merely refers to a direct connection using telephone lines, in most cases, between a terminal device of some nature and a bank computer or computer processor. This on-line method gives the user of that terminal direct access to information stored in the computer. There are currently in existence numerous off-line automated teller/cash dispenser devices using plastic cards that have been on the market for several years; my remarks on card-oriented electronic funds transfer, however, will be limited to on-line concepts.

In a card-oriented system, a bank has the opportunity to offer its customers all of the normal banking functions relating to checking and savings accounts in a more convenient manner. Again, it is most important to emphasize that the consumer understand what a debit card can do for him as a customer of a particular bank. It can be very confusing when a piece of plastic is associated with a banking transaction; however, if the concept is sold without at first including credit services, it is much easier for the customer to understand that the plastic card replaces the paper check or a savings withdrawal slip, or the like. Services to be offered through the use of a debit card or transaction card can include withdrawals from checking or savings accounts, deposits to checking or savings accounts, transfers between checking and savings or savings and checking accounts, payments, and balance inquiries. The type of transaction the customer is able to perform is somewhat tied to the type of hardware or terminal device that a bank is utilizing. For example, many manufacturers have an automated teller with which all the types of transactions I have just listed can be performed. But because of the physical limitations of some point-of-sale terminals, particularly the small devices found in retail stores, many types of transactions cannot be handled.

What have been the results of the card-oriented systems that have been implemented in many parts of the United States? While I am not knowledgeable about all card-based systems, I do know that the Mercantile Bank & Trust in St. Louis, Missouri, for example, is utilizing its plastic cards in an automated teller environment and has had excellent response from its customers. We at the National Bank of Commerce are also utilizing an automated teller environment and are experiencing increased usage each month from our customer base. In August, 1976, we had 3,490 completed transactions. In addition to this, we had 2,955 balance inquiries. After six months of operation in this type of environment, it is our consensus that we do have customer desire to use this type of service.

In order to develop a good card base, it is my belief that the issuance of cards should not be restricted to a select group of people; cards should be distributed among the majority of all checking and savings acount holders. By expanding the card base you should increase your usage. In an on-line environment you will always be protected, because if funds are not available in the account, the transactions are not allowed. If there is a shortage of funds, however, there is no need to reissue the card or do anything on behalf of the bank. Once there are sufficient funds in the bank, the customer can then use that plastic card again to facilitate his banking transactions. Obviously, increased volume will lessen processing costs, for the majority of the transactions taken at an automated teller or at a point-of-sale terminal can be paperless entries, not requiring the labor-intensive handling of the normal paper check.

There is, however, a great deal of bank preparation prior to the issuance of cards. The establishment of a central information file is not mandatory, but it is advantageous to tie into one central location all services currently being utilized by the customer. Such an employee arrangement provides the bank's ease of access to and better control of that customer's total number of transactions. The development of this program can be expensive; most major correspondent banks and computer processors have some sort of service available that can be purchased at a reasonable cost. There is also the issuance of plastic cards, which is not an inexpensive exercise, but the plastic card can last, under normal circumstances, approximately three years. Based on our experience in issuing cards, we estimate that the cost of issuing a piece of plastic to an individual customer is fifty-six cents per card. This includes the price of the plastic, the encoding, the embossing (imprinting the name and number on the face of the card and placing the necessary information in the magnetic stripe on the reverse side of the card), the postage for the mailing of the card and the four-digit security code (the pin number that is mailed separately), and the collateral pieces which include the transaction card agreement, card carrier, security code mailer, and marketing brochure. Theoretically, this cost of approximately sixty cents spread over three years amounts to twenty cents per customer. In general, if the customer can be persuaded to use this piece of plastic, thereby reducing his check volume by twelve checks per year, money can be saved on that particular customer.

In 1976 it cost my bank approximately seven cents to process each on-us debit item. At this rate, the cost of processing twelve checks would amount to eighty-four cents, as compared to twenty cents for issuing the piece of plastic. Based on our experience, a paperless entry can be processed much cheaper than a paper item. Paperless entry processing is not inexpensive, however, for it involves the costs of an electronic banking transaction, of terminals, of telephone lines linking these terminals to computers, and of other sundry items. Terminal prices can range from $25 to $30 a month in rental fees; the purchase price for some automated tellers can run as high as $40,000 or $50,000. But the potential for cost savings in the processing area is apparent to me. It is going to take increased marketing and educating on the part of all bankers to inform their customers if we are going to utilize the advantages that are available in an electronic banking environment.

I have emphasized the advantages of automated tellers because our bank has had more experience with them, but the point-of-sale, or manned teller, terminal is also a reality in many parts of the country. This type of system, in which a third party employee actually operates the terminal, can be somewhat less expensive, but the number of terminals needed in a particular store varies. The capital investment is reduced if there is a customer convenience counter where one terminal can be placed and possibly shared by other banking institutions. Customer convenience counters are generally found only in the grocery store environment, but it is my personal belief that point-of-sale terminals will be utilized in other areas. I feel that the retailer is going to restrict the type of transactions allowed in his particular store. In retail centers (grocery stores excluded) the objective of the sales force is to be selling merchandise, not spending time behind the cash register taking bank deposits and making cash withdrawals that will in no way produce direct revenue for the retail outlet. It is my belief that the point-of-sale terminal system will switch to a type of debit-only function in many outlets. This debit-only function will provide for direct payment of merchandise purchased or will possibly utilize the terminal to authorize charge card credit purchases. Thus the terminal will have a dual use. As far as electronic banking and debit card systems are concerned, however, this type of device is used only for the payments of goods or services.

If a bank is to justify the cost of equipment, it is my belief that we still need to take the deposit dollar. Therefore, the automated teller will continue to play an important role in the development of electronic banking services. The broad range of transactions that may be performed at the automated teller makes it an ideal device as a free-standing, off-premise unit in a shopping center, and in retail stores where the retailer does not have to be a bank, leaving the bankers to provide better services for their customers. A retailer is not going to allow forty-two different terminals at his cash register. There will probably not be physical space for more than one type of machine. If this theory is correct, then sharing between banks will be necessary at some point in time. In a shared usage environment, who is going to gain the benefit of making the capital investment for terminals? Obviously, the cost would be shared equally by the participating institutions either through joint purchases or through a charge made to the card holder's bank for each transaction that his particular customer performs. The advantages are not really in the placing of terminals at your expense, but rather in the processing, paper, and operating costs that can be saved if volume is generated. If we can encourage all of the banks, all of the banks' customers, and all of the major cities to utilize electronic banking, we will have a reduction in the number of pieces of paper flowing through the collection system. We will have a reduction in the amount of float that the banks must carry, and potential profit will be generated because of the cost reductions.

The system of automated teller devices at the National Bank of Commerce includes two on-line machines in operation on the bank's premises. We are in the process of placing a third automated teller in an off-premise location. Our program, called Bank-in-the-Box, has been an experimental process for us in the development of our software and the utilization of hardware. We are finding that customer acceptance has been far greater than we would have anticipated.

To summarize, in every area that I have discussed, the key word is preparedness. Over the next several years, electronic funds transfer systems will greatly affect almost every financial institution in the United States. If the projections on check volume continue to be accurate and we see a doubling effect in the next four or five years in the number of checks being processed, we are going to find ourselves completely overburdened with the labor-intensive functions that will have to be performed in our banks under traditional processing systems. It is necessary for you as a director of your bank, no matter how large or small it is, to insure that a strategic plan be undertaken in your institution. It is important that (a) you study and better understand EFT and (b) that you determine what your involvement should be in a long-range program. You should have three major objectives: (1) to offer services for your customer; (2) to meet competition; and (3) to increase your efficiency and reduce your internal processing costs. Why is the reduction of costs the third objective? Because it is going to take time and cost your bank substantial dollars before you are going to realize the cost-saving potential. We at the National Bank of Commerce established an EFTS committee consisting of representatives from various fund-attracting and operating divisions within our bank. It is recommended that a representative group of your bank's officers be utilized to discuss EFT because the implications affect each area of your bank, not just your computer area, not just your computer processors, not just your commercial department, not just your consumer department. This committee should have the responsibility for analyzing all types of EFT systems to keep in tune with what the industry is doing, to keep up with federal and state legislation in regard to electronic banking, and to be responsible for determining your individual bank's position and for the implementation of any suggested electronic banking system. EFTS is a reality. Be prepared; your bank will be involved sooner than you think.

CHARLES E. RICE

Holding Companies: One- and Multi-Bank

THERE ARE FEW economic institutions more deserving of continued analysis than the commercial banking system. The importance of its position in the economy is unquestioned. Statistics indicate that our nation's banking system is undergoing basic structural changes, the most prominent of which may be referred to as "The Bank Holding Company Movement." Expanded and altered economic requirements, in addition to competition from nonbanking financial institutions, have dictated this change. In a recent speech, a representative of Citicorp gave some very meaningful statistics, stating that at the end of World War II 60 percent of all assets in financial institutions were in commercial banks. At the present time (1975), the relative position of commercial banks in the financial community of our nation has eroded; now only 30 percent of assets in financial institutions are in commercial banks.

Under the law, a bank holding company is regulated by the Federal Reserve Board and is permitted to engage only in banking and in activities closely related to banking. Our own company, Barnett Banks of Florida, Inc., was created to provide banking services to bankless communities in the early 1930s. The organization we now have was created in 1966. I came with an acquisition, so I have been on both sides of the fence. The impetus behind the holding company movement with which I am most familiar, and the only one with which I have had actual experience, is the desire of several banks to create a network where branch banking is limited or prohibited. Of course, there are many other reasons why people have created holding companies, and other reasons why some bank holding companies have grown as they have. Those reasons generally pertain to tax reasons— the ability of dividends to flow on a tax-free basis from the bank to the parent, the ability of the parent to service debt and to flow capital downstream in the form of equity into its banks, and any number of other reasons. But the regulatory climate in our country has been an inducement to the growth of bank holding companies, particularly the regulatory climate as it exists in state legislatures.

As holding companies grew, it became important that they be regulated. Not much was known about holding companies; they were not very significant prior to World War II, yet they are not new in this country. Some understanding of what has transpired in the past is important to an understanding of where we are today and perhaps where we are going in the future with this form of banking structure.

Holding companies first appeared in this country about the turn of the century. The first regulation of bank holding companies was in the Banking Act of 1933. The Federal Reserve Board was empowered by that act to withhold or to issue a voting certificate for corporations owning a majority of the stock of a bank which was a member of the Federal Reserve System. In order to obtain a permit from the Federal Reserve Board to vote the stock of a bank, a corporation had to agree to open up the books of the bank for examination by the Federal Reserve, to establish certain reserves, to publish statements of condition, and to refrain from participation in the securities industry. The first real holding company legislation as we know it today—and we still operate under that legislation—is the Bank Holding Company Act of 1956. This act basically confined bank holding companies to the business of banking and closely related services; and the Congress of the United States in passing this act empowered the Federal Reserve Board to regulate bank holding companies. This applies whether or not those banks in the bank holding company are members of the Federal Reserve System. The act was amended in 1966 and again in 1970. The 1966 amendments basically established uniform standards for bank agencies and the courts in evaluating the legality of bank holding company acquisitions. The amendments also established that previous acquisitions, those that had taken place prior to 1966, were immune from antitrust legislation unless litigation was already in process.

The amendments of 1970 eliminated the exemption, contained in the 1956 act, of the one-bank holding company. It was recognized in 1956 that some people or a person might have a good and legitimate reason for merely wanting the stock of a bank held by a corporation rather than held individually, so that exemption had been written into the 1956 act. By 1970, 33 percent of all bank deposits in the United States were in banks owned by one-bank holding companies. Therefore, the purpose of the exemption of 1956 no longer existed and the one-bank holding companies became a significant factor in the banking community of this country. The one-bank holding company prior to 1956 was not subject to direct supervision by any federal agency, and there appeared to be no restrictions on the kinds of affiliates that it could have, either financial, commercial, or industrial. Because of the amendments of 1970 there is no practical difference today in the regulation of multi-bank holding companies and one-bank holding companies. The 1970 act also modified the provisions of the 1956 act covering activities closely related to banking and allowed the Federal Reserve Board to consider an activity permissible if it meets two tests: (1) The activity must be so closely related to banking or managing or controlling banks as to be a proper incident thereto, and (2) it must reasonably be expected to produce benefits to the public that outweigh possible adverse effects. Neither the 1966 nor the 1970 amendments altered the act of 1956, which preserved the authority of states to regulate bank holding companies. Federal legislation does not supersede the legislation of the states.

To classify generally the laws pertaining to bank holding companies that exist today (1975) in states, there are no limitations on bank holding companies in twenty-six states or in the District of Columbia. Seven states require that the state must give approval for the acquisition of bank stock by a corporation, and seventeen states either prohibit or otherwise severely restrict the acquisition of bank stock by a corporation.

This roughly is the history of the bank holding company movement up to the present time. Since 1956—a benchmark year because that was the year of the first real bank holding company legislation—holding companies have increased from 53 to about 1,700 companies. Now these statistics are not important, but the dynamics of the trends that took place between 1956 and 1973 show what has happened in what we call "The Bank Holding Company Movement." In 1956 there were 1,200 banking offices—this included banks and branches—in bank holding companies. In 1973 there were roughly 19,000 banking offices belonging to bank holding companies. In 1956 the percentage of all banking offices belonging to holding companies was 5.7 percent. The latest figure today is in excess of 45 percent. When the act of 1956 became law, 7.5 percent of the deposits of our commercial banking system were in bank holding companies. Today, 65 percent of bank deposits and the majority of the banking deposits in the United States are in bank holding companies.

What are the advantages or the disadvantages of bank holding companies? There are no rules, no standard set of criteria that would apply in all situations. All we can hope to do in discussing the advantages and disadvantages of bank holding companies is try to crystallize or perhaps categorize the arguments for and against them. If certain factors are recognized as being advantageous or disadvantageous per se, careful consideration would then have to be given as to whether or not these factors apply to individual situations. I would not be able to confirm or refute any particular argument that might be advanced about the validity of bank holding companies; I can only tell you of our experience in this area. Such things as the expanded legal limit of a bank's lending capacity by way of a network of credit participations might be categorized as an advantage. I think it is an irrefutable fact that an expanded legal lending limit can be created. This factor might be completely irrelevant if you have demand for loans in excess of your own legal lending limit, or if you anticipate such a demand.

Perhaps a year ago the argument might have been advanced that this vehicle would not be needed for expanding your legal limit because of the network of correspondent participations. But I doubt that I would be given that argument today because of experiences people have had in trying to participate loans to correspondents during the historically high interest rates of 1974.

There are many arguments relative to the economies of scale that could be advanced in favor of bank holding companies. In the area of marketing, for instance, the use of a common logotype permits an institutional approach to advertising. Because of the high costs, it is very expensive to advertise a unit bank in a newspaper that covers a service area much greater than that of the bank. But like the central purchasing of supplies, some consolidation of advertising—what we call the overview or the umbrella approach to advertising—creates tremendous economies of scale.

The consolidation of the investment function eliminates the need for numerous and varied correspondent arrangements and the payment for such arrangements. In a multi-bank holding company this consolidation is a necessity because of the repercussions that various investment portfolio activities might have on the filing of a consolidated tax return, and on profits after securities transactions. You would probably find that if a number of banks in a holding company consolidated the investment function, the need to increase already existing bank balances at the lead bank would be less because of the many transactions that could be closed as the result of the safekeeping function being handled by the lead bank. Another factor in the investment area is, again, group purchasing or economies of scale. The sheer size of volume in the investment portfolios should lead to price concessions that would not be possible on smaller purchases.

An extremely apparent advantage of holding companies or any other multilocation banking system is the mobility of funds. It is natural to have an insufficient supply of funds in some areas of a state and an oversupply in others. We have banks that are seven hundred miles apart. We have banks that are very cyclical during the year because they are tourist oriented. We have banks that are cyclical on a different cycle because they are agriculturally oriented. We have banks that are very stable because they are military oriented. Through the participation of loans we are able to equalize the supply of funds and create a mobility of funds just as in a branching system. Loan diversification, if the banking offices are not all in the same service area, seems to be a valid advantage to consider. It is just simply the spreading of risk.

We found that attracting management into a holding company was easier than trying to attract management into individual banks; that is, the function of recruiting and hiring is better performed by the holding company than by the individual bank. This is because a larger organization has a greater incentive to train and hire, to make possible management succession and lateral moves. Career paths have more alternatives in any multi-banking organization than in a single banking organization. It takes a great deal of time and money to train promising people, and it is a very costly exercise if they have to decide to look for better opportunities elsewhere because their career path is being blocked in their present situation.

In making bank acquisitions, a reason we have often been given for the availability of the bank is that the principal owner or president of the bank has not provided for management succession and feels that the holding company, because of its training program and its having a large number of qualified people, is in a better position to supply personnel for management succession than he is.

A reason that I would have given a year ago, but one that I am not sure is valid today, is the visibility and marketability of holding company stock and the resulting advantage that there might be in capital markets. The condition of the capital markets today does not make that observation a particularly valid one, although, if the economic conditions that have existed until 1975 can be called normal, I do believe that we will eventually return to normal times. Perhaps today the unit bank can meet its capital needs from its local community more easily than we can meet ours in the national markets.

There are, of course, many reasons to be considered for not going into a bank holding company. Again this depends on individual situations. Most of the reasons I have heard for objecting to the holding company structure have to do with some variation on the theme of autonomy—the loss of autonomy or the fear of the loss of autonomy. It can be expressed in many different ways, and a careful analysis of a unit bank's objection to the bank holding company structure would come back to that central theme. A bank belonging to a bank holding company is not as autonomous as a unit bank. Yet most of the holding companies with which I am familiar do recognize the areas in which a bank must remain autonomous if it is to serve the optimum needs and convenience of the people of a community.

A variation of this anti-holding-company, antibranching theme would simply relate to bigness. A better definition of this type of objection would be antibigness, and this might very well be a valid objection to a particular situation after consideration has been given to the impact that it would have on a community, especially if holding companies are in the infancy of their development in a particular community. When the bank with which I was first associated went into the holding company, our largest competition began to advertise as "your homeowned bank." This caused us great concern. We were very much aware of it, but in retrospect I think it did little or no damage. However, it certainly is a factor to consider.

There is the feeling that a bank holding company can become impersonal in its approach to a community, unaware of the needs of a local community, and unresponsive to the direction that can come from the local board of directors or the local president. This, of course, would be no different from the type of concern any multi-banking organization could generate. Much depends on the responsiveness of the bank holding company to the local boards of directors and its having enough flexibility to know what functions can be centralized, and which functions should be centralized and which decentralized; the latter basically are the people-contact functions.

The structure of banking in the future is uncertain. There have been many suggestions in 1975, particularly as the equity markets have eroded and analysts and others have looked for reasons for this erosion, that bank holding companies are overextended. While this may be true of some situations in holding companies, the same would be true of any other category of banking structure. I do not believe that it is valid to single out bank holding companies for that type of concern. There have been many articles about bank holding companies being involved in mortgage companies, in factoring, in leasing, or as advisers to REIT's, etc.; and there is some debate or concern over whether or not these are proper activities for banking. But for a great many years these activities have taken place in banks that are not holding company banks; they are not peculiar to bank holding companies. They are familiar to bankers in general.

In the April 1974 issue of *Barrons*, there was an article entitled "Beautiful Balloon? Bank Holding Companies Embark on Frantic Expansion." It seemed to be the first of a series of articles critical of bank holding companies. But a careful reading of the article revealed that there are really very few references to bank holding companies; the references are to banks in general, which of course include banks that belong to bank holding companies and the bank holding company structures themselves. Yet bank holding companies are singled out in the title.

An article in the November 15, 1974, issue of *American Banker* is another example of the type of publicity that bank holding companies had in 1974. The headline is "Judge Sees Travel Unit as Threat to Bank Holding Companies." This has to do with a controversy that has existed for several years about whether or not a travel agency is an appropriate function of a bank or a bank holding company. The article, which is relatively brief, states that "public confidence in the banking industry could be shaken if bank reputations become dependent on efficient operations of travel clubs and tours." The judge's first comments on banking confidence came in testimony stating that the

Bank of America maintains control of tour offerings of Pathways International, an outside tour contractor, because it recognizes that dissatisfaction with poorly operated tours could cause bank cusomers to become dissatisfied with other banking services. A question was asked: Did that mean the bank's reputation would suffer? My point is that bank holding companies are not mentioned in the main body of the article—only in the headline. The article refers to banks. We have a travel agency in our organization. We inherited it when we acquired a bank, and it belongs to the bank and not to the holding company. So these activities existed in banks and are not recent inventions of bank holding companies.

Recently there have been four highly publicized problem banks. Perhaps those who have a depth of knowledge of these situations might feel that the press was inaccurate. Of the four banks, only the Beverly Hills Bank Corporation had a bank holding company problem. The holding company went bankrupt, but Beverly Hills National Bank was merged successfully and, it has been reported, with little or no inconvenience to the depositors. There was not a bank holding company involved in the case of U.S. National Bank or Security, and while there was bank holding company ownership of Franklin, it was the bank that was in trouble and not the holding company.

We see this year of 1975 as one of consolidation and of retention of earnings. There should be at least two basic reasons for that. We need to digest the expansion that has taken place and the acquisitions that have been made in recent years. There has also been a lack of funds industry-wide for further expansion because of the state of the capital markets. In the long run this pause for digestion will be very beneficial to the banking industry and particularly to the holding company structure. This period of consolidation can build a healthier base for the future growth that will be necessary for an expanding economy.

The financial legislation for the 94th Congress is very uncertain. We have new chairmen for the House and Senate banking committees and twenty of the forty-three members of the House Banking Committee are freshman. The overall atmosphere in the House has changed because of changes in the rules and the seniority systems. Any very long-range forecasting is difficult. Any of us can do it but it would probably be rather meaningless. Legislation that might be likely in the 94th Congress would probably have to do with the ability of the bank to cross state lines where the acquired bank is deemed to be a problem bank. The Federal Reserve has been working on this for some time and is sympathetic with letting a banking organization acquire a problem situation in another state. In fact, the Association of Registered Bank Holding Companies, a national organization headquartered in Washington, D.C., has filed a statement with the Holland Committee concerning a proposed amendment to the Bank Holding Company Act to approve bank acquisitions by bank holding companies across state lines in emergency situations. It is my understanding that the Holland Committee consists of Governors Holland, Mitchell, Bucher, and Coldwell.

My point is that the industry is in sympathy with the possibility that it will be necessary for holding companies to cross state lines in an emergency situation. Perhaps even those who would like to protect the integrity of the state lines of a banking organization find this to be a desirable alternative to foreign banking interests being permitted to acquire a troubled bank.

Who will be the successful banker of the future? There have been so many changes just in the last couple of years that this is really looking into the crystal ball, but I think the change will take place at the top. Traditionally, executive officers of major banking institutions have come from the ranks of lending and have been the allocators of resources. Until very recent times this had been the most critical function that had to be performed within a bank. But that function is no longer as important; and the days of acquiring business as a result of social friendships are gone. No longer can bankers do more business on the golf course on Wednesday afternoon than the other fellow who stays in and works.

Customers as well as banks dealing with larger banks are more interested in what can be done for them and the services that can be provided by the financial institution than they are in friendships for the purpose of forming lasting liaisons; and they are willing to pay for those services.

The day of the professional manager is here, and he is one who can accumulate deposits from consumers, understand people, organizations, and particularly important for the future, the information he is given. By 1970, consumers had already become the major suppliers of funds to the banking system; by 1980 consumers will have replaced governmental bodies and corporations as the major users of funds. These are the types of trends that we must recognize, trends that are going to continue. This is the kind of awareness that the successful banker of the future must have.

The bank of the future will be a marketing organization that will introduce products and understand and serve consumers. The successful banking organization of the future will sell data and the computing methods to utilize the data. Perhaps the most important thing for the future in banking will be an understanding of the payments system and the ability to take advantage of the opportunities to streamline that system. There were forty billion debit transactions in our banking system in 1970; there will be eighty billion by 1980 if our present trend of 7½ percent growth on a straight-line basis annually continue. Eighty billion debit transactions a year is more than we feel the banking system can handle under the present methods of moving funds. I assume that we will continue to have a fragmented banking structure, which has been and probably will remain a viable one in our type of society. That banking structure consists of state banks, national banks, member and nonmember banks, unit banks, branch banks, and chain banks.

Assuming this environment continues, the holding company on balance is the structure that will permit banking institutions to reassert themselves in the future in some of the areas that have been lost in the past; it will restore banks to a position in the financial arena where they can function in a meaningful way in modern times.

HARRY W. ALBRIGHT, JR.

National and International Banking Structures

THESE ARE MOMENTOUS TIMES in the world of finance; money markets around the globe and in the United States have been buffeted by powerful forces. The cost of money moved to record heights. Our great securities houses experienced a special recession all their own and many firms are joining forces for survival. The structure of international finance has been wrenched, and the new alignment of currency values that has emerged is creating opportunities and problems for the private businessman and the public regulator alike.

At the same time, a welcome spirit of reform is abroad in the world finance community. Negotiations for a basic overhaul of the world money mechanism are well underway. Congress, the Securities and Exchange Commission, and Wall Street leaders—while not always in agreement—are making some progress in their consideration of the future share of the securities markets. Finally, there is a gathering momentum to encourage regulators and legislatures—at the Federal level recently, and, we hope, in New York State in the near future—to focus renewed attention on possible reforms in the structure of our deposit institutions.

It was in this spirit of possible reform that, several months ago, I suggested a proposal for reciprocal banking privileges across state lines in the United States. Since the time I made that proposal, which was endorsed and supported by Governor Rockefeller, we have had a most encouraging response—far beyond my most optimistic expectations—both from the other governors and the regulators of the states principally involved and from the banking community itself.

The most frequent questions I have been asked are, "What form will the statute likely take?" and "*When* do you think reciprocal legislation can be implemented?"

In preliminary discussions with my fellow regulators, we considered whether legislation should authorize (1) interstate bank branching on a reciprocal basis; or (2) interstate bank acquisitions by out-of-state or foreign bank holding companies on a reciprocal basis; or (3) both of the above.

At this juncture, the above policy issues are completely open, since no significant legislation has taken place at the state or federal level which would fill the field. As far as I can ascertain, only the state of Iowa has enacted a limited statute permitting interstate bank acquisition by bank holding companies. In considering the alternative routes available, the present pattern of federal legislation is such that enabling legislation on the federal level would be required before interstate branching, as such, could be available to national and state member banks.

We in New York State have decided to focus on the holding company route as the more readily attainable approach because (1) we have been seeking opportunities to reassert our leadership as a state with the ability to forge solutions to difficult banking problems; and (2) because federal action in our view would be extremely unlikely or difficult to come by.

Interstate banking through the medium of bank holding company expansion, either *de novo* or through acquisition, is permissible under the Bank Holding Company Act when it is expressly authorized by state statute and when it essentially serves the same purpose as branching. It has the added virtue from my point of view of assuring that state supervisors will retain a key role in the development of interstate banking.

In seeking a feasible and desirable formula for an interstate banking operation, we were fortunate in having former Superintendent Dentzer's study bill as a good starting point. His approach was to permit statewide branching on a basis of complete reciprocity. The arguments and reasoning advanced with this study bill enabled us to advance to the present stage of our thinking.

Before going to the drawing board to implement our holding company concept, we were aware that the leap over state boundaries inevitably raises certain problems. Would not such an enabling statute open the door to statewide branching by giant out-of-state banks all across the state of New York? Could we realistically expect to gain support for legislation which would permit BankAmerica Corporation to charter a New York State bank and open offices in downtown Manhattan, suburban counties, and upstate cities? Our upstate bankers, girding for the shock of statewide branching in 1976, would be forgiven for not relishing a network of Bank of America affiliates populating their bailiwick. And I am sure California bankers might view with equal concern a statewide invasion of their territory at this time by New York based banks.

Accepting the premise that reciprocal statewide branching on a broad statewide basis is neither practical nor legislatively feasible at this time, it was next suggested that we limit reciprocal banking powers to wholesale type banking—large customers only.

I cannot state too strongly my opposition to such a limitation. I firmly believe in the principle that a bank ought to provide a full range of banking services whenever possible and should not be hobbled at the outset in its banking powers. We do not want a half-baked facsimile of a bank, and we would expect that the banks organized in other states by New York-based holding companies would have the same banking powers as local banks.

Another issue raised has been that acquisition by holding companies, as opposed to branching, increases banking concentration and is anticompetitive. Our response to that argument is that if bank holding companies are forced to proceed by acquisition of *de novo* subsidiaries, then the effect on competition is no more deleterious than it is from branching. Secondly, even when a bank holding company acquires an existing bank in another state, strengthened competition may result by virtue of the increased banking conveniences and competition that may be generated.

If the new banks we envisage were to receive full banking powers but not be permitted to spread geographically across the entire state of New York or California, what limitations, for example, should be fairly imposed? The thought that first came under serious consideration was what we might call a City-of-London type of geographical limitation; that is to say, the subsidiary of an out-of-state holding company would locate only within a defined area where the major money market banks had traditionally located. Recent legislation in Illinois, authorizing foreign banks to locate in the Chicago loop area, illustrates how this type of limitation could be applied.

Unfortunately, the matter cannot be settled by laying out a single money market area in the leading financial centers of each major state.

Although we can do that easily enough in New York—in Manhattan, perhaps, below Sixteenth Street—what do we do about California, a state which has two money market cities, Los Angeles and San Francisco?

California Superintendent of Banks Pearson has advanced a most sensible solution to the problem posed by the unusual existence of two major money market cities in his state. His suggestion is that, where interstate reciprocity has been established, a bank's entrance to the receiving state would be limited to either two unit banks or one bank with a maximum of one other branch. Accordingly, the offices of these banks, which would have full banking powers, could be established anywhere in the state.

Realistically, the sites selected by the entering institution will undoubtedly be within the bounds of the money market center or at key locations in expanding suburban areas. With only two offices, site selections would obviously be based on maximum potential. Holding companies coming to New York State would probably give priority to New York City, and possibly to Westchester County or Long Island for a second office. New York holding companies entering California would surely consider Los Angeles and San Francisco as logical office locations.

The two-for-two concept of interstate banking office reciprocity is not always possible. Two offices could be established in California, a branch banking state, but presumably not in Illinois, Texas, and Florida, which are unit banking states. In interstate relationships of this kind, we hope that a two-for-one situation will be accepted by the branch banking state. If not, we could probably be willing to fall back to a one-for-one basis.

The interstate branching proposal is, of course, only a threshold experiment in breaching the barriers now imposed by state lines. Whether it is an experiment that should later be broadened and expanded to allow wider interstate banking, no one can say at this point.

In addition to the questions posed by *interstate* barriers and by experiments in reciprocity, there are other issues relating to reciprocity on an international scale. I believe American bankers of late have been overly preoccupied with the possible existence of advantages foreign banks have in the United States market as compared with those of our domestic banks. The major advantage cited is the foreign bank's ability to operate full service banking offices in more than one state.

(Actually, only a handful of states are open to foreign banks, but these are among the largest states—California, Illinois, Massachusetts, and New York.)

Our proposal on interstate banking, as we intend to develop it, would go a good deal of the way toward equalizing the interstate banking capabilities of foreign and domestic banks. But the interstate banking proposal can hardly be expected to bring about the millenium of perfect equality between domestic and foreign-based banks. It is only a threshold experiment.

Even if our interstate banking proposal gains acceptance, there would still remain other supposed advantages enjoyed by foreign banks, such as their ability to operate affiliated securities companies which can engage in underwriting activities (though in a depressed market, this advantage may not be too great).

But foreign bank operations in the United States are only one side of the international banking picture. To keep the question of relative advantages and disadvantages in proper perspective, one must consider the latitude American banks have in operating abroad. In many of the commercial nations of the world, American banks have been allowed to operate flexibly and profitably, and have attracted a very significant portion of these nations' banking business. On balance, I feel that American bankers should do some very hard thinking before urging regulators or the Congress to take drastic action to eradicate the supposed advantages enjoyed by foreign banks in the United States.

First, the question should be asked whether the advantages enjoyed by foreign banks have not been somewhat exaggerated in our minds. And second, we should ask whether the elimination of these advantages is worth running the risk of creating an unfavorable retaliatory climate among bank regulatory authorities abroad. Actually, I would be less than candid if I did not note what I consider to be an already disturbing increase in the restrictions on banking opportunities in certain overseas markets. The continuation of such a trend both here and abroad could do great violence to the concept of international banking reciprocity.

Protectionism moves quickly to an eye-for-an-eye approach which would cause the international banking system to atrophy just when it has become a potent force for increasing world commerce and strengthening economic ties between nations. Nothing could be more devastating to the concept of international banking development than letting reciprocity degenerate into a synonym for retaliation.

I believe that national and international economics should start with the initial premise, at least, of minimum barriers and maximum access. Only for the most persuasive reasons—and then only in the most limited circumstances—should restrictions be established. Essentially, the natural hydraulics of international economic trends should be allowed to shape the structure of international markets.

Thus I believe that we should seek to break down artificial or historical barriers wherever and whenever we come upon them. I am pleased to report we have done so in New York State by eliminating the artificial barriers of district lines to permit statewide banking in 1976. Our interstate banking proposal represents another effort to eliminate the artificial barriers of state lines. But finally, our greatest challenge clearly remains the international arena, an area where some Americans have also been indulging in the temptations of "protectionism."

But to me, at least, each day presents increasing evidence of our international interdependence—one nation upon another whether it be for sources of food, sources of energy, or sources of credit. One day's advantage turns out to be tomorrow's disadvantage. No nation can be so astute as to be able to foresee the real harmful effects of protectionist policies in the long range. Thus the real challenge is to break down artificial barrriers at all levels, to allow credit to be allocated where it is most needed, and in this way to foster the true spirit of international banking reciprocity.

APPENDIX A

Codes of Conduct

BANK DIRECTORS' CODE OF CONDUCT,
LOUISIANA NATIONAL BANK

DIRECTORS of Louisiana National Bank are chosen on the basis of their ability to contribute to the management of the bank; safeguard its deposits; enhance its profits; and, generally, improve this community and provide an opportunity for its citizens to enjoy vital and meaningful lives.

Our directors must manage their business and personal affairs so as to avoid situations where personal interests may conflict or appear to conflict with the interest of the bank or its customers. Specifically, Louisiana National Bank directors should recognize that:

1. Confidential information with respect to the bank, its customers, and suppliers, acquired in the course of duty, is to be used solely for banking purposes.

2. Confidential information which might reflect favorably or adversely upon the investment value or future market value of any business enterprise is not to be used in any manner for personal advantage.

3. Information of and about competitors will not be available to them, nor will they be present when loan information or other confidential matters concerning a competitor are to be discussed.

4. They are compensated for their services and the use of their names by the direct method of directors' fees and committee fees. In the case of loans, trusts, and other services, their rates and fees will be commensurate with those charged other customers.

5. There is a legal prohibition governing the sale of bank property to directors, officers, or employees. Furthermore, directors selling products or services will be treated in the same manner as any other vendor.

We are sure that all LNB directors are aware of these principles, but this is just an effort to reduce them to writing.

CODE OF CONDUCT FOR ALL EMPLOYEES,
LOUISIANA NATIONAL BANK

Preamble

A bank is judged by the collective and individual conduct of its directors, executive personnel, and employees. Thus, bankers traditionally have recognized that their first duty to the bank, its customers, and its shareholders is to act in all things in a manner that merits public trust and confidence.

The code of conduct formalizes in writing the policies which already guide all of us in our business and personal affairs. The adoption of this code and its periodic review will help crystallize in the minds of our bank directors, executive personnel, and employees the principles to which we are all dedicated. It will help us in a continuing effort to better serve the public and more fully meet the needs of our community.

Bankers' Code of Conduct

A bank's reputation for integrity is its most valuable asset and is determined by the conduct of its executive personnel and employees. Each must manage his personal and business affairs to avoid situations that might lead to a conflict or even suspicion of a conflict between his self-interest and his duty to the bank, its customers, and shareholders. One's bank position must never be used, directly or indirectly, for private gain, to advance personal interests, or to obtain favors or benefits for himself, a member of his family, or any other person. The following guidelines should help in the exercise of personal judgment to avoid conflicts of interest or the appearance of conflicts.

I
CONFIDENTIAL INFORMATION

1. Confidential information with respect to the bank, its customers, and suppliers, acquired in the course of duty, is to be used solely for banking purposes and under no circumstance revealed to unauthorized persons. It is imperative that we keep all information about customers in the strictest of confidence.

2. Confidential information which might reflect favorably or adversely upon the investment value or future market value of any business enterprise should not be used in any manner for the purpose of personal advantage or to provide advantage to others. For example, confidential information coming to the Commercial Banking Department about a customer cannot be used by the Trust Department in making investments for fiduciary accounts.

II
PERSONAL INVESTMENTS

1. Executive personnel and employees should disclose to the Executive Committee when he or his family has any ownership or beneficial interest in customers, suppliers, or competitors of the bank. If a conflict of interest with the bank exists, then appropriate action can be determined by the Executive Committee.

2. Executive personnel and employees should not borrow excessively for the purchase of stocks and bonds or other investments.

3. Executive personnel and employees should be prudent in their investments and not speculate in securities, real estate, or commodities. Executive personnel and employees may not have a margin account with an investment firm.

4. Executive personnel and employees may not accept from a broker an opportunity to buy a security during a distribution before the security becomes generally available to the public.

5. Executive personnel and employees should not accept offers which come to them because of their bank position to buy a security at terms more favorable than that available to the general public.

III

GIFTS, FEES, LOANS, ETC.

1. Executive personnel should not accept excessive entertainment, gifts, or price concessions from bank customers, suppliers, or competitors.

2. As a general rule, gifts should not be accepted from any persons dealing with the bank. Entertainment should not be accepted unless you are in a position to reciprocate on a personal basis or be reimbursed from the bank through the filing of a proper expense report.

3. It is realized that some of you will receive, at Christmas and at other times, gifts from customers or others who furnish supplies, equipment, or services to the bank. The following is our policy regarding the acceptance of gifts:

A. Any gift with a value of $25.00 or more received from a customer or a supplier must be reported to the Executive Committee within 15 days of receipt. The Executive Committee shall have the responsibility of determining whether the gift can be retained or returned to the donor.

(a) Regardless of value, a gift should be declined if your good judgment indicates you would be obligated in any way to the donor, or if there is the slightest implication of influence. Although some embarrassment may be involved, a tactful explanation of bank policy will enable you to decline the gift.

(b) It is not possible for you to know the identity of every bank customer or supplier. However, if a gift is involved, it is your obligation to make the necessary inquiries to determine whether or not the donor is a customer or supplier.

B. Bank personnel may accept fees, gratuities, or honorariums for bank-related speaking engagements or from outside teaching activities with prior approval by the Executive Committee.

C. It is a federal criminal offense for *any* bank employee to accept "any fee, commission, gift or thing of value" for procuring or endeavoring to procure any loan or extension of credit (18 United States Code 220). This statement should be of particular concern to lending officers, although it applies to any bank employee.

4. Executive personnel, other employees, and all retired personnel and members of their immediate families shall not accept directly or indirectly any bequest or legacy from a bank customer or prospective customer except where such customer or prospective customer is a close relative. If a member of executive personnel or employee or a retired person learns of such a legacy in a customer's or prospective customer's will, they should report all facts to the Executive Com-

mittee. Circumstances may exist which dictate an exception being made to this general policy.

5. Executive personnel and other employees shall not borrow from bank customers, prospective customers, suppliers, or other persons or companies with which the bank does business, except those engaged in lending in the usual course of business and then only on terms offered to others under similar circumstances.

IV

OUTSIDE ACTIVITIES

1. Executive personnel and other employees shall not engage in business activity or employment which interferes with their duties to the bank or its stockholders, divides their loyalty, or allows a possibility of conflict of interest.

2. No member of executive personnel and no employee may serve as a director, official, or member of any other business organization (other than one affiliated with the bank) unless he shall have the prior consent of the bank's Executive Committee.

A. One of the principal reasons for this provision is the fact that, when a member of executive personnel or an employee of the bank appears as a director, officer, or employee of some outside company, it may give the impression that the bank is financially interested in the enterprise or is financially supporting it. In general, the bank does not approve of its executive personnel and employees being in any way associated with outside commercial enterprises. As a result, Executive Committee approvals under the section are granted only in special circumstances.

3. Executive personnel and other employees are encouraged and urged to participate in civic organizations and political activities provided that such participaton does not unduly interfere with their duties or bring detriment to the bank.

V

OTHER GENERAL CONSIDERATIONS

1. No loans will be made to corporate officers, correspondent banks or bankers, or any others because of balances which may be controlled at rates of less than the prime rate of interest charged by the bank to prime borrowers.

2. Any doubt on the part of any employee about any part of this code should be referred to the Executive Committee.

3. Federal law prohibits the making of loans for political activities. Therefore, no lending officer should violate this section of law.

VI

ADMINISTRATION

For the purpose of implementing this code, each member of executive personnel and all employees should review it annually, setting out any information called for by the code. Notwithstanding the disclosures required by the annual statement, each member of executive personnel and all employees are expected to report promptly to the Executive Committee for approval the existence of any relationship or interest as of June 14, 1971, which might involve or appear to involve a conflict of interest.

Memorandum

To: Executive Committee

Recognizing that the Code of Conduct formalizes in writing the policies which already guide all of us in our business and personal conduct, I acknowledge that I have received and read a copy of the Code of Conduct dated June 14, 1971, as provided in Section VI.

Within its meaning, expressed and implied, I am not and have not been aware of any circumstances of a personal or family nature which would conflict with the interest of the Bank. I further recognize my responsibility to report promptly any such circumstances which may develop in the future.

Signature: _____

Department: _____

APPENDIX B

Specimen of a Statement of Lending Policies and Procedures

THE OFFICERS of this bank, in making loans, shall be guided by the following memorandum.

1. The management of the bank believes that sound loans are a desirable and profitable means of employing funds available for investment. Authorized bank employees are expected to make, and seek to develop, all of the sound loans that the resources of the bank permit and that opportunity affords. In the allocation of resources available for loans, primary consideration shall be given to existing or potential customers with economic interests in the Dayton area.

2. The Board of Directors realizes that the lending of money by the bank necessarily includes reasonable business risks. Some losses are to be expected in the lending program, and it is the policy of the Board of Directors to maintain a reserve for future loan losses as large as is allowed by pertinent banking and tax laws. Any officer may request of the Senior Loan Officer that a loan be charged off, but such credits shall be reduced to judgement on or before the decision to charge off when such action is consistent with good banking practice. It shall be the responsibility of the officers who approved the credits to continue to follow their loans after charge-off proceedings.

3. The administration of the bank's lending activities will be supervised by the Senior Loan Officer of the bank, and he shall follow the policies set forth in this resolution. The Senior Loan Officer shall seek the advice and counsel of the Executive Committee of the Board of Directors when in doubt as to credit decisions or questions involving the interpretation or application of loan policies.

4. All loans in excess of the limits hereinafter provided for the various lending officers, and not to exceed the legal limit of the bank, shall be approved prior to consummation by one of the following:

    A. The Executive Committee of the Board of Directors, or

    B. An officer whose authorized limit is great enough to allow his individual approval of the loan, and/or

    C. The Officers Loan Committee, which shall have the combined author-

---

Reproduced with permission of Robert J. Barth, President, First National Bank, Dayton, Ohio.

ity of all officers appointed thereto, the members and chairman of which shall be designated by the Executive Committee, ratified by the Board of Directors.

5. All loans shall be reported to the Executive Committee following disbursement; and in addition, loans and credit lines of $_____ and over, not specifically approved by the Executive Committee at its next meeting following such approval. Any loan to an individual or company which would place the total credit extended to a related group of individuals and/or companies in excess of the bank's legal lending limit must receive approval of the Executive Committee prior to disbursement.

6. The members and responsibilities of the Officers Loan Committee are set forth in Exhibit A which is attached hereto. The Executive Committee of the Board of Directors shall review these responsibilities no less than one time during each calendar year and the Executive Committee is authorized to make such changes in the Loan Committee and its responsibilities as it may consider prudent.

7. The lending representatives of the bank shall have the authority up to the amount as is indicated by their names, without the approval of any committee, provided such loans are in accordance with the policies and principles herein expressed. It is intended that the total liabilities of a borrower to the bank, including real estate, installment, and commercial loans, are not to exceed the authority of the lending representative approving the loan.

8. The Chief Executive Officer of the bank may, without specific authorization of the Board of Directors, grant lending authority of not more than $_____ to officers and/or employees. Such action must be reported to the Executive Committee at its next meeting and recorded in the minutes.

9. Loans of the following types are considered desirable by this bank. Each loan must meet the tests of a prudent loan:

A. Unsecured loans to business concerns and individuals on a short-term basis, supported by a satisfactory balance sheet and earnings statement, usually for a term not to exceed 90 days, and

B. Loans to business concerns and individuals secured by a security interest in marketable equipment, such loans to be amortized over a period of time generally not to exceed 36 months, and

C. Loans to companies against assignment of accounts receivable. Loans against assigned accounts receivable shall be supervised by an officer of the bank appointed by the Officers Loan Committee, and procedures for servicing the loan must be approved in advance by the Officers Loan Committee.

D. Loans collaterally secured by marketable bonds, and

E. Loans collaterally secured by securities listed on a recognized stock exchange; such loans must comply in *all respects* with regulation U of the Federal Reserve System, and

F. Loans collaterally secured by unlisted securities which are readily marketable in the "over the counter" market, and

G. Loans against the cash surrender value of life insurance, such loans not to exceed the cash surrender value plus the accumulated dividends, and

H. Loans secured by the assignment of savings accounts in the bank, or other banks, or secured by savings accounts or share accounts of federally insured savings and loan associations, and

I. Loans under $_____ in amount secured by first liens on improved business or residential properties, such loans to qualify as follows:

    1. Real Estate loans shall be in the form of an obligation secured by a first mortgage, and

    2. Real Estate loans shall generally not exceed, in amount, _____% of the appraised value of the real estate offered as security, and

    3. Real Estate loans shall generally not exceed a term of _____ years, amortized in equal installment payments, and

    4. Real Estate appraisals upon which mortgage loans are based shall be made by appraisers who are approved by the Executive Committee.

J. Real Estate loans, in excess of $_____, governed by the principles as set forth in Section I, above, and approved in advance by the Executive Committee.

K. Installment loans, governed by Exhibit B of this "Statement of Lending Policies."

L. Commodity loans secured by warehouse receipts in bonded warehouses or by field warehouse receipts.

It should be recognized by each lending representative of the bank that it is to the advantage of the borrower and to the bank that each loan have a program of repayment, agreed upon at the time the loan is made.

It is evident that certain loans—due to the nature of supporting collateral—may, in reality, be less liquid than others. All loans, excluding real estate loans, shall be reviewed at least each quarter by the lending representative who initiated the loan, and when changes in the economy, the securities market, or the commodities market warrant, loans shall be reviewed more often.

All loans shall have an ample margin of safety between the advance and the current market value of the collateral. When insurance on the collateral or on the life of the borrower is warranted, it shall be obtained and periodically reviewed by the officer initiating the loan.

10. Loans of the following type are not considered desirable loans for the purposes of the bank. Such loans will ordinarily be declined unless they are specifically approved by the Officers Loan Committee or the Executive Committee of the Board of Directors for reasons which appear to justify an exception to the bank's general policy:

    A. Capital loans to a business enterprise where the loan cannot be repaid within a reasonable period except by borrowing elsewhere or by liquidating the business.

    B. Loans to a new enterprise if the repayment of the loan is dependent upon the profitable operation of the enterprise.

    C. Loans to parties whose integrity or honesty is questionable.

    D. Real Estate mortgage loans secured by property out of the bank's recognized trade area.

    E. Construction mortgage loans, except in cases where the building is being supervised by an architect and/or a contractor having financial responsibility and where the borrower has produced a satisfactory take out commitment.

F. Loans to be paid from the proceeds of the settlement of an estate, unless these loans are fully collateralized or guaranteed by the estate and approved by bank counsel.

G. Loans secured by stock in a closed corporation which has no ready market.

H. Loans for the purpose of enabling the borrower to speculate on the future market of securities or commodities.

11. A written application must be prepared for all loans, in order that the bank will have a written record of the representation upon which the loan was based and the agreed upon term of repayment.

12. Interest rates shall be in accordance with the schedule adopted by the Officers Loan Committee. The Officers Loan Committee shall review the interest rate schedule when deemed appropriate and shall make required changes.

13. All unsecured loans in excess of $1,000 must be supported by a current financial statement. Such financial statements shall contain sufficient information to support the loan, shall be signed by the borrower, or shall be certified by an acceptable independent public or certified public accountant to the extent determined by the Officers Loan Committee and/or the approving loan officer. Whenever possible fiscal statements are to be supplemented by interim statements and other financial information.

14. It shall be the duty of the credit manager to see that an appropriate memorandum for the credit file is prepared on each loan. The memorandum shall recite the circumstance under which the loan was made, the factors which justify it, and the borrower's plan of repayment.

15. Description and classification of collateral. (Note: The state of the economy and the susceptibility of the stock market to change may make the following advances imprudent. Each member of the lending staff shall take the full responsibility for appraising the original and continuing advisability of certain percentage advances against the following types of collateral. The following percentage advances are subject to change by the Executive Committee.)

DESCRIPTION AND CLASSIFICATION OF COLLATERAL

Class A

1. U.S. Government securities (___% of market).
2. Securities of Federal Agencies (___% of market).
3. Stocks listed on New York Stock Exchange or American Stock Exchange (___% of market).
4. Municipal bonds rated by Moody's "A" or better (___% of market).
5. Cash surrender value of life insurance (full cash surrender value including accrued dividends).
6. Savings accounts in our bank (___% of amount on deposit).

Class B

1. Stocks listed on other security exchanges (___% of market).
2. Other bonds rated by Moody's or listed on a security exchange, or quoted in the Wall Street Journal (___% of market).
3. Mutual funds (___% of market).
4. Stocks quoted over the counter (___% of market).
5. Savings accounts of other banks, or share accounts of insured building and loans (___% of account).
6. F.H.A. Title I—maximum to any one borrower (including spouse) limited by law.

Class C

1. Chattel mortgage and/or security agreement with appropriate filings.
2. Assigned accounts receivable.
3. Warehouse receipts on marketable commodities.
4. Unquoted stocks.
5. Real estate mortgages.
6. All other collateral.

EXHIBIT A

Officers Loan Committee

1. The Committee shall consist of the following members:

_____, Chairman

_____, Vice Chairman

_____

The Chief Executive Officer of the bank shall be Chairman of the Committee and the Senior Lending Officer shall serve as Vice Chairman. Two members of the Committee shall constitute a quorum, and one of the two members shall act as Chairman in the absence of the Chief Executive Officer and the Senior Lending Officer.

2. All commercial loans and approvals of credit shall be reviewed or approved by the Committee. The Officers Loan Committee shall meet at least three times each week.

3. The authority of the Committee shall be equal to the combined authorities of the members in attendance.

4. Loans and credits of $_____ or more should, whenever practicable, be made or committed only after approval of the Executive Committee.

5. The Credit Manager or his appointed representative will act as Secretary of the Committee and will be responsible for arranging the flow of material to meetings. Officers wishing to present matters to the Committee should so notify the Credit Department in advance.

EXHIBIT B

Installment Loans

It is the purpose of this exhibit to establish a uniform and proved approach to installment lending. The following comments and point evaluations will offer guidance and set standards for the granting of such credit. All consumer loans *must* be evaluated according to the point system currently in use and wherever possible the signatures of both husband and wife should be obtained. Any loan made where the total points indicate excessive risk must be fully justified *in writing* at the time the loan is made. All installment loans made which do not conform to both the bank's "Statement of Lending Policies" and this Exhibit B shall be reviewed by the officer in charge of installment loans. If the loan does not conform, the member of the lending staff approving the loan shall so indicate on the application.

1. *All loans*, both direct and dealer, will be point scored using the current tables as approved by the Installment Loan Department. Any loan not meeting the score requirements will be rejected unless written reasons for approval are shown on the application or investigation sheet.

2. Personal loans:
    A. Must score 60 points.
    B. Get complete listing of all debts.
    C. *No* personal loans to be extended to individuals having household goods loans at loan companies.
    D. No personal loans if the total of *all* monthly payments (excluding home mortgage) will exceed 25% of net income.
    E. Get signatures of *both* husband and wife on note.

3. Automobile loans:
    A. Must score 50 points.
    B. Complete description of car, including engine and major accessories, must be on application or investigation sheet.
    C. Yegen Guide figure or Red Book loan value must be shown.
    D. Advances on new cars—Yegen Guide with 10% *leeway*.
    E. Advances on used—loan value with 10% *leeway* subject to inspection of car.
    F. All used cars to be inspected on direct loans and on indirect where advisable.
    G. Maximum maturities: new cars—36 months; used cars—30 months. Loans must be fully amortized in substantially equal payments. *No balloons.*

4. Collateral loans on household goods:
    A. Must score 60 points.
    B. Get signatures of *both* husband and wife on note and security agreement.

5. Property improvement loans:
    A. Must score 60 points.
    B. Applications must be complete in every detail.
    C. No advances for funds to be used for purposes other than improvement of the subject property.
    D. No mortgages.
    E. Husbands and wives must sign the note.